THE FALL AND SIN

THE FALL AND SIN

What We Have Become as Sinners

Marguerite Shuster

WILLIAM B. EERDMANS PUBLISHING COMPANY

GRAND RAPIDS, MICHIGAN / CAMBRIDGE, U.K.

© 2004 Wm. B. Eerdmans Publishing Co.
All rights reserved

Wm. B. Eerdmans Publishing Co.
255 Jefferson Ave. S.E., Grand Rapids, Michigan 49503 /
P.O. Box 163, Cambridge CB3 9PU U.K.

Printed in the United States of America

09 08 07 06 05 04   7 6 5 4 3 2 1

Library of Congress Cataloging-in-Publication Data

Shuster, Marguerite.
The Fall and sin: what we have become as sinners / Marguerite Shuster.
p. cm.
Includes bibliographical references and index.
ISBN 0-8028-0994-4 (pbk.: alk. paper)
1. Fall of man. 2. Sin. I. Title.
BT710.S53 2004

233'.14 — dc21

2003060240

www.eerdmans.com

In memory of Paul,

Who loved righteousness and hungered for it

Contents

Preface   xi

I. THE FALL OF HUMANKIND

1. Introduction: Primal History Viewed as Covenantal   3

   Creation and Fall   3

   God's Covenant Relationship with Humankind   6

   Excursus: Primal History, Time, and Space   8

   Parties to the Covenant   12

   Conditions of the Covenant   17

   The Threat of Death   24

   The Promise of Life   26

   The Ongoing Status of the Covenant of Works   27

   "On Doing What We Can" — A Sermon   30

2. The Root of the Fall   37

   The Fall and Human Freedom and Responsibility   38

   The Fall and the Idea of Tragedy   44

3. The Nature of the Fall   49

   The Significance of the Insignificant   49

   The Problem of Authority   51

   The Fall as Pride and Unbelief   52

   Objections to Understanding the Fall as Pride and Unbelief   55

   Roman Catholicism and the Donum Superadditum   59

4. Consequences of the Fall   62

   Humankind's Attitude toward God   62

   Excursus: Clothing, Modesty, and Nudity in Art   66

   God's Attitude toward Humankind   70

   Humankind's Environment   72

   Fallen Human History   80

5. The Divine Purpose and Moral Evil   84

   Divine Sovereignty   85

   Is God Responsible for Sin?   87

   Is Evil Necessary for Good?   90

II. THE DOCTRINE OF SIN

6. The Nature of Sin   99

   Sin as Act   102

   Sin as Condition   113

   "Sin" — A Sermon   128

7. Sin and Sins   135

   Degrees of Sin and of Culpability   137

   Categories of Sins   143

8. Original Sin   159

   Original Sin as Radical Depravity   160

Original Sin as Universal   167

The Biblical Basis of the Doctrine of Original Sin   171

"Shadows" — A Sermon   175

9. Problems of Freedom   182

    Moral Inability   182

    Pelagianism   188

    Free Agency   190

    Solidarity in Sin   199

10. Civil Righteousness   212

    "I'd Rather Do It Myself" — A Sermon   221

APPENDIX 1: Physical Death as Existential Reality   230

    Death as Curse and Mystery   230

    Death Avoided   232

    Death Shaping Life   238

    Death Embraced   243

    Death, the Funeral, and the Grave   252

    "Private Enemy #1" — A Sermon   255

APPENDIX 2: Biblical Vocabulary Relating to Sin   263

Subject Index   266

Name Index   271

Scripture Reference Index   275

Preface

Somehow it seems fitting to be inscribing this preface to a volume on the Fall and sin on Christmas Eve, anticipating the coming of the One who delivers us from their fatal effects and whose final victory we await with longing. True, at the close of the fateful year 2001, the minds of many citizens of the United States are fixed more on their offended innocence in the face of terrorist attacks, than on the overwhelming guilt that marks them as members of a universally fallen humankind. Yet apart from the Fall and the pervasiveness of sin, wars and rumors of wars, cruelty and deceit, suffering and loss, and our final helplessness before all of these, would be all the more baffling. And so, again, we ache for our Savior.

This volume is in its design the third in the series of theology texts begun by Paul King Jewett with *God, Creation, and Revelation* and *Who We Are: Our Dignity as Human*. However, ten years have elapsed since Jewett died. He had not begun work on this volume before his death, and hence I have taken responsibility for its content. Surely, it is not in any meaningful sense what it would have been had he written it himself. He did, however, leave transcripts of his lectures and an immense collection of notes and references to research extending over a lifetime. I have consulted all of these and have made much use of them, though I have also, of course, profited from other works published in the last decade. It would be next to impossible to separate out Jewett's work from mine, or to identify where I have diverged from the way he would have wished to state things. Sometimes, I have left sentences or (rarely) even brief paragraphs of his notes virtually intact; more usually, I have recast and expanded them. While the outline of the volume is more or less his, I have also changed the order and the emphases from time to time, even as he did himself with his earlier volumes. Thus, this is a book that could not have been written without him, one in which use of the editorial "we" seems indubitably justified, yet one for the final form of which Jewett may not be called to account. I offer it as an act of gratitude for a long friendship, and with endless admiration for Dr. Jewett's courage, faithfulness, wisdom, and passion for justice. He had an uncompromisingly realistic view of human weakness and corruption, yet these seemed in him to foster not bitterness or cynicism but a certain matter-of-fact attitude toward the faults he saw so clearly, mixed with generosity and compassion toward all who suffer from the effects of sin.

I also extend my thanks to Fuller Theological Seminary, where Paul Jewett taught for almost his whole career, and whose generous sabbatical policy has enabled me to give attention to this project.

MARGUERITE SHUSTER
Pasadena, California

Part I

The Fall of Humankind

'Twas but one little drop of sin
We saw this morning enter in,
And lo! At eventide the world is drown'd.

John Keble, *The Christian Year*

Introduction:
Primal History Viewed as Covenantal

Creation and Fall

God made this world, made it in such a way that he exulted in it and repeatedly approved it as *good*. Moreover, the human beings God made for himself and for one another, he made in his own image — as great a dignity as could be bestowed upon a creature (Gen. 1). What could augur a more glorious future? And yet — and yet. . . . Even in our contemplation of the good creation of the world and humankind, we cannot avoid reflecting repeatedly on the painfully obvious fact that the world as we know it staggers under suffering and evil.[1] The natural world, even apart from humankind, is stunningly brutal. We human beings defile our God-given dignity not just when we commit crimes, but in our everyday relationships with the opposite sex, with persons of different racial or ethnic backgrounds, and in our exercise of dominion over our environment. Something has surely gone desperately wrong, so wrong that no effort to discuss goodness in an unqualified way can be sustained for long. Theologians have traditionally spoken of what went wrong in terms of the Fall.

1. See the extended discussion in Paul K. Jewett, *God, Creation, and Revelation* (Grand Rapids: Eerdmans, 1991), and Paul K. Jewett with Marguerite Shuster, *Who We Are: Our Dignity as Human* (Grand Rapids: Eerdmans, 1996).

Despite the time-honored credentials of this approach, we must acknowledge that the contemporary predilection of many biblical scholars and theologians to give short shrift to the Fall — even at a time when there is a renewed interest in sin — does not lack reasons. It is true that the Bible itself does not speak directly of a "fall," nor does the rest of the Old Testament or the Gospels refer to the events of Genesis 3 as such as the source of human ills.[2] What we know about the vast drafts of time involved in evolution and about violent death long before humans entered upon the scene makes the picture of an idyllic Eden seem simply incredible.[3] The specifics of what is at most "prehistory" could not even hypothetically, by any reasonable reckoning, be retrieved (apart, of course, from the way they are depicted in the biblical account itself). And surely we have gotten beyond the naïve hope that if only we understood what went wrong, we would be able to undo it: nothing but redemption can achieve that. In the meantime, we had best get busy and fight evil as well as we can, rather than spending our energies on fruitless speculation.[4] With such complaints we are in broad sympathy.

2. There is, however, the idea of a "fall" of Adam in late Judaism, as seen in 2 Esdras 7:118. While it may well be that the apostle Paul had such interpretations in mind as he wrote his epistles (especially Romans 5 and 1 Corinthians 15), surely it does not follow that this understanding must be a *faulty* appropriation of the Genesis narrative. Furthermore, see Henri Blocher, *Original Sin: Illuminating the Riddle* (Grand Rapids: Eerdmans, 1999 and Cambridge: Apollos, 1997), pp. 42-48, for argument that the early chapters of Genesis are by no means so completely ignored by the rest of Scripture as is sometimes supposed.

3. Indeed, it seemed incredible as early as Philo (d. A.D. 50), who took it as figurative, though the later prevailing view was that Eden should be viewed historically. See Jean Delumeau, *History of Paradise: The Garden of Eden in Myth and Tradition,* trans. M. O'Connell (New York: Continuum, 1995), pp. 15-21.

4. Take Rauschenbusch as an example: "The social gospel is above all things practical. . . . It would have no motive to be interested in a doctrine which diverts attention from the active factors of sin which can be influenced, and concentrates attention on a past event which no effort of ours can influence. Theology has made the catastrophe of the fall so complete that any later addition to the inheritance of sin seems slight and negligible. What can be worse than a state of total depravity and active enmity against God and his will? Consequently theology has had little to say about the contributions which our more recent forefathers have made to the sin and misery of mankind. The social gospel would rather reserve some blame for them, for their vices have afflicted us with syphilis, their graft and their wars have loaded us with public debts, and their piety

Nonetheless, the fall narrative has a kind of prominence due to its position in the Bible, its familiarity, and the power of the story itself that requires us come to grips with what the story (and its place in the primal history) means: when Jesus speaks of blood shed "from righteous Abel to Zechariah son of Barachiah" (Matt. 23:35), anyone with even a little biblical awareness understands the first reference, but few indeed know the second. Furthermore, we demur from the conclusion that it does not matter whether anything that can be called a "fall" occurred in the chronological past, but only that we recognize now that things are out of joint.[5] What is at stake theologically is, first, the nature of God himself; and, second, who human beings are, not in themselves, if such a thing could be conceived, but before God. To suggest that evil is intrinsic to the creation (or to say that humankind fell not *in,* but *into,* history) impugns the Creator: it implies that he lacked the power or the will to make a world and human beings that were simply good, as Genesis 1 proclaims — whether because of the limitations imposed by finitude or the recalcitrance of matter or whatever.[6] He may have created the best of all *possible* worlds (Leibniz), but he could not create one that a naïve observer could affirm as wholly good. This proposition we deny. We insist instead that something intruded, in space and time, upon what God made. Furthermore, to suggest that our primary duty is to recognize and deal with the fact that things are not now as they should be provides a subtle temptation to leave God out of the discussion, to focus on ourselves and the bad things we do. But we do not rightly understand that duty if we implicitly see it as a sort of soliloquy in which our higher self addresses our lower self. Rather, the ethical imperative is and always has been a matter of our being addressed by God. Just as our human identity as those creatures

---

has perpetuated despotic churches and unbelievable creeds. . . . In so far as the doctrine of the fall has made all later actions of negligible importance by contrast, it blocks the way for an important advance in the consciousness of sin" (*A Theology for the Social Gospel* [New York: Macmillan, 1919], pp. 42-43).

5. For this view see, for instance, Ted Peters, *Sin: Radical Evil in Soul and Society* (Grand Rapids: Eerdmans, 1994), p. 28.

6. We will take up certain aspects of the problem of evil below, pp. 83-95. On human nature as created faultless, see, e.g., Augustine, *Treatise on Nature and Grace,* chap. 3 (Nicene and Post-Nicene Fathers [NPNF], first series, ed. Philip Schaff [Grand Rapids: Eerdmans, 1956 (reprint)], vol. 5, p. 122).

who are made in the divine image essentially involves relationship with God,[7] so our sin is fundamentally against God and involves a broken relationship with God, to which truth the doctrine of the Fall points.[8]

Because God's decision in making humankind was a decision to make a free and responsible creature to whom he would be uniquely related, and because God himself has set the terms of the relationship throughout the whole of human history, from the First Adam to the Second, from creation to the covenant of grace, we will unapologetically use the theological perspective of *covenant* as a means of viewing that relationship. This perspective fittingly emphasizes the kind of God with whom we have always to do, even when covenant as such is not in the forefront of particular passages. (We thus signal that we do read the primal history in the light of Scripture as a whole, while also wishing to give due weight to the narrative as it stands.) Other particular difficulties we shall take up in due course.

God's Covenant Relationship with Humankind

To speak of God's relationship to humankind as covenantal is to speak of God's sovereign ordering of human history in accord with his own purposes for human salvation, in accord with his own holy will. It provides a way to conceptualize and unite various strands of revelation, related to humankind as created in the divine image, that constitute the background for the idea of the Fall. Creatures uniquely endowed with

---

7. See *Who We Are*, pp. 18-19 and passim.

8. For treatment of sin defined as being against God, see below, pp. 102-4, 264-65. Brunner, who rejects the idea of a definitive historical fall (and, in our view, slips into certain persistent inconsistencies of language in doing so), nonetheless insists that loss of the concept of the Fall has disastrous effects for the whole of Christian doctrine: "Only a *fallen* humanity needs a Redeemer." Every conception of sin apart from a Fall "makes sin either a fact of nature, or merely the moral concern of the individual" (*The Christian Doctrine of Creation and Redemption,* trans. Olive Wyon [London: Lutterworth Press, 1952], p. 90). Also, Quell: "The point of the portrayal is to make it clear that our whole destiny as men is supremely shaped by this event" (Quell, Bertram, Stählin, and Grundmann, "αμαρτανω, κτλ," in G. Kittel and G. Friedrich, eds., *Theological Dictionary of the New Testament (TDNT)*, 9 vols., trans. and ed. G. W. Bromiley [Grand Rapids: Eerdmans, 1964-74], 1:281).

the image of God, made to be uniquely related to God and beginning their existence in the goodness and security of this relationship, must by definition have as their highest end and obligation to enjoy God forever in a free and voluntary submission to his will in all things. God being who he is must demand as much, and humankind being who they are must owe as much and render it. The primal history tells what came of this obligation. And to view this primal history as covenantal is also to set it firmly in the context of God's actions in time and space, not in a realm outside of them or solely in a "depth dimension" that pervades history but has no particular location of its own.[9]

Of course the opening chapters of Genesis do not refer explicitly to a covenant, though the narrative in Genesis 3 gives details that would fit nicely enough into the terms of a covenant: God created the man and the woman in a garden; forbade them to eat of the Tree of the Knowledge of Good and Evil upon pain of death; and, when they failed the test, expelled them from the garden. However, it is actually by working back from the comparison between Adam and Christ — Christ, the Second Adam, the mediator of the covenant of grace — particularly as Paul develops it in Romans 5 and 1 Corinthians 15, that theologians came to see the original condition of the first human pair in covenantal terms.[10] The First Adam and the Second Adam are both uniquely related to the human race as a whole, with the work of the Second Adam contrasted with that of the First: "'The first man, Adam, became a living being'; the last Adam became a life-giving spirit. . . . Just as we have borne the image of the man of dust, we will also bear the image of the man of heaven" (1 Cor. 15:45, 49); "as all die in Adam, so all will be made alive in Christ" (1 Cor. 15:22); "just as one man's trespass led to condemnation for all, so one man's act of righteousness leads to justification and life for all. For just as by the one man's disobedience the many were made sinners, so by the one man's obedience the many

9. Contrast the disjunction made by Albertus Pieters in *The Seed of Abraham* (Grand Rapids: Eerdmans, 1950), pp. 11-12, between Genesis 11 and Genesis 12: he asserts that everything preceding Gen. 12 is introduction, not organically related to what follows, while the redemptive enterprise starts with the call of Abraham.

10. For a very early pointer in this general direction, see Irenaeus, *Against Heresies*, 3.11.8, in Ante-Nicene Fathers (ANF), vol. 1, ed. Alexander Roberts and James Donaldson (Grand Rapids: Eerdmans, 1950 [reprint]). Of course he is well known for his larger theory of "recapitulation."

will be made righteous" (Rom. 5:18-19). Theologically speaking, the two Adams constitute the beginning and the end of the human story.[11]

In speaking of neither Adam nor Christ, neither Genesis nor the Gospels, however, can we get behind the narratives to a secure grasp of the historical details — as, in the case of Christ, the successive quests for the "historical Jesus" demonstrate (granting, of course, despite the parallel we have made, that Genesis 1-11 and the Gospels are not the same kinds of literature, even though both are shaped by their theological purposes). With reference to both, our understanding comes through the theological perspective we take, which is in our case, as we have said, a covenantal perspective.

Excursus: Primal History, Time, and Space

Because the New Testament as well as the Old refers to the primal history in a way that assumes its continuity with the rest of history (especially in the Lukan genealogy of Jesus, which goes back to Adam [Luke 3:38]; but see also, e.g., Matt. 23:35; Luke 11:51; Heb. 11:4; 12:24; 1 John 3:12; all of which refer to Abel and/or Cain), it could be argued that the question of the historicity of Adam parallels the question of the historicity of those aspects of the life of Jesus deemed implausible by later

---

11. Many have found direct biblical support for the idea of an original covenant with Adam in Hos. 6:7 ("like Adam they transgressed the covenant"), which is certainly a possible reading, though the translation of the critical term כְּאָדָם, "like" or "at" Adam, is debated (the same term appears in Job 31:33, where "like Adam" is also plausible; but there, the translation of both the preposition and the noun is debated). In any case, the earlier Reformed theologians referred to the relationship of God to humankind before the Fall as the "covenant of works," by contrast to the covenant of grace. (Note that one moves from the covenant of works to the covenant of grace in Genesis 3: the covenant of works should not be confused with the Old Testament, nor the covenant of grace with the New. That both parts of our Bible are called "testaments" or "covenants," however, does show the prominence of the covenantal idea as a whole.) Humankind were created good, upright, with knowledge of the divine will and with conformity to that will as a positive reality. By implication of the affirmation that God is just, humankind would have continued in favor with God had they continued to act in conformity with his will. As Scripture says, the one who does the things enjoined in the law shall live by them (Rom. 10:5, quoting Lev. 18:15). The commandment is indeed ordained to life (Rom. 7:10) and brings death only because things have gone wrong.

interpreters. What complicates matters, however, is not just that the events of Genesis 2 and 3 take place before physical artifacts or written sources; but also that the narratives have a particular sort of literary artistry about them that signals a kind of universal intent — as, to take the simplest instance, in the well-known fact that אדם can serve either as the personal name Adam or as a general term for humankind. For the translation problem this poses, note the difference between the KJV and the NRSV in the first five chapters of Genesis, with the KJV using the personal name much more frequently, but the NRSV not being able to avoid it entirely.[12]

We are not wrong if when we hear Genesis 3:9 read — God calling out, "Where are you?" — we hear ourselves being addressed. Thus far the existentialized view is proper. We argue only that it should not be so pressed as to deny the historical givenness and definitiveness of the original event. In Von Rad's moving words, the primal history "tells a story, a part of a traveled road that cannot be traversed again."[13] We have access to that primal event through the symbols of the narrative. The problem comes not when we acknowledge that these are indeed symbols, but if we should deny that they point to any reality at all, or should set them up in place of such a reality.[14] Similarly, we should not press our use of existential language when we say that in Christ all die, that his death is our death, in such a way as to deny the historical character of the salvation event.[15]

Actually, to affirm the historicity of the Fall is not fundamentally

---

12. In Gen. 1-5, the Hebrew word occurs twenty-two times with the article, with meanings ranging from "humankind" to a sort of titular usage, "the Man." Of the twelve additional occurrences without the article, R. S. Hess, in an informative and nuanced discussion, argues that only five, beginning with Gen. 4:25, should be taken as a personal name, with the others having meanings similar to the articular uses ("Splitting the Adam: The Usage of 'ĀDĀM in Genesis i-v," in J. A. Emerton, ed., *Studies in the Pentateuch, Supplements to Vetus Testamentum*, vol. 41 [Leiden, New York, København, Köln: E. J. Brill, 1990], pp. 1-15). The NRSV follows this pattern, though with three marginal notes offering the proper name. In 1 Cor. 15:45, however, Paul speaks of "ὁ πρῶτος ἄνθρωπος Ἀδάμ" ("the first human, Adam"): he obviously understands "Adam" as a proper name.

13. Gerhard von Rad, *Genesis*, rev. ed. (Philadelphia: Westminster, 1961), p. 75.

14. See Olov Hartman, *Earthly Things*, trans. Eric J. Sharpe (Grand Rapids: Eerdmans, 1968), p. 202.

15. See Claus Westermann, *Genesis 1-11*, trans. J. Scullion (Minneapolis: Augsburg, 1984), pp. 64-68, for a sophisticated and subtle treatment of the link of Genesis 1-11 to history.

different than to affirm the historicity of other central aspects of our faith. For instance, that humans are in some important sense different from animals, most people agree; yet the idea of the divine image is notoriously controverted; and that *God* is somehow involved in what makes humans human, after long evolutionary development, cannot be demonstrated. That Jesus died in history is generally conceded. Many believe, and many deny, that he rose from the dead. But that this death and this resurrection have something to do with forgiveness of our sins and our future hope can only be asserted and taken on faith. We cannot read the meaning off of the brute facts.

To say that the essential events to which the primal history refers took place in time and space is not, however, to suggest that we can date and locate them, or that we should assume the details of the account correspond literally to historical events that we could have recorded if only we could have supplied a video camera. We would eschew, that is, a wooden concordism. At the crassest level, it is not a particular skeletal form, however much God may through evolution or otherwise have prepared a suitable form, that makes a creature human, but God's own act, which we may hardly suppose left skeletal traces. And if it is in some sense by the divine address that Adam and Eve were constituted human, and by the divine purpose that that essential humanity was passed on to their heirs; it is not less plausible that their turning from the One who addressed them was likewise constitutive for their descendents. We cannot see the "how" in either case: insofar as it happened, it happened because God decided that it should. As Romans 11:32 bluntly puts it, "God has imprisoned all in disobedience."[16]

The problem of place is at least as difficult as that of time, for nothing in the geological record would lead us to believe that creation was ever marked by something other than the deadly preying of all upon all that we see today. That is, the brutality in nature that other ages attributed to our first parents' sin seems clearly to have predated our first parents' arrival upon the scene at all. What, then, of Eden, the pristine context in which Adam and Eve were said to have been tested and to have fallen? Is this "place that all mankind remembers" built up from

---

16. Obviously, we grant the vast periods of time involved in prehuman and human development. For brief reflection on some of the chronological problems of Genesis 1-11, see *Who We Are*, pp. 390-91.

our longing, and actually to be reached only "at the end of the enormous journey"?[17]

First of all, it is vital to repeat that we do not see these early chapters of Genesis as containing empirical, scientific reporting, or information about geography or botany or zoology or scientific anthropology. Here we do not follow Calvin, the first to place in his commentary on Genesis a map locating paradise.[18] Rather, these chapters give theological insight about the nature and destiny of humankind. For instance, if we assume — as we do — that on the empirical evidence, human beings probably first emerged somewhere in Africa, we cannot by any stretch of the imagination harmonize such a conclusion with the plain statements in Scripture about the location of the Garden of Eden, which seems obviously to have been placed somewhere in the Tigris-Euphrates Valley, the cradle of civilization and specifically of that civilization of which the Semitic family were heirs. Naturally, the writers of Genesis wrote in terms of what they knew. Thus, we no longer consider it meaningful to ask, as did theologians of an earlier age, Where is the Garden now? What happened to it?; or to put the classic answer, It was destroyed in the Flood (as does Milton in *Paradise Lost*, bk. 11), having remained until the Flood as a kind of uninhabited park to memorialize human folly and doom.

It is, however, meaningful to insist that God not only acts redemptively in time, as biblical theologians have emphasized when they have spoken of *Heilsgeschichte,* salvation history, in contrast to a Greek Idealist realm of eternal, unchanging ideas; God also acts in space, in the world of sense perception, of visible, tangible reality; not only in a divine "now" but also in a divine "here."[19] That the particular setting in which our first parents were placed is described as a garden

17. See Dorothy Sayers's "Introduction" to Dante's *Purgatory,* trans. D. L. Sayers, *The Divine Comedy,* vol. 2 (Baltimore: Penguin, 1955), pp. 18-19. Dante would not, of course, have denied an actual Eden; but he also placed it at the top of Mt. Purgatory, the destination reached at last by those purified through purgatorial penances.

18. Delumeau, *History of Paradise,* p. 143; see the whole volume for a fascinating account of changing views of Eden.

19. See Thorleif Boman, *Hebrew Thought Compared with Greek,* trans. J. L. Moreau (New York: Norton, 1960), p. 162. Boman uses the precise topographical information the New Testament gives about the life of Jesus, the Savior made flesh, to illustrate the importance of place to the Hebrews.

no doubt symbolizes what gardens have symbolized from time imme-
morial in literature: harmonious, beautiful, ordered, and peaceful existence, a conclusion fortified by the name *Eden,* which means *delight.*
(We recently noticed a modern volume, not on theology but on horti-
culture, entitled *Visions of Paradise: Themes and Variations on the Garden.*)
Since humankind were created in harmony with God, their neighbor,
and themselves, it is fitting that their existence should be represented
at the spatial level as existence in a garden. Indeed, the rest of Scripture
takes up the theme of Eden or the garden of the Lord as an ideal (Gen.
13:10; Isa. 51:3; Ezek. 28:13; 31:8, 9, 16, 18; 36:35; Joel 2:3; plus numerous less
specific references to gardens and vineyards); and the tree of life and
great river appear in the New Jerusalem, Revelation 21-22.

Parties to the Covenant

The parties to the covenant are God and humankind as created by God.
But in speaking of parties to the covenant, we must disassociate ourselves immediately from all thoughts of equality or parity between
these parties. A covenant is not a contract, à la Rousseau and the social
contract, but rather a relationship constituted by God as its supreme
Disposer. The Creator does not ask the creature if the creature agrees
to the terms; he does not consult Adam and Eve and ask them their
opinion. Nor does he consult their descendants and get their consent
to have Adam and Eve act on their behalf. No; they are established as
head of the race, and given their representative capacity, simply by the
act of their Maker. The sheer brevity of the account, with terms stipu-
lated and command given, focuses the divine sovereignty of the arrangement.

Throughout Scripture, the idea of "covenant" has this sense of au-
thoritative divine ordering.[20] It is, we should say, the consequence of
the fundamental difference between Creator and creature, and
creaturely rebellion against the whole idea has something to do with
creaturely rebellion against the truth that the creature and the Creator
are not on the same level. Likewise, the principle of representation,
both in sin and in grace, that is so closely tied to the covenant, pervades

20. See G. Quell and J. Behm, "διατίθημι, διαθήκη," *TDNT* 2:104-34.

Scripture, with particular emphasis on Adam and Christ, as we have already noted. If we deny the public character of Adam's act, trying to say that he acted for himself alone, we undercut the principle of representation which is basic for understanding the work of Christ. But it is a mistake to say that we have to go to the New Testament before we can see the sin of Adam and Eve conceived as having fundamental significance for all of humanity: in the original story, the way back to the Garden was obviously barred not just to Adam and Eve but also to their posterity.

Liberal theologians have been more consistent in regard to the role of Adam and of Christ than have those who would not call themselves Liberal but have complained against the idea that we are condemned for Adam's sin, while being very willing to accept the thought that we are justified by Christ's righteousness. Liberals and Humanists, by contrast, have repudiated vicarious ethical action of either kind. They have insisted both that we cannot be guilty for Adam's sin and that we must render our own obedience. Adam, as Pelagius argued, had the power of a bad example that may lead to our demise; Jesus provides a good example that may inspire us. Others argue against the legitimacy of comparing our relationship to Adam with that to Christ, noting that while our appropriation of the work of Christ involves personal exercise of choice, belief, commitment, faith; no one was there to choose the first Adam as her representative. But even though a certain difference between the two cases must be acknowledged, it is less large than may at first appear — we might call it a secondary rather than a fundamental difference. We must recall that the Lord works with the same sovereignty as Redeemer as he does as Creator, choosing the redeemed from before the foundation of the world, before the first Adam (Eph. 1:4). Thus an individual decision to trust in Christ reflects a prior decision of God and the gift of his enabling grace.[21]

We must affirm, however, that to say that God sovereignly constituted Adam and Eve head of the human race and to say that they acted in a representative capacity must not be taken to deny their human individuality, as if they were a cipher for a group, all of whom behave in the same way because "that is just what people are like." We are given our humanity as individuals and so must think of human origins in

---

21. We will expand on the idea of human solidarity in sin below, pp. 199-211.

terms of individuals.[22] Even though we have granted a certain limited validity to the existential approach to the primal history, the persons of that history are not simply "Everyman" and "Everywoman": note, for instance, that the story of Cain and Abel emphasizes the different behavior of the two brothers.[23]

The affirmation that, as parties to the initial covenant, Adam and Eve were created upright (cf. Eccles. 7:29; and hence not faced from the outset with impossible demands)[24] has naturally led to much speculation concerning of what this original state of integrity *(status integritatis)* in which they existed, this original righteousness *(justitia originalis)* with which they were endowed, might have consisted. This side of the theory of evolution, it is difficult indeed to conceive of the original pair as blessed with every excellence of mind and body that the artistic and literary imagination can bestow. Pannenberg, among many others, states flatly that any historical claim about a harmonious original state represents an "outdated worldview" and "is incompatible with our currently available scientific knowledge." Calvin, by contrast, asserted confidently, "man in his first condition excelled in these pre-eminent endowments, so that his reason, understanding, prudence, and judgment not only sufficed for the direction of his earthly life, but by them men mounted up even to God and eternal bliss."[25] We would seek to move between these extremes, retaining the historical moment without modernizing our first parents. We would not follow Niebuhr in locating original righteousness in the "perfection before the act" we recognize repeatedly in ourselves, when we know a good that we cannot

---

22. For reflections on the theme of human individuality and also on the way in which racial prejudice substitutes the mass for the individual, see *Who We Are,* pp. 23-25, 104-5.

23. A. M. Dubarle, *The Biblical Doctrine of Original Sin,* trans. E. M. Stewart (London: Geoffrey Chapman, 1964), p. 66.

24. In the words Milton put in God's mouth, "I made him [Adam] just and right,/ sufficient to have stood, though free to fall" *(Paradise Lost* 3.98-99). Matt. 19:8 at least suggests a primal state of integrity. For cautions against a too quick assumption that Eccles. 7:29 actually is intended to refer to the Genesis account of the Fall, however, see Dubarle, *Biblical Doctrine of Original Sin,* pp. 90-91.

25. Pannenberg, *Anthropology in Theological Perspective,* trans. Matthew J. O'Connell (Philadelphia: Westminster, 1985), pp. 20, 57. Calvin, *Institutes of the Christian Religion,* ed. John T. McNeill, trans. Ford L. Battles (Philadelphia: Westminster, 1960), 1.15.8; the Reformed confessions are much more modest.

perform.[26] Without speculating on the length of the stay in Eden, we would nonetheless note that the story makes it at least long enough to name the animals and recognize Eve with joy, which we would understand to be actions, and actions not tainted by sin. Pascal notes movingly that even our consciousness of our wretchedness is an evidence of our greatness and of what we have lost: "For who is unhappy at not being a king, except a deposed king? . . . Who is unhappy at having only one mouth? And who is not unhappy at having only one eye? Probably no man ever ventured to mourn at not having three eyes. But any one is inconsolable at having none" (*Pensées*, #409).

Idyllic pictures of humankind's original blessed state may, in a sense, be thought of as a reading back of the creation as restored by Christ into the original creation (and it may be that pictures of the Garden of Eden as a vegetarian "peaceable kingdom" where the lion and lamb lie down together are a similar reading back of that which is yet future).[27] The idea of original righteousness does not require such exalted views of the first pair's capacities. All it requires is that God had indeed made them in his image, with awareness of a relationship to him, of his command, and of right and wrong as related to that command. It requires only that primitive awareness of self and of God that

---

26. See Niebuhr, *The Nature and Destiny of Man* (New York: Scribners, 1941), 1:276-80. Niebuhr found a kind of support for his position in the view of Irenaeus, that Adam's very first act was marked by sin, so that that righteousness which preceded the Fall was of exceedingly short duration. 2 Enoch 32 allowed 5½ hours (chapters 30 and 31 attributed to Adam vast excellencies).

27. To speak of a reading back of what will be restored in Christ is emphatically not to posit a paradise to be achieved at the end of history by evolution or human "progress" (see, for the popularity of the latter view, George Vandervelde, *Original Sin: Two Major Trends in Contemporary Roman Catholic Reinterpretation* [Amsterdam: Rodopi N.V., 1975], p. 43; contrast the less-than-sanguine discussion of "progress" in *Who We Are*, pp. 372-73). Surely it would take an extreme optimist to suggest that human moral excellence shows any signs of increasing. R. S. Nye, who sharply doubted Coué's cheerful motto, "Day by day in every way we are getting better and better," while taking the quality of people produced to be the sign of any real progress, remarked, "We have nailed that standard [Coué's] to the masthead, deserted the helm and gone below to speed up the engines, happy in the thought that all motion must necessarily be onward, and that the only requisite is speed" (quoted in Wayland Maxfield Parrish, *Reading Aloud* [New York: Thomas Nelson, 1936], pp. 107-8). My judgment is equally pessimistic. Humankind is, however, restored to the Second Adam, not to the First; restored by grace and not by human progress.

can differentiate between turning one's will toward God in obedience and turning it away from him in disobedience; it involves conscience as an essential aspect of humanness.[28] As long as the relationship to God is fully intact, relationship to the human other will also be intact. In any case, moral excellence is not a matter of intelligence, technical achievement, and sophistication, but of purity of the will. Similarly, moral obligation rests not upon the completeness of one's knowledge of the consequences of one's acts, but upon the relationship that brings the obligation.[29]

Despite the goodness of the original creation and the gift of an initially positive orientation toward God,[30] which is original righteousness, something was yet to be desired in this original relationship with God. Even though it was a positive disposition and not a case of the will poised neutrally, so to speak, between good and evil, it still came short of perfection.[31] It had about it an aspect of contingency, of mutability. That is, two possibilities lay before the first couple: they could continue in obedience and be confirmed in goodness, thus attaining a

28. See *Who We Are,* esp. pp. 78, 86.

29. We might note by way of analogy that those who "make history," lack the perspective of history and in the critical moments are generally wholly unaware of the long-term repercussions of their acts. Luther, for instance, in nailing his Ninety-Five Theses on the church door at Wittenberg — the town bulletin board — intended simply to prompt debate. It is hardly as if he had thought it over, decided that the time had come for reform in the church, and marched off with his hammer and nails to post notice that the Reformation had begun. Similarly with Calvin's arrival in Geneva. From his point of view at the time, he just chanced to stop over in the city on his flight from France; and little could he realize at the time the significance of his decision to stay there and take up the cause of the Gospel.

30. Note that this positive disposition may be construed as being already a gift of grace — indeed, the whole creation is such. Augustine wanted further to guard against any kind of pre-Fall Pelagianism and insisted that right from the beginning, the possibility of obedience depended upon grace; in his *Enchiridion* (106), the point is made in a way that is quite general and does not entail the opposition between flesh and spirit implied by the developed idea of the *donum superadditum.*

31. Jonathan Edwards, among others, differentiated between disposition and act: the first couple were endowed with righteousness, which he identifies with innocence, at the level of disposition — a sort of potential perfection — but were obligated to act in accord with this disposition; which, until the Fall, they did (*Original Sin,* ed. Clyde A. Holbrook, *The Works of Jonathan Edwards,* vol. 3 [New Haven: Yale University Press, 1970], pp. 228-36).

goodness even beyond that with which they were endowed by the Creator; or they could desert the path of rectitude and lose the good that they had.[32]

Conditions of the Covenant

Probation

The fundamental requirement of the covenant is obedience, obedience to be rendered under the double circumstance of, first, a specific test or probation; and, second, as the narrative unfolds, the surprising intrusion of temptation. In the story the test takes the specific form of a command not to eat of the fruit of the Tree of the Knowledge of Good and Evil.[33] We should not hear this prohibition as a kind of arbitrary taboo with magical disasters attending its breaking, as if the required obedience were a sort of cultic conformity lacking in true moral quality, and as if our first parents could do whatever they pleased as long as they avoided eating the forbidden fruit. Against this sort of thing the prophets protested vehemently as they inveighed against the people of Israel who cried, "the temple of the LORD, the temple of the LORD," but failed to amend their ways and act justly (Jer. 7:4, 5). Nor was the Tree bad in itself. Nor, most certainly, was God indulging a petty jealousy of his creatures, after the manner of a modern cartoon that shows Eve sitting in a garden furnished with an Apple computer and the Serpent whispering in her ear, "Of *course* he told you not to touch it — then *you'd* have access to

---

32. Augustine was the first major theologian to reflect on this distinction as he read the opening chapters of Genesis in the light of the rest of the biblical revelation. He said that humankind was created so as to be able not to sin *(posse non peccare)*. Fallen humankind, by contrast, is in a lost and alienated condition, not able not to sin *(non posse non peccare)*. Humankind as restored by grace in Christ will be confirmed in righteousness, not able to sin *(non posse peccare)*. (See, for instance, Augustine's *Treatise on Rebuke and Grace,* chaps. 31-33.) This handling of the data, followed by later theologians, involves a covenantal approach to the primal history.

33. It is worth noting that while the Tree of Life has parallels in the literature of the ancient East, no parallel to the Tree of the Knowledge of Good and Evil has been found (Delumeau, *History of Paradise,* p. 5).

all the data *he* does." Such an idea goes against everything Scripture reveals to us of God's nature. Instead, we should understand the prohibition as intended to focus human obedience in terms of the will of God alone.[34] The first couple were to obey when there was no obvious reason for the obedience other than the express commandment of God their maker. (Abram, similarly, was commanded to leave Haran [Gen. 12] and did so simply because he was overwhelmingly persuaded that God had told him to — a sobering reminder in a day when many are inclined to submit everything to the bar of their own reason alone and to reject what that reason cannot encompass, as if not God but human reason were the measure of all things.) Further, the prohibition reveals human life as a task to be undertaken in free responsiveness to God, rather than as the mechanical playing out of a predetermined destiny.[35] Thus, though it does constitute a test, the command to Adam and Eve may be seen not as gratuitous provocation by a God whom, under such circumstances, it is difficult to see as acting benevolently, but rather as a gracious reminder of the true state of affairs: that they were not independent but subject to God, and that they must not stray in their fidelity.[36] God's will is the highest expression of the good in human life. Bonhoeffer remarks suggestively that the Tree is placed in the center of the Garden as an indication that that is where God belongs with respect to human life: human limits are found not on the edges, leaving a potential inner boundlessness, but right in the middle.[37]

The Tree itself we might think of as sacramental, as a physical object used to convey a spiritual reality. We are familiar with this idea

---

34. The view is classically expressed by Augustine, *City of God* 13.20.

35. This is the way Barth answers his own query as to why God should have placed a DO NOT ENTER sign over an open door; why not just close the door? (He, however, rejects the idea of probation or testing. See *Church Dogmatics,* ed. G. W. Bromiley and T. F. Torrance, trans. J. W. Edwards, O. Bussey, H. Knight [Edinburgh: T&T Clark, 1958], III/1:263.) A certain poignancy remains in the question as to why the command could not have been made more effective, a question that is heightened when one carries the principle over into redemption and is sometimes led to marvel less at the positive evidences of sanctification than at the paucity thereof; but that is an issue for a later volume.

36. See Thomas Boston, *Human Nature in Its Fourfold State* (Edinburgh: Thomas Nelson, 1840), pp. 23-24.

37. Dietrich Bonhoeffer, *Creation and Fall* and *Temptation,* trans. John C. Fletcher and Kathleen Downham (New York: Macmillan, 1959), pp. 51-53.

from the New Testament, where we have the use of water in baptism and of bread and wine in the Lord's Supper. But such usage is also common enough in the Old Testament, as when, for instance, the bow in the clouds is a kind of sacrament of God's covenant never again to destroy the earth by flood (Gen. 9:12-13). Indeed, all of the blood sacrifices of the Old Testament, and most particularly the Passover, can be looked upon as conveying the spiritual truth that without the shedding of blood there is no forgiveness of sins (Heb. 9:22) — a truth finally fulfilled in the sacrifice of Christ on Calvary.

When we speak of the Tree as sacramental, we do not have in mind merely a kind of negative sacrament, whereby humankind indeed became aware of good and evil when they partook of the Tree, but in a disastrous way: aware of good in the loss of it and of evil in the experience of it. Rather, we suspect that even had our first parents sustained the test, they would have become aware of good and evil, though in a very different way. We can suggest this positive outcome only by the use of analogy, since we have no direct experience of it. Consider, though, that any test with a moral edge, any struggle between right and wrong, produces an ethical awareness, deepens and heightens the meaning of right and wrong. Such knowledge would, again, not have been identical with the knowledge our first parents actually obtained, yet it would truly have been a knowledge of good and evil, and it would have been a knowledge connected with a higher blessedness than they had had before they were tested and had encountered the Tempter.[38]

What, exactly, "knowledge of good and evil" (הַדַּעַת טוֹב וָרָע, Gen. 2:17) means has been subject to long and largely inconclusive debate. Some have suggested that it refers to alternate outcomes of the pro-

---

38. As Dante put it: "'Twas not the tasting of the fruit that hath,/My son, earned of itself such banishment,/But solely the transgression from the path" (*Paradise,* trans. D. L. Sayers and B. Reynolds [Baltimore: Penguin, 1962]: 26.115-18; see 19.46-48 for a related remark about Satan) — not knowledge in the sense of abstract understanding but disobedience is the key thing. C. S. Lewis remarks that it is possible to think of evil without being evil, just as it is possible to think of a triangle without being one (*Preface to Paradise Lost* [London: Oxford University Press, 1942], p. 83), a seemingly obvious truth. However, it may well be that thinking of evil without in some sense participating in it is possible only to unfallen humanity and to God (Gen. 3:22), as the insidious influence of exposure to evil on the actual human psyche shows. Thus Paul solemnly adjures us to think about the things that are good (Phil. 4:8).

bation: if humankind pass the test, they will be confirmed in righteousness and know a more lasting and higher good than they had
known before; if they fail, they will come to know evil in the loss of
the good that they had and in an increasing spiral of actual evils.
Such a reading is plausible and easy but implies that the text puts
good and evil as alternatives, as good *or* evil. But actually, the text
puts good and evil in a relationship of mutuality, so that the Tree me-
diates both rather than one *or* the other. Those who suppose that the
Tree imparted some particular *content* have suggested everything
from sexual knowledge to universal knowledge or omnipotence, with
a kind of secular knowledge of what is useful or helpful versus what
is harmful, and a capacity for moral judgment, in between. All of
these suggestions are problematic. Genesis 2:23-24 and 3:22 would
seem to imply sexual knowledge before the Fall. Extremes can indeed
express totality, as in 2 Samuel 14:17, 20; but humankind certainly did
not achieve omniscience. The text gives no indication of an increase
in worldly knowledge. One can hardly imagine a Hebrew asserting
that God wished to prevent moral judgment; and besides, how can
there be such a thing as disobedience unless one already has a moral
sense or conscience?[39] We would incline to the view that the Tree offered the power of rational and ethical discrimination, a power for
which, apart from the simplest awareness of themselves as rightly oriented toward rather than away from God, Adam and Eve would have
had no need before their disobedience;[40] but which could, as one can
see from our exposition above, come as a positive good out of the
process of undergoing probation. (As a positive good, it could con-
note a kind of maturing; and we do see this sense in Greek literature
of an admittedly later date, as in Telemachus's comment in the *Odyssey,* "I am grown up now to the knowledge of good and evil and understand what is going on.")[41] When Adam and Eve disobeyed, however, this power of discrimination became the will to decide for

39. For this summary, see Brevard Childs, "Tree of Knowledge, Tree of Life," in
George A. Buttrick et al., eds., *Interpreter's Dictionary of the Bible,* 4 vols. (New York:
Abingdon, 1962), 4:695-97; see also Westermann, *Genesis 1-11,* pp. 242-45.

40. See James Barr, *The Garden of Eden and the Hope of Immortality* (Minneapolis: Fortress, 1992), p. 62.

41. Homer, *The Iliad* and *The Odyssey,* trans. Samuel Butler, *Great Books,* vol. 4 (Chicago: Encyclopaedia Britannica, 1952), 20.299.

themselves what is good and evil in independence from God, which could only yield further disaster.[42]

Temptation

Now comes the great mystery of these opening chapters of the Bible — indeed, among the greatest mysteries to be found anywhere in Scripture (and a mystery that we will take up in various ways below, pp. 38-42): not only must our first parents undergo probation; they must do so under conditions of temptation, of a solicitation to do evil. Temptation must be sharply differentiated from probation, which can be described as a trying or testing or proving. Probation has as its purpose not destruction but strengthening, confirmation in righteousness. Temptation, by contrast, intends destruction by seducing, weakening, and degrading humankind.[43] Obviously, temptation cannot be God's work: the Scriptures say that God tempts no one and no one should accuse God of such an act (James 1:13).[44]

42. See Berkouwer, *Sin,* trans. Philip C. Holtrop (Grand Rapids: Eerdmans, 1971), pp. 271-72; see also Barth, *Church Dogmatics,* III/1:287. This interpretation is found also in Aquinas, *Summa Theologica,* Part 2-2, Q. 163, Art. 2. Christof Gestrich, however, denies that ability to discriminate good from evil eventuates from the Fall, arguing instead that involvement in sin makes proper discernment impossible — a conclusion that differs more in form than in substance from what we have affirmed, insofar as we have agreed that moral judgment apart from God is no proper judgment (*The Return of Splendor in the World: The Christian Doctrine of Sin and Forgiveness,* trans. Daniel W. Bloesch [Grand Rapids: Eerdmans, 1997], p. 173).

43. For a description of the tragedy that ensues all around when probation and temptation are confused, see the story "The Novel of the Ill-advised Curiosity" in Cervantes' *Don Quixote,* trans. John Ormsby, *Great Books,* vol. 29 (Chicago: Encyclopaedia Britannica, 1952), pp. 120-37.

44. The issue here is complicated by old English usage, which sometimes uses the word "tempt" in the sense of "test" or "try": hence one finds the KJV speaking of God tempting Abraham (Gen. 22:1), though elsewhere it translates the same word as "prove"; and the psalmist can even ask the Lord to "try" him in the sense of proving him (Ps. 26:2). The Hebrew root נסה, like the Greek πειράζω, can be translated either way; and it may indeed sometimes be the inner intention leading to the act that differentiates the two: the same overt act could be motivated by entirely different intentions. As with many translation problems, context is everything in these matters (though context will not always suffice, as the debate about how to render a petition in so central a text as the Lord's Prayer shows [Matt. 6:13]). Furthermore, while the key term does not occur in the

In Genesis 3, temptation confronts humankind as a superior, master intelligence in the form of a serpent. And while we could not possibly think of the serpent as sacramental in a positive sense, we could perhaps see it as a symbol of evil, as a sort of counterfeit sacrament, like the counterfeit miracles in the book of Revelation. On the natural level the serpent is simply said to be subtle or crafty, more so than any other wild animal the LORD had made. So, when we associate it with that Tempter of superior intelligence that is Satan, we are of course reading the narrative in the light of subsequent biblical revelation (e.g., Rev. 12:9; 20:2; see also John 8:44).[45]

From the narrative itself, we learn something of the nature of temptation. It is, first of all, artful and designing; it raises doubts and questions about what God said, putting a fatal gap between hearing God's command and obeying it, a gap in which one's own reasonings reign supreme. It pulls one away from the simple and immediate relationship with God. More particularly, it involves distortion of the truth: this is the factor of subtlety underscored in the story. The serpent told Adam and Eve that their eyes would be opened when they ate of the fruit, and indeed they were. Only they did not see what they thought they would see. And so it is with temptation: it presents as good something that is actually evil. So it is, in fact, with evil in general: it has the appearance of good. A lie would not work unless it contained a great

MT or the LXX of Genesis 3:1-19, the idea of temptation is unequivocally present. Clearly, then, one must use theological judgment in one's choice of vocabulary and one's exposition. See Heinrich Seesemann, "πείρα, κτλ," *TDNT* 6:23-36; and for complexities in the relationship of testing and temptation, see Marguerite Shuster, "The Temptation, Sinlessness, and Sympathy of Jesus: Another Look at the Dilemma of Hebrews 4:15," in Marguerite Shuster and Richard A. Muller, eds., *Perspectives on Christology: Essays in Honor of Paul K. Jewett* (Grand Rapids: Zondervan, 1991), pp. 195-209.

45. The identification was made by Justin Martyr in the second century, an identification that has persisted ever since (Jeffrey Burton Russell, *The Prince of Darkness: Radical Evil and the Power of Good in History* [Ithaca, NY: Cornell University Press, 1988], p. 63). Only slightly later Irenaeus (*Against Heresies* 3.23.7) brought together the serpent of Genesis, that of Revelation, and those of Luke 10:19. A significantly earlier instance, however, may be found in the Wisdom of Solomon 2:24: "Through the devil's envy death entered the world" (see Barr, *Garden of Eden*, p. 17). Even apart from a direct original identification, which can be argued against on the grounds that the developed idea of Satan belongs to a later period than that of Genesis 3, the demonic, anti-God character of the serpent makes interpreting it in terms of Satan a sound intuition (Walther Eichrodt, *Theology of the Old Testament*, 2 vols., trans. J. A. Baker [Philadelphia: Westminster, 1967], 2:405).

deal of truth. Traditional rat poison seduced its prey by being 96 percent good corn meal and only about 4 percent arsenic.

We also learn from the introduction of the Tempter that sin did not originate with humankind but was suggested to them from without — an observation that does not solve but only pushes farther back the larger problem of evil, but which does in some sense mitigate the fault of our first parents. To be seduced to sin is not quite the same thing as inventing it. Also, their acquiescence constituted their sin, not the external suggestion itself: insofar as there is no inner resonance to the suggestion, it is no sin to be presented with temptation. As the line in the old gospel song goes, "Yield not to temptation, for yielding is sin." However, this hymn line, which we affirm as good pastoral advice to those plagued with a scrupulous conscience, may yet be accused of not quite probing the depth of the temptation problem. Part of the trouble is that we use the same phrase — "to be tempted" — to refer both to recognition of the act of one who would seduce us and to the inner struggle we may experience in response; but these are neither the same thing nor necessarily concomitants of one another. Someone can "tempt" me by passing me a joint of marijuana without my feeling "tempted" to smoke it. Another problem is that, from our fallen perspective, we tend to attribute virtue to one who *overcomes* a strong inner impulse rather than to one who does not experience the impulse in the first place; but surely that judgment is mistaken.

Many have argued that it is impossible to succumb to temptation unless there has been some prior inclination to turn away from God's will.[46] Even to experience a suggestion as internally tempting involves this departure from simple and cheerful responsiveness to God. In some sense, that is, sin presupposes sin. In that sense, the yielding to temptation occurs before one commits any overt act — and the New Testament is quite clear that wrong attitudes and impulses, not just overt acts, are sins (take Jesus' condemnation of lustful thoughts in Matt. 5:28, for instance). For the purposes of our argument here, we need not deny that inner resonance to an evil suggestion is key. We claim only that, in this first instance, the suggestion came from the outside, as the story says.

46. E.g., Wolfhart Pannenberg, *Systematic Theology*, 3 vols., trans. G. W. Bromiley (Grand Rapids: Eerdmans, 1988-93), 2:213, noting earlier work by Schleiermacher.

The Threat of Death

Adam and Eve underwent probation and temptation in the context of a clear warning of the consequences of disobedience: "in the day that you eat [of the Tree] you shall die" (Gen. 2:17).[47] In Scripture "death" has a threefold meaning, being a judicial, a spiritual, and also a physical reality; and theologians speak of it in all of these ways. Each evidences in a different manner the essential quality of death as separation from God, which renders life meaningless, wretched, and miserable.

As a judicial reality, death means that we are under the wrath and curse of God, as were our first parents once they had fallen. The fellowship they had hitherto known with God was lost. God's countenance was changed toward them (Luther); God had become the angry God. And this judicial sense carries over to hell as the second death. Hell is the final form of that misery in which people are aware of God as angry and relate to him in terms of his wrath and condemnation instead of his grace and mercy. They are at enmity with God. They are not apart from God in a neutral sense but are God-forsaken in the sense that they experience his penal displeasure (see Rom. 1:18).

As a spiritual reality, death refers to the change of attitude toward God on the part of humankind. One might consider it a sort of inevitable counterpart to the change in God's attitude toward them. As sinners, humans have lost the inner conformity of their minds and wills to God and hence are at enmity with him. This condition is called "spiritual" death because it has its seat in the essential being, the spirit, of the person.[48] And it is called "death" not because persons have become inactive as spiritual agents but because they have become incapable of restoring and renewing their inner conformity to the will of God. To be "dead through trespasses and sins" (Eph. 2:1; see also Rom. 7:9-10; Col. 2:13; 1 Tim. 5:6) is to live in a state of opposition to God beyond any remedy one can devise. The sinner's heart is alienated and separated from God, and she has become depraved and guilty. This condition is

---

47. For further discussion, see below, pp. 230-62, on death as an existential reality. We consider it fruitless to speculate about what a threat of death could mean to Adam and Eve, who had never encountered death. Putting that sort of question is like asking who was Cain's wife — not an issue the writer of the narrative had in mind.

48. For a basically dichotomistic understanding of humankind, see *Who We Are,* pp. 26-99.

reflected in the biblical narrative in the awareness of guilt and shame that leads our first parents to flee from God, to hide, to cover themselves — all things that they had never done before.

Finally, death as a physical reality refers, of course, to the meaning of which we are most aware, since here we are talking about an empirical fact. People die. But theologically speaking, this sense of the word is the least significant.[49] It is, as it were, a parable at the physical level of the deeper reality of judicial and spiritual death. The rupture at the judicial-spiritual level whereby humankind are rent asunder from God, their highest good, is symbolically set forth in the judgment of physical death, whereby humankind are physically rent asunder, soul and body. As such, even though it is not the essential thing, still it is not nothing, not neutral, not an illusion, but a curse, the grim reaper and the last enemy to be destroyed. Thus, the words of God to the fallen pair, "you are dust, and to dust you shall return" (Gen. 3:19), should be read not as mere description but as judgment.[50] Conversely, only in the overcoming of death can we

49. Augustine and Aquinas (and many others) stoutly denied that Adam would have experienced biological death had he not sinned (e.g., in *On the Merits and Remission of Sins, and on the Baptism of Infants*, 1.2; *City of God*, 13:3; *Summa Theologica*, Pt. I, Q. 98, art. 1). Rather, at a fitting time, he would have been removed "to a better place" without biological death (Augustine, *Enchiridion*, 104). However, it is sufficiently clear that biological death is not the main issue, as evident in Jesus' words (Matt. 10:28; Luke 12:4; John 8:51), that others have not thought it necessary to hold with confidence to the idea that an unfallen humanity would be naturally immortal. It is sin that gives bodily death its dreadful aspect, 1 Cor. 15:56. (See, e.g., Dubarle, *Biblical Doctrine of Original Sin*, pp. 133-34, 234-35.) We would yet caution that speaking in this way should not be taken to imply that death as we know it is "natural." We prefer Milton's poetic conception, that it is a monster brought forth by a union of Satan and Sin (*Paradise Lost*, 2.760-89; see Roland M. Frye, *God, Man, and Satan* [Princeton: Princeton University Press, 1960], pp. 36-38).

50. Note that the threat of judgment and destruction by God is common in Scripture, Old Testament and New, though we would, of course, take later instances to be a playing out of the effects of failure to heed this first warning. As just one example, consider Paul Ricoeur's remarks on the prophets' announcements of impending destruction of the people: "It is, then, under the sign of a total threat and in a sort of aggression of God against his people that man is revealed to himself. One must not weaken this disconcerting 'announcement,' but take it in its initial fury: you shall be destroyed, deported, ravaged. . . . To be a sinner is to find oneself subject to that wrath, involved in that enmity" (*The Symbolism of Evil*, trans. Emerson Buchanan [Boston: Beacon, 1967], p. 54). However, it must also be admitted that death as such is not necessarily seen in the Old Testament as intrusion or punishment, most especially if the deceased has died at a good old age (see Lloyd R. Bailey, Sr., *Biblical Perspectives on Death* [Philadelphia: Fortress, 1979], pp. 23-61).

have assurance of the overcoming of sin: "If Christ has not been raised, your faith is futile and you are still in your sins" (1 Cor. 15:17).[51]

The Promise of Life

The promise of life is implied in the whole covenantal arrangement we have been discussing. Surely if humankind are tested under the threat of death for disobedience, we may infer that a higher blessedness in life will be bestowed if they sustain the probation, having retained their integrity. We would take the Tree of Life in the Garden as sacramental of this higher form of life. And, of course, when we look at the narrative in the context of the Bible as a whole, we perceive that the obedience of Christ as the Second Adam secures for us life in the highest sense of confirmation in righteousness. Furthermore, where the book of Revelation symbolizes and pictures the final state of blessedness, we find no Tree of the Knowledge of Good and Evil, but we do find the Tree of Life (Rev. 22:2), as we have already mentioned in passing. In fact, we find a whole row of trees on either side of the River of Life, bearing fruit monthly. Even the leaves of these trees have healing efficacy.

We can hardly be surprised, then, that Adam and Eve, having failed their probation, are prevented from eating of the Tree of Life by being expelled from the Garden. Note, though, that *before* their failure, no prohibition was attached to this tree, nor is there any sense that those who were in possession of life felt a compelling urge to fortify their grasp of it. Nothing indicates whether or not the first couple actually partook of this tree before the Fall (though the grammar of Gen. 3:22 would appear to make it unlikely that they had). In fact, one of the striking features of the story is the relatively small role this tree has in the development of the narrative.[52] We might compare what happens

---

51. It has sometimes been argued that, at least at the physical level, the threat of death was empty. The serpent was right, it is averred, in his supercilious assurance, "You will not die" (understood to mean, "you will not die immediately," as "in the day that you eat of it" is taken to imply). Westermann, however, denies that בְּיוֹם means "on the very same day": the threat describes a penalty, not an immediate physical consequence (*Genesis 1–11*, p. 224).

52. So both Westermann, *Genesis 1–11*, and Childs, "Tree of Knowledge, Tree of Life." By contrast, Barr, as the title of his book, *The Garden of Eden and the Hope of Immortality*,

after the Fall, however, to certain strictures pertaining to the sacraments of the covenant of grace. Since it is their function to be both sign and seal of the blessing of salvation, life restored in Christ, it would be at best a meaningless and at worst a sacrilegious act to partake of the outward sacraments in hopes of gaining the blessing when one has no inner conformity of heart, no faith to bring to the sacrament (note the warning in 1 Cor. 11:27-29). Similarly, it would have been a mockery if God had allowed our first parents to remain where they had access to the Tree of Life when they had forfeited the right to this life by their sin. This, then, may be the way we should understand the difficult passage Genesis 3:22, where the LORD God says, "'See, the man has become like one of us, knowing good and evil; and now, he might reach out his hand and take also from the tree of life, and eat, and live forever' — הֵן הָאָדָם הָיָה כְּאַחַד מִמֶּנּוּ לָדַעַת טוֹב וָרָע וְעַתָּה פֶּן־יִשְׁלַח יָדוֹ וְלָקַח גַּם מֵעֵץ הַחַיִּים וְאָכַל וָחַי לְעֹלָם. — and the Hebrew breaks off. Whether the text is faulty or whether the author intended this structure, we cannot say. But we might take it to mean that now that humankind are much more fully aware of good and evil and the contrast between what they sought to gain and what they actually lost, God thrust them out of the Garden lest they attempt to steal the blessing surreptitiously by laying hold on the Tree of Life. Such would have been an act of superstition and folly that would only aggravate their guilt. If so, then the phrase, "he might . . . eat and live forever," should be interpreted in terms of Adam's *hope* of living forever. (It would be difficult to suppose that we have here in the Bible an actual presentation of a superstitious and mechanical view of grace that would teach that the fruit of the Tree of Life had in itself the kind of magical potency the explorers vainly sought as they searched for the fountain of youth.)

The Ongoing Status of the Covenant of Works

We have already remarked that, given the representative character of the First Adam's disobedience and the universal quality surely intended

---

would suggest, construes the whole story in its final form as mainly about the loss of a chance for immortality that humankind could conceivably have attained.

in the composition of the story, it is not only proper but necessary to read the narrative existentially as well as in terms of a past event. All of us are involved in Adam and Eve's folly and in their destiny; thus we do not limit our appropriation of the text to interest in it as a piece of history of which the significance is fixed and finished, no matter how serious the ongoing consequences of that piece of history. Similarly with the narrower concept of the covenant of works: though humankind have fallen and have been expelled from the Garden, it does not follow that the theological content of this strand of revelation has no further relevance. To be sure, we are no longer born in any context in which we are put on probation with respect to the fruit of any tree; neither are we starting with a clean slate. But even though we are born sinners and are sinful from our youth upward (Gen. 8:21), we nonetheless are obligated as those created in the divine image to obey God, to love him supremely, and to love our neighbor as ourselves. That our first parents failed to obey the specific divine commandment relating to the Tree removed neither their nor our responsibility to obey God in all things. To say that no human being will be *justified* by deeds prescribed by the law, since by the law is knowledge of sin (Rom. 3:20), is not to imply that we are relieved of our duty to *observe* the law.

Hence when we think about salvation and consider salvation as a covenant of grace, we must remember that the covenant of grace does not simply set aside the conditions of the covenant of works. Rather, Christ himself obeyed for us and suffered the sanctions of the law in our place. He did not undergo probation in the specific form in which our first parents faced it, but he did undergo it representatively, vicariously, in just as real a sense. In fact, he rendered whole-souled and perfect obedience, fully conforming his life both outwardly and inwardly to the will of his Father, under circumstances that were even more difficult than those the First Adam faced. He identified with us in our sinful humanity (Heb. 4:15), he came in the likeness of sinful flesh (Rom. 8:3), and he countered the Tempter (Matt. 4:1-11; Luke 4:1-13). He lived in a world already vitiated by sin, wherein the force and power of Satan are everywhere apparent; so in keeping his integrity under temptation, his achievement was vastly greater than what was asked of the First Adam. The concept of vicarious obedience (and the death of Christ as a vicarious satisfaction offered in obedience to God, fulfilling the demands of the divine justice on our behalf) presupposes that the fundamental structure of human existence as one in which we humans owe such absolute obedience to our Maker, has not been abrogated. Rather, it is now graciously fulfilled by another on our behalf — our Savior, our Second Adam.[53]

---

53. It would be a reasonable implication of this position that, as Jonathan Edwards held, the covenant of works remains in force as the basis of Christ's final judgment of the wicked: see the sermon, "The Excellency of Christ" in his *Discourses on Various Important Subjects Nearly Concerning the Great Affair of the Soul's Eternal Salvation* (Boston: S. Kneeland and T. Green, 1738), p. 257.

On Doing What We Can

A Sermon Preached by Marguerite Shuster
at La Verne Heights Presbyterian Church, La Verne, California
Lord's Day, January 12, 1997

Now the serpent was more crafty than any other wild animal that the
LORD God had made. He said to the woman, "Did God say, 'You shall
not eat from any tree in the garden'?" The woman said to the serpent,
"We may eat of the fruit of the trees in the garden; but God said, 'You
shall not eat of the fruit of the tree that is in the middle of the garden, nor
shall you touch it, or you shall die.'" But the serpent said to the woman,
"You will not die; for God knows that when you eat of it your eyes will be
opened, and you will be like God, knowing good and evil." So when the
woman saw that the tree was good for food, and that it was a delight to
the eyes, and that the tree was to be desired to make one wise, she took of
its fruit and ate; and she also gave some to her husband, who was with
her, and he ate. Then the eyes of both were opened, and they knew that
they were naked; and they sewed fig leaves together and made loincloths
for themselves.

GENESIS 3:1-7 (NRSV)

"Just do what you can," we say, understanding that there are, after all, limits in life, but wishing it were not so. "I did what I could," we protest, admitting less than perfect results and hoping to be excused for at least trying. "I'll do what I can," we promise ourselves — hoping, perhaps, that by stating this year's New Year's resolution in somewhat less than absolute terms, we will manage to feel less utterly defeated than we did last year. "Do what you can": the phrase is tinged with hope and with regret, but especially with regret for what lies beyond our reach, beyond our strength, beyond our competence or knowledge. "Something there is that doesn't love a wall,/That wants it down," wrote Robert Frost; and we know what he means in more arenas of life than just the relationships between neighbors.[1] Something in us resists restrictions, period. So we admire those who crash through barriers: the Olympic athletes who, some six months ago, broke long-standing records; the Nobel Prize winners who a few weeks ago were rewarded for breaking new ground in their respective fields. These people expand our view of what can be done, maybe give us new hope of what even we can do (as burgeoning sales of sports and exercise equipment after the Olympics always demonstrate). Sometimes it seems as if no limit at all could really prove permanent. Do what you can. You'll be amazed at what you can achieve. True enough, as far as it goes.

And yet. . . . A doubt creeps in. Do we, really, *always* want to do all we can, or to have it done on our behalf? Consider. If you have accompanied someone to the hospital recently, or have had surgery yourself, you probably know that most hospitals today will ask you right at the registration table if you have a living will or a durable power of attorney for health care. Why? Because, when they think about it, a rather large number of people want to make as sure as they can that under certain dire circumstances in which they cannot speak for themselves, someone else will *not* decide to do all that current medical technology can provide. We *can* do more than a great many people think we *should* do, or than it is *good* that we do. Or, if you have children, are you entirely pleased at all the options open to them today that might not have been open a few generations ago? Sure, they *can* do all kinds of things, try all kinds of things. But most of you will do everything in your power to make certain that they don't. Once in a while a few brave or foolhardy souls, mildly and tentatively, ask questions even about the endeavors of our scientists and technicians, wondering if entering into certain arenas and breaking certain barriers might not do more harm than good. Yet raising such questions makes many of us anxious, for we have been well taught that nothing must inhibit our restless search for more knowledge; which, we somehow suppose, is what promises to deliver us from our human ills. And thereby hangs a tale.

It's a very old tale, set in a time before there were human ills to worry about. Even then human freedom chafed at limits, even then when limits didn't threaten to thwart the expected triumph over some

---

1. From "Mending Wall," in Robert Frost, *Selected Poems* (New York: Park Lane Press, 1992), p. 88.

disease or other evil. Even in Paradise the serpentine voice inquires, "Did God really say you couldn't . . . ?" suggesting, by the way, that more was off limits than really was, and all the while managing to insinuate that this whole business of "this far and no farther" was hardly reasonable. Surely *God* wouldn't say anything like that? What *kind* of God would say that? "Oh no," said Eve, presumably with Adam close at hand; "he didn't say that. Not all of *that*. He mentioned just this one thing, along with something that sounded odd if we disobeyed — death, whatever that is." "Hrrumph," goes the voice. "You won't die" ["you don't have to believe that old fuddy-duddy God," that is]. (And, of course — and here's a hard part — in one sense, the crass, immediate, physical sense, the serpentine voice was right. Whatever happened to their spirits, the first couple's bodies kept right on going for the time being. It's still true: you can break all kinds of rules and not drop dead immediately, no matter what your mother or your pastor or your teacher seemed to imply; and everybody who has taken Psychology 101 or taken her puppy to dog school knows that postponed punishment doesn't work very well.) "You won't *die*," said the voice. "No indeed-y. You'll just learn some things that God of yours doesn't want you to know because then you'll be just like him — knowing about good and evil and all." It sounded pretty tantalizing, especially to folks who didn't know anything about evil. (But then, you never know ahead of time the full results of your choices and never suppose the evil could outweigh the good.) After all, the argument made sense. Why should anyone want — for good motives, anyway — to keep us from knowing things and from being all we can be? What is this — cosmic censorship? That's even worse than Internet censorship! Isn't it a good thing to grow up, become independent, be able to decide for yourself? In fact, how could you keep your self-respect if you just kept submitting meekly, without even knowing what the alternative was? Get a life! Do what you can.

They bit. And we keep right on biting, still not quite clear on just where the lie is in all of this. Because the arguments still sound pretty persuasive. And more than a little up-to-date. The mystery of human freedom, you see, is that we *can* do more than we *should* do. It is not the powers we lack, but the powers we have, that do us in.

We mustn't — we *mustn't* — do all we can. "Try it, you'll like it," the serpentine voice wheedles, without adding the relevant footnote that once we've tried it, it won't matter if we like it, because the way back to the Garden is barred by a fiery sword. The pregnant teen tells the truth when she says she only tried it once. But there's no going back. No matter what choice she makes now, her life has changed forever. With the best scientific will in the world, our scientists discovered that in the course of their efforts, they had made us some plutonium; and then, with a somewhat less good will, we kept producing more plutonium; and now what? Have you followed the news stories? How do we get rid of the fifty tons of weapons-grade plutonium we would like to dispose of (not to mention keep "safe" the remaining tens of tons we want to have on hand "just in case")? Shall we burn it? Shall we encase it in glass and bury it? Because the trouble is, you see, that a single microgram of the stuff can produce lung cancer; and it does not lose its toxicity for 250,000 years. It's almost a parable of sin: the tiniest amount is deadly; and once it has entered in, you can try to contain its effects, but there is no way to get rid of it. There's no going back.

The other thing (the thing we understand, if anything, even less well, recognize even less clearly) is that, paradoxically, we *can't* do all we can. What I mean by that seeming contradiction is the simple fact that every choice we make excludes, and often excludes permanently, many other possible choices. You can't go to the ball game and the party at the same time. You can't be a Trappist monk and a politician and an experimental physicist, even if you theoretically have gifts for them all. You can't have both all the joys of motherhood and all the freedom of a single person, even though both are perfectly honorable choices. Don't let those who tell you (in a wheedling voice?) that you can have it all deceive you, whatever examples they may give of persons who have achieved remarkable breadth. There is always a cost, which usually leaves those who have been seduced by the promises baffled at what went wrong.

And this point is even more critical when we stop talking just about choices that are indifferent or good in themselves, and turn to those that are between a lesser and a greater good, or, most important of all, between good and evil, or between ourselves and God. Put it bluntly: we cannot focus on God and on ourselves and our presumed rights and privileges at the same time. Think about how it was in the Garden of Eden: the problem really came not with the bite of fruit: that just clinched matters. It came when the first couple, with the help of the

wheedling voice, conceived the possibility that there might be goods
outside of God, and that they should look to themselves and their desires and daring and ingenuity instead of to God for good things. As
soon as that thought arose, the whole disastrous train of doubt and
unbelief and pride that produced the fatal disobedience was set in motion.

The forbidden tree was in the center of the Garden. As such, it
points to the truth that God's will as he has revealed it to us — whether
we understand all the reasons for what he tells us or not — must be at
the center of our lives. The limit is not at the edges of our experience, as
if we were trapped in a larger or smaller cage, but at the center: if we are
rightly related to the center, we will not have to worry about the edges.
Once we turn away, no edge will hold; for there is no convincing way of
saying why the boundary should be placed here rather than there.

Or change the figure. Consider the mirror, and our fascination with
mirrors — with looking at ourselves. In one of his folk sermons, James
Weldon Johnson pictured Satan flattering Eve in the Garden and presenting her with a mirror — a powerful insight into the deadly dynamic
of turning one's attention toward oneself.[2] I am told that in the literature of the occult — that prime way of getting power without God —
there is a striking preoccupation with mirrors. In seventeenth-century
churchman Jeremy Taylor's famous devotional work *Holy Living*, he
wrote, "Let thy face like *Moses* shine to others, but make no looking-
glasses for thyself."[3] Anything morally worthy in ourselves is corrupted
if we wish to admire ourselves. And someone else remarked that there
are no mirrors in heaven. There couldn't be, for the mirror is the symbolic antithesis of a glad, free offering of our full attention to God and
his purposes.

God's will at the center of life; God as the only real source of good;
the fact that there is nothing that is finally good that we can seize in opposition to God's will, no matter what the latest seducer may try to tell
us: that's the point. But even so we *can* turn away, turn to ourselves and
our own ways. To do so is in our power. That is the terrible possibility of
our freedom. And if the truth were to be told, we would have to admit

2. James Weldon Johnson, *God's Trombones* (New York: Viking, 1957), p. 32.
3. Jeremy Taylor, *Holy Living*, ed. P. G. Stanwood (Oxford: Clarendon Press, 1989),
p. 91 (italics in original).

that we already have turned away, many times. And we will again, because the way back to the Garden is barred and the wheedling voice of the ruler of this world, that old serpent, retains its terrible plausibility.

The way back is barred. Barred utterly and finally. No one with the slightest spiritual insight will suppose herself to be able to regain her innocence, much as she may be rightly instructed by the fault of our first parents. The loss is irreversible. But not unredeemable. The way forward is open, and open because of One who, tempted in every way as we are, yet did not do all that he could have. Do you remember? The first time it was in a desert, not a garden, but the voice was the familiar serpentine one. "Turn these stones to bread," it said to the desperately hungry Jesus. Food again. Bodily desires can be compelling. And Jesus replied that we do not live by bread alone: even the most natural, the most necessary, the most surely good things can be wrongly taken — most surely wrongly taken if we think even for a minute that they can ultimately satisfy. "Throw yourself down from the pinnacle of the temple," said the voice. "Don't you believe it where it says that angels will bear you up? You won't die." Sound familiar? But Jesus knew the difference between believing God and testing him; and he refused. "Rule all the kingdoms of the world. Be all you can be, more than anyone ever dreamed of being before. All you have to do is turn away from God and worship me," the voice offered, with oppressive reasonableness. And Jesus sent him away (Matt. 4:1-11). That was the first time. The last time it was a Garden again, and someone accompanying Jesus tried to use a sword to ward off those who had come to arrest him. Jesus said, "Do you think that I cannot appeal to my Father, and he will at once send me more than twelve legions of angels? But how then would the scriptures be fulfilled, which say it must happen in this way?" (Matt. 26:53-54). He didn't do what he could. Instead, he obeyed God, and he died. Not the way, by our lights, it should have come out. But that is the trouble with second-guessing God. For death is not the last word. The apostle Paul tells us that this One who (unlike our first parents) did *not* consider equality with God something to be grasped, and who was obedient even unto death, was therefore highly exalted by God, and given the name that is above every name, so that at the name of Jesus every knee should bend, in heaven and on earth and under the earth, and every tongue should confess that Jesus Christ is Lord, to the glory of God the Father (Phil. 2:6-11). And all because he didn't do all that he could.

This is the One who holds our future in his hand. To come to him is to admit once and for all that nothing we can do can save us from our spiraling futility; that many things we can do will destroy us and others in ways we cannot foresee or imagine; and that we desperately need a limit at the center of our lives. It is to come in humility and belief and the desire to obey, knowing that that means we must often refuse to do all that we can. Then, and only then, may we begin to glimpse the real secret: when the limit at the center holds steady, in the profoundest sense the limits that trap us are gone. For we are held by the God who is able to work in us more than all we can ask or imagine (Eph. 3:20). As John says, "We are God's children now; what we will be has not yet been revealed. What we do know is this: when he is revealed, we will be like him, for we will see him as he is" (1 John 3:2). What we can never seize will be given us as a gift.

2

The Root of the Fall

Humankind, created in the image of God, endowed with an inner self conformed to the will of God their Maker, transgressed the divine will. But why? How could such a thing be? No answer to that question can be given at the level of causality (a philosophically controverted enough idea in any case, though here used in the rough-and-ready sense of that which is sufficient to produce a particular effect), as if, given the conditions they faced, our first parents could have done nothing other than fall. Temptation did not cause the Fall, though it certainly offered the opportunity for it. Our first parents' immaturity, innocence, and finitude did not in themselves make it inevitable that they would stumble; nor did they simply "fall short" of an ideal they might have attained rather than "fall away" from a state of holiness.[1] The Fall was not really "upward," as if a rising consciousness vital to true humanity could appear only along with self-assertive choice over against God: Jesus, the exemplar of true humanity, was without sin, obedient to his Father in all things. No; we may find occasions and make excuses for the Fall, but we do not find a cause.

---

1. This last alternative was the view of Jonathan Edwards's opponent John Taylor, among others; see Hilrie Shelton Smith, *Changing Conceptions of Original Sin: A Study in American Theology Since 1750* (New York: Scribners, 1955), p. 17.

The Fall and Human Freedom and Responsibility

No external power or suggestion coming upon a person from the outside can compel that person, insofar as she is a free and rational agent, to commit a voluntary and responsible act of sin — the all too familiar sort of sin regarding which we say, or would say if we were being strictly honest, "Yes, I knew better, but I did it anyway." We have tried to put that affirmation carefully, for, a fortiori after the Fall, there are always factors of environment and genetics, not to mention impositions of physical force, that compromise freedom and rationality. Those wishing to change the behavior or commitments of others may use everything from mind-altering drugs to extremes of torture, and in a significant percentage of cases they will succeed in producing, say, the "confession" they are seeking. The problem here, though, is not whether to maintain the traditional view; but rather, in the light of the obvious truth of the traditional view, how to discern to what degree a person remains a free and responsible agent when she has been submitted to extremes of coercion.

Psychologists have probed the question of why some people are "survivors" and manage to hold out when others break down. The moral question, however, cannot be answered at this observable level, for one cannot necessarily tell from the outside at just what point a given person has been destroyed as a moral agent. (Hence judgment rests with God, Deut. 32:35; Rom. 12:19; Heb. 10:30.) In an early study of techniques used on prisoners in China, Robert Jay Lifton sought to disabuse people of seeing "brainwashing" as an "all-powerful, irresistible, unfathomable, and magical method of achieving total control over the human mind." He continued, "It is of course none of these things, and this loose usage makes the word a rallying point for fear, resentment, urges toward submission, justification for failure, irresponsible accusation and for a wide gamut of emotional extremism."[2] He acknowledged, however, that "the experiences had such magnitude that they affected every prisoner in some measure, no matter what his background and character."[3] One may be struck particularly by the testimony of

2. Robert Jay Lifton, *Thought Reform and the Psychology of Totalism: A Study of "Brainwashing" in China* (New York: W. W. Norton, 1961), p. 4.

3. Lifton, *Thought Reform*, p. 67.

priests who explicitly sought to rely upon God in the midst of their torment, but yielded significantly all the same.

Even so, experts are inclined to doubt that the human will can *permanently* be overpowered by psychological techniques. During the Korean War, for example, thousands of Americans were incarcerated and subjected to "brainwashing," and about half of them collaborated to one degree or another with their captors; but when the war was over, only twenty-five of the some 2,500 who remained alive refused repatriation — fewer than the number of Confederate and Union soldiers who refused to come home after the Civil War.[4] Not a very impressive success ratio even with the application of extreme pressure; and this relative failure takes place with respect to those already vitiated by the Fall. Absent captivity and physical pressure, the power of "brainwashing" is still more questionable: in such cases, even the American legal system has been increasingly reluctant to see people as prone to be so coerced psychologically that they cannot act freely.[5] The view that resists seeing the human will as hopelessly vulnerable and malleable echoes the classic Puritan concept of the integrity of the self which we find in Milton's *Comus*. In the poem, the villainous sorcerer seeks to divest a virgin of her chastity by bringing her to a stately palace, presenting her with dainties, and putting her in an enchanted chair; yet he does not succeed in his design:

Comus. Nay Lady sit; if I but wave this wand,
Your nerves are all chain'd up in Alabaster,
And you a statue; or as *Daphne* was
Root-bound, that fled *Apollo.*
La. Fool do not boast,
Thou canst not touch the freedom of my minde
With all thy charms, although this corporal rinde
Thou haste immanacl'd. . . .[6]

---

4. H. Newton Malony, "Brainwashing and Religion: A Current Problem," lecture given at Fuller Theological Seminary, Jan. 17, 1996.

5. See, e.g., Dick Anthony and Thomas Robbins, "Negligence, Coercion, and the Protection of Religious Belief," *Journal of Church and State* 37:3 (Fall 1995): 509-36.

6. John Milton, *Comus, Great Books,* vol. 32 (Chicago: Encyclopaedia Britannica, 1948), ll. 659-66.

Similarly Bunyan, speaking of the allegorical town of "Mansoul" as Lucifer is planning his attack: "*Mansoul* were a strong people, . . . nor can they by any means be won but by their own consent."[7]

Let there be no mistake: Adam and Eve were subjected to no coercion. Nothing in the serpent's suggestion made Adam and Eve its helpless victims. They were, however, seduced and deceived by a mastermind of evil. The presence of the serpent gives a sort of depth dimension to moral evil: the fall of humankind is part of a larger conspiracy which in traditional theology has been associated with the fall of Satan and certain of the angels (an obscure event that nonetheless has a clear promised outcome, with Satan, the Beast, the False Prophet, and all who follow after them being irrevocably destroyed by the victorious Christ [Rev. 20]). Thus, human sin is a manifestation in the human realm of a larger kingdom of moral evil; and so we find throughout Scripture the thought that salvation involves much more than simply overcoming our own weaknesses. "Our struggle is not against enemies of blood and flesh, but against the rulers, against the authorities, against the cosmic powers of this present darkness, against the spiritual forces of evil in the heavenly places" (Eph. 6:12). Thoughts of this kind are so endemic to the whole New Testament — Gospels, Acts, Epistles, Apocalypse — that we should hesitate to set them aside as belonging merely to the primitive mythology of another age. Everywhere the work of Christ is set forth as a destruction of the powers of the demonic (e.g., John 12:31; Col. 2:15; Heb. 2:14, 15; see also the so-called *protevangelium,* Gen. 3:15, which surely suggests that deliverance from the Tempter will come from one who, though born of a woman, is more than a human being). And of course it must be set forth in this way, for humankind's ruin came through the Tempter. In short, we reject a reductionistic, purely horizontal understanding of sin. We understand it first in terms of our relationship to God and our responsibility to him, but secondarily in terms of Satan and the demonic, the personal forces of evil behind the evil manifested in human history.

In our judgment, the reason the Gospels give prominent place to the temptation of Jesus by the Devil (Matt. 4:1-11; Luke 4:1-13; cf. Mark 1:12-13) is to contrast the experience of the First Adam and the Second. Nor was this key instance the only one. It would seem that the whole

---

7. John Bunyan, *The Holy War,* ed. Roger Sharrock and James F. Forrest (New York: Oxford University Press, 1980), p. 12.

narrative of the Gospels suggests that Jesus lived constantly under the temptation of failing to achieve his messianic mission, especially with respect to the supreme obedience required of him, that he submit himself to the will of the Father even unto death. Thus, when he speaks of his death and of the cross, and the disciples are shocked and Peter makes what would seem to be a perfectly natural response — "God forbid it, Lord! This must never happen to you" (Matt. 16:22) — Jesus immediately answers, "Get behind me, Satan!" (Matt. 16:23). We should hear this response not as a rebuke exceeding all bounds, but as Jesus recognizing the subtle voice of the Tempter behind Peter's loving and solicitous words. And Jesus was instantly on his guard to resist the suggestions of the Evil One. As we have said, temptation does not constitute sin; and Jesus, constantly bombarded by satanic suggestions, consistently maintained his integrity.

From what we have already said, it will be evident that we do not excuse, much less condone, the behavior of our first parents on the grounds of their immaturity, as if a little more strength or a longer period of evolution were required before they could be expected to act morally; but that growth was God's intention from the beginning.[8] Recall that sophistication is the initial property of the serpent, and succeeding history gives us little encouragement to believe that increasing human sophistication brings increasing virtue or self-control or genuine piety. Beyond a certain minimum, the effects of greater powers of body or mind are determined not by their quantity but by the direction

---

8. See, for instance, John Hick, *Evil and the God of Love*, rev. ed. (San Francisco: HarperSanFrancisco, 1977). Hick, while explicitly not intending a full exposition of Irenaeus, gets the inspiration for his "Irenaean theology" from certain passages in that church father in which he comments on Adam and Eve's infantile incapacity for perfection; see especially *Against Heresies* 4.38 (ANF, vol. 1). Jeffrey Burton Russell thinks Hick made altogether too much of Irenaeus's weakness theory and took it in a direction inconsistent with the rest of Irenaeus's theology (see his *Satan: The Early Christian Tradition* [Ithaca: Cornell University Press, 1981], p. 82 n. 10). However, the general idea was common enough in the early centuries of the church: Clement of Alexandria also posited Adam and Eve's childishness and spoke of them as adapted for the reception of virtue but not as created possessing it; see his *Stromata* 6.11, 12 (ANF, vol. 2). We might remark the curious anomaly that an idea of our first parents as being in an early stage of development that mitigates their fault has a rather modern ring to it and seems to fit in with an evolutionary point of view; and yet contemporary theologians drawn to this view are highly unlikely to think of the Fall as taking place in time and space.

in which they are applied. Nor would we judge that, before the Fall, finitude by definition puts a person in a position in which doing evil is inevitable. It is true that limits provide opportunities to try to over-reach the limits, but nothing necessitates that one will seek to do so. It is also true that certain choices exclude others, but that does not mean that an unfallen creature must experience choice as entailing painful loss. Presumably one may be simply happy with what one has gained. (The situation is very different after the Fall: we take very seriously both the structural aspects of evil and the myriad situations in which no simply good choice is available.)

In a sense, the problem of consciousness is similar to the problem of finitude: whereas finitude divides by setting limits, consciousness divides by separating the subject from the object. We certainly agree with those who make consciousness in the sense of awareness of self and other essential to our humanity, which we have described in terms of our relationship as an "I" to God as our supreme "Thou" and also to our neighbor as "thou."[9] Where we would differ from those who identify the Fall as the birth of consciousness — and hence as a fall "upward," since without it nothing we know as human could have developed — is, first, that we consider anything that could be construed as the Fall to be possible only for those who are already human, conscious, and responsible; and second, that we do not consider the division intrinsic to consciousness to be *essentially* productive of evil (any more than is finitude as such), but only so as a result of the Fall: Adam recognized and delighted in Eve before the Fall; the two covered themselves and engaged in blaming after the Fall. The Fall, that is, is not a moment in natural history taken alone, but a culpable act by those who are accountable for their actions.[10]

The sin of our first parents — not the suggestion of the sin, but the sin itself — originated with them. It was a conscious, voluntary re-

9. *Who We Are,* pp. 16-23.

10. Thus we would consider such a view as that of Nicolas Berdyaev to be both rather romantic and also somewhat confused. He writes: "Man rejected the bliss and wholeness of Eden and chose the pain and tragedy of cosmic life in order to explore his destiny to its inmost depths. This was the birth of consciousness with its painful dividedness" (*The Destiny of Man,* trans. Natalie Duddington [New York: Harper & Row, 1960], p. 36). But, of course, one who is not yet conscious is not capable of this sort of agency.

sponse to the Tempter's suggestion. It was a mysterious change within their own being which was not forced upon them, not compelled by the Tempter or by the environment, not made inevitable by something in their own constitution as created by God.[11] In a way that is beyond our discovery, there was a free movement of their spirits that contradicted the disposition to love God and serve and obey him with which they were originally endowed. About this event hidden in darkness, the Bible gives us no further information, no theoretical explanation. It simply tells the story of how it came to be. (And the same is true of the mystery of the love of God that saves us.)

Some will have observed that we have made nothing of the Serpent's approach to Eve rather than to Adam, and the reason is not far to seek: so far as we can see, the narrative makes nothing of it — a remarkable enough fact for a text written in an incontrovertibly patriarchal culture. The focus of the narrative at the point of the fatal disobedience is on humankind over against God, not on man and woman in relationship to one another. The text, prior to the Fall, suggests nothing about Eve stepping out of her place with respect to a putative God-given role in creation or in marriage. Similarly, the motives attributed to Eve are, it would appear, generically human motives, not ones peculiarly identified with women. The point is that both Adam and Eve succumbed to temptation and fell; God in no way ratified Adam's attempt to put the blame on Eve. If the results of the Fall are played out somewhat differently in the two sexes, that is another matter.[12]

By frankly admitting that we can offer no explanation of the Fall, much less a cause, we underscore the irrationality of all moral evil. Moral evil is a surd, an irrational act, an irrational fact. To "explain" it would be to give it a sort of justification for being that it does not have. It is simply inexplicable: "Only he who understands that sin is inexplicable knows what it is."[13] We can see this truth in our own experience

11. Interestingly enough, Kant comes to much the same conclusion in his remarkable essay on radical evil, in which he says, "evil does not start from a propensity thereto as its underlying basis, for otherwise the beginning of evil would not have its source in freedom . . ." (*Religion Within the Limits of Reason Alone,* trans. Theodore M. Greene and Hoyt H. Hudson [New York: Harper & Row, 1960], p. 37).

12. For detailed rejection of the hoary tradition that *would* make much of the Serpent's approach to Eve, see *Who We Are,* pp. 136-76.

13. Emil Brunner, *Man in Revolt,* trans. Olive Wyon (London: Lutterworth, 1939), p. 132.

as moral agents, especially when we try from within grace to analyze our own sin candidly and frankly. Ultimately, we come up against the question, Why did I do this or that? And that question drives us back to an even harder question, How could I *possibly* have done this or that? Oh, we will offer some secondary reasons and extenuating circumstances — the deceitful human heart is very adept in finding excuses — but as these are stripped away by the grace of God and by the insight which the Spirit of God brings when he leads us into repentance, we become more and more appalled at the awful mystery that we have done things for which there is no final excuse; and we do not really know why we did them; and we cannot even believe that we did them. The root was deeper than temptation, deeper than weakness, deeper than ignorance. Thus the great apostle Paul could never escape the haunting memory of the wickedness of his past, so much so that at the end of his life he could still refer to himself as the chief of sinners (1 Tim. 1:15). Anyone who had not grappled existentially with the problem of moral evil in her own life may smile at this judgment as incontrovertible evidence of a distorted perception of reality, of an inordinate and misplaced sense of guilt, and wish that such a person could go to a psychologist and gain a better self-image. But the Christian knows that this is impossible. We cannot provide our own solutions for moral evil but only repent of it and accept the solution offered us in the grace of God.

The Fall and the Idea of Tragedy

The Fall and the idea of a tragically structured existence are alternative, essentially incompatible visions of the source of our human dilemma.[14] The doctrine of the Fall roots our misery in the culpable disobedience of our first parents: they were free, they were responsible, they had sufficient knowledge of their duty, and they could have done differently.

14. This conclusion is reached not only in classic treatments such as Reinhold Niebuhr's *Beyond Tragedy* (New York: Scribners, 1957) and Edmond Cherbonnier's "Biblical Faith and the Idea of Tragedy" in Nathan A. Scott, Jr., ed., *The Tragic Vision and the Christian Faith* (New York: Association Press, 1957); but also by more recent authors who prefer the tragic vision, like Wendy Farley, *Tragic Vision and Divine Compassion: A Contemporary Theodicy* (Louisville, Kentucky: Westminster/John Knox, 1990).

Their reaching for the fruit was neither noble nor heroic, not an admirable but doomed Promethean effort to aid humankind, but simply sinful. A righteous God justly punished them.

By contrast, in classical tragedy, heroes suffer not for their fault but for or at least in spite of their virtue, as they pursue worthy goals but are thwarted by the inevitabilities of fate and the savagery, capriciousness, or mischievousness of the gods. Yes, they may overreach themselves (hubris) — a "tragic flaw" is doubtless involved — but the overriding sense is that their punishment is disproportionate for a guilt that arises fundamentally not from a choice between good and evil but from a blindness posited with their very existence.[15] Tragedy is the Greek substitute for sin: the Greek "never even imagines that it is he himself who absolutely and essentially is incapable of obedience to the law. . . . He traces back the contradiction [in conflicting mandates] to deity itself."[16]

One can sense the attractiveness of the tragic vision when one ponders the sheer magnitude of undeserved suffering in the world, or at least suffering wholly incommensurate to the victim's offense, and perceives further that virtue does not guarantee happiness. One may be an extraordinary individual and yet fail. In Sophocles' *Antigone*, for instance, the heroine is driven by the very laws of heaven to bury her brother, but the laws of the state — also presumed to be given by the gods — conflict, leading to her doom; in the *Iliad*, Agamemnon can protest, "It was not I that did it: Jove, and Fate, and Erinys that walks in darkness struck me mad."[17] Factors of conflicting mandates, fate, and transcendent spitefulness that a human being could not possibly over-

---

15. See Stählin and Grundmann, "ἁμαρτάνω," *TDNT*, 1:298.

16. H. Kleinknecht, "νόμος," *TDNT* 4:1027. Spengler's idea of tragedy rested on the irreversibility of time, the fixedness of the past. (See Karl Heim, *God Transcendent*, trans. Edgar Dickie [London: Nisbet and Co., 1935], p. 121.) But for the Christian, time is lived between two fixed points: the First Adam, in whom we are sinners, and the Second, in whom we are redeemed. Both are "past" to us; yet the Second holds our future. Their acts on our behalf cannot be undone, yet we have not tragedy but fault and redemption. A "redeeming of time" is, then, possible. Our fall has been established and yet we continually confirm it anew; our redemption is past and yet not complete. In both realms, we become what we are — the first temporally, the second eternally.

17. Homer, *The Iliad, Great Books*, vol. 4 (Chicago: Encyclopaedia Britannica, 1952), 19.94.

come determine the outcome. "Man is not the chief problem: man is merely the vehicle of destiny, and that destiny is the real problem."[18]

Transposing the matter into modern terms, one might speak of the myriad vulnerabilities and contradictions to which humans are subject in a finite world, the realities of the laws of nature, the bafflement and frustration good people face as they wrestle with recalcitrant problems, and the constraints the Creator faces once he has created anything (even apart from positing indifference or ill will on the part of the deity). She might then hope that a candid recognition of these circumstances would generate an embracing compassion having more promise for alleviating human suffering than does a schema emphasizing sin and, hence, blame. And she might argue that only misguided and perhaps even unconscious commitments to theodicy (justification of the omnipotent God's righteousness in the face of evil) blind theologians to the inexplicably tragic dimensions of our existence.[19]

An insight from the tragic vision that the Christian must not lose, even if she rejects that vision as a whole, is that there is indeed a kind of irreducibility of evil that must be faced somehow and not just tidied up. As we have implied above, evil is prior to human sin and not only a consequence of it: the serpent was in the Garden prior to the Fall. There is something wrong with theodicies that leave us on the sidelines, as if we could watch the fray coolly rather than fighting for victims and against a real Enemy (though theodicy is not the only or perhaps the main culprit here: Augustine opposed watching tragic drama precisely because the spectator is "not called on to relieve, but only to grieve").[20] There *is* a gnawing torment and overwhelming magnitude to suffering that cannot be rationalized away. There *is* something transcending the merely human in evil. Furthermore, as we shall discuss further below, it is quite true that after the Fall, burgeoning evil engulfs the comparatively innocent and may spare the comparatively guilty, such that fault and suffering are by no means neatly coordinated (Job; Luke 13:1-4; John 9:1-3); many times there is no simply good choice, but

18. As Jaeger put it, referring to the plays of Aeschylus, in his *Paideia: The Ideals of Greek Culture*, 3 vols., trans. Gilbert Highet (New York: Oxford University Press, 1945), 1:254.

19. See Larry D. Bouchard, *Tragic Method and Tragic Theology* (University Park, PA: Pennsylvania University Press, 1989), pp. 1-2 and passim.

20. Augustine, *Confessions* 3.2.

only a choice between evils; and faithfulness may be counted on to lead to suffering (as Jesus said repeatedly; see also 2 Tim. 3:12).

However, it is a mistake, as we have said, so to existentialize the Fall as to assume that it changed nothing but instead merely reveals the situation of Everyman and Everywoman at the moral crossroads; and that we can therefore simply identify current conditions with those that always and necessarily prevailed. God's laws are not internally or intrinsically inconsistent: the ethical dilemmas we face are post-Fall dilemmas. And, at the risk of manifesting theodicy-induced blindness,[21] we further deny both that the Fall itself was tragic, and even that contemporary life is marked by those essential marks of classic tragedy, inexorable fate and divine malevolence. Certainly the Cross, at the heart of Christian faith, is, because of the Resurrection, a sign not of tragedy but of triumph, a sign not of God's indifference or malice but the supreme manifestation of his love. The Resurrection confirms the conviction that this world is governed not by obscure necessities and malignant gods but by the personal providence of the one God made known to us in Jesus Christ. As Charles Williams put it, after Christ:

The idea of social justice became important. The idea of tragedy lost its importance — almost its nature. In this world all was, in the end, under Providence, however detestable the enemies of Providence; as when, in one of his loveliest passages, Dante speaks of Luck as being one of the primal creatures, who forever enjoys her own beatitude, while fools blaspheme her below. Nor could the other world be tragic, since there could hardly be tragedy, whatever grief, in a man's obstinate determination to be damned.[22]

In such a context, human sin can only be a human responsibility, and all attempts to evade blame are variations on Adam's excuse to God that the woman God gave him handed him the fruit (Gen. 3:12). Indeed, our consciences inform us that all such attempts to shift blame simply increase our guilt: whatever an observer may say about forces pressing in on us, even now we know in the secret of our hearts that, in the mo-

21. On theodicy, see further pp. 83-95, below.
22. Charles Williams, *He Came Down from Heaven* (1938; Grand Rapids: Eerdmans, 1984), p. 85; for the discourse on Luck, see Dante, *Divine Comedy: Hell*, 7.73-96.

ment of decision, we could have done differently.[23] Furthermore, it would be a serious mistake to allow the tragic vision to obscure the real difference between good and evil (which all systems based on hard necessities do), to push human beings to the periphery of a drama that only incidentally concerns them, and to confuse legitimate human aspiration with fatal hubris. In the end, it seems to us to be the idea of final tragedy that robs human suffering and indeed the whole human enterprise of meaning, as the last stanza of W. H. Auden's poem, "Musée des Beaux Arts," suggests:

> In Breughel's *Icarus*, for instance: how everything turns away
> Quite leisurely from the disaster; the ploughman may
> Have heard the splash, the forsaken cry,
> but for him it was not an important failure; the sun shone
> As it had to on the white legs disappearing into the green
> Water; and the expensive delicate ship that must have seen
> Something amazing, a boy falling out of the sky,
> Had somewhere to get to and sailed calmly on.[24]

Contrast the parable of the Good Samaritan (Luke 10:25-37) and the biblical injunction that we act in such a way as to manifest love to our neighbors, as a witness to the truth in an evil world.

23. See Karl Heim, *Jesus the Lord,* trans. D. H. van Daalen (Philadelphia: Muhlenberg, 1961), p. 88; and Heim, *Jesus the World's Perfecter,* trans. D. H. van Daalen (Philadelphia: Muhlenberg, 1961), chaps. 1 and 2.

24. W. H. Auden, *Collected Poems,* ed. Edward Mendelson (New York: Random House, 1976), p. 147.

3

The Nature of the Fall

While we cannot — must not — explain the Fall, we can reflect descriptively upon its nature, as laid out in the biblical story. As an act, the seizing of the fruit[1] was an act of disobedience to the express divine command, a disobedience that the narrative implies involved both disbelief in the divine word and a coveting of the divine prerogatives (pride).

The Significance of the Insignificant

On the surface, the disobedience seems paltry, inconsequential. How could the source of human ills be found in so petty a thing as the eating of an apple? Surely there is a wild disproportion between the seriousness of the offense and the magnitude of the result?[2] But so to ar-

---

1. The traditional identification of the fruit with an apple rests on a play on the Latin for "apple tree" *(malus)* and "apple" *(malum)* and the masculine and neuter forms of the adjective "evil" *(malus* and *malum,* respectively) (Richard A. Muller, *Dictionary of Latin and Greek Theological Terms* [Grand Rapids: Baker, 1985], p. 183).

2. So has gone an argument with a long history, taken up recently by James Barr, *The Garden of Eden and the Hope of Immortality* (Minneapolis: Fortress, 1992), p. 12, who uses this interpretation in support of his view that the whole story is really interested in something other than the origins of sin and evil. Augustine, by contrast, argued that in this one act all sins entered in: "For there is in it pride, because man chose to be under his own dominion, rather than under the dominion of God; and blasphemy, because he

gue may well be to take the Devil's part: in Milton's *Paradise Lost,*
Lucifer, returning to Pandemonium, boasts how he ruined God's creature with so simple a thing as an apple — a wonder worthy of the fallen
angels' laughter. Then, in the great surprise scene of the poem, the den-
izens of the lower world all turn into serpents who crave fruit; which, as
they eat it, turns to ashes in their mouths.[3] Not a moral absurdity but a
great truth about the nature of moral evil lurks here: the significance
of the seemingly insignificant. Satan's master stroke is always to make
sin in its beginnings to appear of little consequence, to make every
transgression to appear of no moment.[4]

The nature of sin is such that the seemingly inconsequential leads
almost inexorably to the highly consequential. In the Fall, the fundamental issue is the authority of God as Creator over humankind, his
creatures. That authority is enshrined in the commandment forbid-
ding the fruit of the Tree of the Knowledge of Good and Evil, a fruit
forbidden not, as we have said, because is was in itself bad (nothing created by God is evil in itself) but, in Augustine's classic view, simply to
command a pure and simple obedience.[5] The command thus constitutes the relationship between God and humankind as a relationship
of a particular kind, one in which humankind are given their blessedness not in a declaration of their own maturity and independence but

---

did not believe God; and murder, for he brought death upon himself; and spiritual for-
nication, for the purity of the human soul was corrupted by the seducing blandishments of the serpent; and theft, for man turned to his own use the food he had been forbidden to touch; and avarice, for he had a craving for more than should have been
sufficient for him; and whatever other sin can be discovered on careful reflection to be
involved in this one admitted sin" (*The Enchiridion on Faith, Hope and Love,* ed. Henry
Paolucci [South Bend, IN: Regnery/Gateway, 1961], pp. 54-55).

3. Milton, *Paradise Lost,* book 10.

4. Surely we have seen something of this principle at work in our experience as a nation with the war in Vietnam, a war whose consequences are still being reaped now in
the destroyed lives of so many of our veterans and in society's inability to deal with their
trauma. But we started out simply by giving a bit of aid to the South Vietnamese. Then
we sent technical advisors, followed by military advisors and personnel. Finally we committed troops, and eventually hundreds of thousands of troops, and vast expenditures
for armaments, only to lose everything — not only billions of dollars spent, not only the
good will of the family of nations, but hundreds of thousands of lives of our young citizens. And we did not lose nearly so much as our allies the South Vietnamese, who went
down in defeat and destruction with and even far beyond us.

5. Augustine, *City of God* 13.20; 14.12; see above, pp. 17-18.

in submission to the will of their Creator. It means that true humanity is *not* to be found by human beings doing whatever they are capable of doing — a statement which sounds so odd to the modern ear that it demonstrates how far we have indeed fallen from what God intended for us.[6] The key thing is not that we should understand the reason for the command, as if we could stand apart from it and judge for ourselves its validity (James 4:11), but that we be so related to the God who gave it as to receive it gladly as the expression of his will for the structuring of our lives.

The Problem of Authority

Given objections that arise immediately in a culture taught to "question authority," it may be important to note here that we as fallen creatures can hardly conceive being rightly, freely, and gladly subject to any authority — God's or anyone else's. All of our relationships to authority are now corrupt, including our most earnest attempts to be obedient to God. We misconstrue as well as disobey his will. We use God's holy law in ways that damage ourselves and others (e.g., brutal truthtelling, when silence would suffice, to take a simple example), which gives point to the charge of those who complain that we *must* make judgments; we *must* bring what we are doing before the bar of reason and experience if we are not to wreak havoc. But reason is also corrupt and will often mislead us. To say that we cannot escape this morass is again to say that we cannot on our own undo the Fall.

Another intriguing aspect of the problem of authority is that, as a matter of fact, submission is necessary precisely in order to know[7] — quite contrary to the serpent's claim that superior knowledge would come with disobedience. For instance, to learn a language, one must submit to the usage of those who already speak it. One might make an analogy between speaking one's native tongue, which one learns natu-

6. See Joseph Ratzinger, *In the Beginning . . . : A Catholic Understanding of the Story of Creation and the Fall*, trans. Boniface Ramsey, O.P. (Grand Rapids: Eerdmans, 1995), pp. 64-71; also the remarks on technology in *Who We Are*, pp. 418-45. Milton presciently gave the Tempter to call the Tree "Mother of Science" (*Paradise Lost* 9.680).

7. See Michael Polanyi, *Personal Knowledge: Toward a Post-Critical Philosophy* (New York: Harper & Row, 1962), p. 208.

rally and in which one converses easily, and the original relationship of humankind to God. By contrast, when one learns another language as an adult, one is conscious of complexities, rails against rules and irregularities, and in general feels strain, even when one seeks to submit — as do fallen humankind before God. To refuse to submit to the authority of one who knows the language, however, is to decline to learn it at all.

To reject God's authority is indeed to transgress the law (the character of the first and of all subsequent sins, 1 John 3:4), but not just the law as abstract principle. Rather, the sinner rejects God's right to rule.[8] Behind the law is the word of the One who gave it — as we continue to see in the Ten Commandments (Exod. 20:3-17), where the law takes the form of personal address, "thou shalt." Thus, the Fall is an act of revolt[9] against One toward whom the proper relationship is love and the loyalty and obedience that come from love. And before the revolt culminated in the actual seizing of the fruit, there must already have been some turning of the will away from God, so that the fatal error preceded the actual eating. This turning of the will is a Janus-like sin: one underlying fault with two faces. One of those faces is unbelief, and the other is pride.

The Fall as Pride and Unbelief

In emphasizing pride and unbelief, we speak from an Augustinian and Reformed perspective.[10] By way of acknowledging alternatives, we might note that the Eastern Church, by contrast, stressed sensuousness, and particularly sexuality, as both source and result of the Fall (and, with its somewhat more optimistic anthropology, gave rather less attention overall to these matters than did the West). For instance, Origen proposed that the Serpent physically infected Eve; and Gregory of Nyssa argued that humankind had been created as two sexes in anticipation of the Fall.[11] One can, of course, see in the narrative certain elements that suggest the role of sensuality — in particular, reference to the fruit as be-

8. See William F. May, *A Catalogue of Sins* (New York: Holt, Rinehart and Winston, 1967), p. 12.
9. Thus the title of Emil Brunner's volume on anthropology, *Man in Revolt*.
10. See, for instance, the treatment by Calvin, *Institutes*, 2.1.4.
11. Gregory of Nyssa, *On the Making of Man*, 17 (NPNF, series 2, vol. 5).

ing "good for food and . . . a delight to the eyes" (Gen. 3:6) and the immediately following reference to our first parents' new awareness of their
sexuality as problematic (Gen. 3:7). That many sins do involve sensuality
hardly requires illustration. However, insofar as sensuality is simply a
matter of the animal or instinctual, it lacks the character of sin: animals
do not sin. When it is not simply a matter of the instinctual, it already
engages the person in her spiritual aspect. But neither is reason as such
the source of the Fall, but rather that will, that self, that lies deeper than
reason but expresses itself through it, even as it expresses itself through
sensuality. As Niebuhr put it, following Hobbes, "the self is always the
master, and not the servant, of its reason. . . . The self, in short, could use
reason to justify its ends as well as to judge them, and there was evidently no power in reason to limit the desires and ambitions of men."[12]
Sin in its essence, that is, is an act of the whole person and not of a particular aspect or faculty of the person.

A more recent rejection of the Augustinian and Reformed view of
sin as prideful, unbelieving rebellion against God comes from Marjorie
Suchocki.[13] In what she explicitly identifies as an exercise in natural
theology, from a relational (process) perspective, that reverses the theological tradition, Suchocki claims that sin should be understood as
"participation through intent or act in unnecessary violence that contributes to the ill-being of any aspect of earth or its inhabitants."[14] Sin
is against God only secondarily, as God experiences the world. What is
curious about this often-astute analysis is not so much its neglect of
Scripture in general, apart from reference to the Adam story (after all,
it is intended as "natural theology"; and Suchocki's dialogue partners
are Niebuhr and Tillich rather than the Bible), as its ignoring of the
very specific importance of violence in the primal history with which it
is at least indirectly engaged. Genesis 4 — Cain's murder of Abel, pro-
gressing to Lamech's boast of unlimited vengeance — could hardly be
in more immediate proximity to Genesis 3. The biblical writers themselves, that is, do not ignore but highlight violence, but they highlight
it as the inexorable *result* of the primal disobedience of God. Suchocki

---

12. Reinhold Niebuhr, *The Self and the Dramas of History* (New York: Scribners, 1955),
pp. 17-18.

13. Marjorie Suchocki, *The Fall to Violence* (New York: Continuum, 1995).

14. Suchocki, *The Fall to Violence*, p. 12.

fears that emphasizing the vertical dimension obscures the actual circumstances of sin and reduces the significance of the creation; we would counter that we can see sin's terrible seriousness and creation's actual importance only in the light of the holy God who loves what he has made. We have also insisted above that when the relationship with God is fully intact, so is the relationship with others. Therefore, we continue to hold pride and unbelief to be fundamental.

To suggest that unbelief and pride are not only fundamental but also closely interrelated rather than separate faults is simply to say that disbelieving God implies the pride constituted by trust in oneself instead of God; and the more one trusts oneself in one's independent decision-making, the more distrustful of God one becomes.[15] The Serpent starts by raising doubt. After engaging Eve in a discussion about what God had actually commanded, he simply denies the veracity of what God had said: no, they will not die if they eat the fruit (Gen. 3:4); thus suggesting to our first parents that they need not take God's command seriously and sowing the seed of unbelief. Of unbelief as the root of all sin, the source both of the Fall and of the murder of Jesus, Charles Spurgeon preached:

> [Unbelief] is the monarch sin, the quintessence of guilt, the mixture of the venom of all crimes; the dregs of the wine of Gomorrha; it is the A 1 sin, the master-piece of Satan, the chief work of the devil. . . . [I]t may be said of unbelief that it not only sins itself; but makes others sin, it is the egg of all crime, the seed of every offense; in fact everything that is evil and vile lies couched in that one word — unbelief. . . . A Christian's life is always walking on water — mine is — and every wave would swallow and devour him but faith makes him stand. The moment you cease to believe, that moment distress comes in, and down you go. . . . Once make a giant unbelieving, and he becomes a dwarf: Faith is the Samsonian lock of the Christian; cut it off, and you may put out his eyes — and he can do nothing.[16]

15. Brunner suggests that from the point of view of dogmatics, separation from God's word (unbelief) comes first; but from the point of view of psychology, precisely this severance from the word is arrogance (*Man in Revolt*, p. 130 n. 1).

16. C. H. Spurgeon, "The Sin of Unbelief," New Park Street Pulpit, January 14, 1855 (quoted from The C. H. Spurgeon Collection, Ages Digital Library, 1998). Quite a re-

Then, after raising doubt, in the very next breath, the Serpent holds out the prospect of becoming like God (Gen. 3:5), a prospect quintessentially expressing pride[17] — and one which, later, the Second Adam explicitly rejected, counting equality with God *not* a thing to be grasped (Phil. 2:6-11). It was Nietzsche who coined what we might call the motto of original sin as pride: *"if* there were gods, how could I endure not to be a god!"[18] Camus's protagonist in *The Fall* expressed what is essentially the same sentiment in mundane terms when he said, "Even in the details of daily life, I needed to feel *above."*[19] What are such desires but the refusal of creatureliness? And what is the refusal of creatureliness but the denial that we are who God says we are, and the denial that God is who God says he is with respect to us? Unbelief and pride.

Objections to Understanding the Fall as Pride and Unbelief

Objections to characterizing the Fall in this way come from all sides — from that part of the scientific community that rejects curbs on human exploration of whatever kind, from that part of the psychotherapeutic community that emphasizes high self-esteem as a fount of both virtue and happiness, and from that part of the feminist community that claims that the sins we have associated with the Fall are typically masculine rather than feminine sins and ignore the particular temptations of women. These are important complaints, for each sees in the way we and others like us have handled the Fall a threat to some

---

markable statement, especially considering that Spurgeon was hardly twenty-one years old when he delivered this sermon.

17. Because pride has so many possible connotations and is so often used in a positive sense in our culture, it is helpful to note William May's careful distinctions: "pride is neither an overestimation of one's talent (egoism), nor a flutter of delight that goes with accomplishment (vanity), nor an inner firmness of identity that is essential to integrity (self-respect); it means, rather, man's self-exaltation into the position of God" (*Catalogue of Sins,* p. 175).

18. Friedrich Nietzsche, *Thus Spoke Zarathustra,* in *The Portable Nietzsche,* ed. and trans. Walter Kaufman (New York: Viking Press, 1954), p. 198.

19. Albert Camus, *The Fall,* trans. Justin O'Brian (New York: Alfred A. Knopf, 1957), p. 23.

significant truth about humankind. Fears arise that a traditional understanding of the Fall fosters many evils rather than setting men and women on a good and true path.

The question of the scientific community that concerns us here is the question of limits: can we really say, "This far and no farther," to the inquiring human mind? Surely curiosity and desire for mastery are part of our endowment as human? Yes indeed; and we would have to acknowledge that in our historical experience, those who have sought to restrict the freedom of others to know have most often proved servants of tyranny. Nonetheless, the Genesis narrative tells us that limits are also part of what it means to be human, and refusal of limits will not finally liberate us but leave us enslaved to forces beyond our control that we have set loose.[20] Despite the difficulty of drawing lines once the original line has been crossed, we do insist that there are certain things we should not do with our minds, as with our bodies, even though we can do them. It is still possible for the cost to be too great.

An indication of the subtlety of sin in this matter of limits is observation of how easy it is to say that we will "never" do something that we doubt we will ever be able to do, and how much clearer it may be to us that we should not do it when we are not being seduced by its possible benefits. For instance, not many years ago, ethicists declared with confidence that we would never clone human beings. Today, certain scientists declare equally confidently that if the laws of the United States of America make doing so illegal, they will simply go elsewhere, and we may safely assume that those interested in their services will follow them.

An objection of a different kind comes from those who have observed that efforts to counter the sin of pride by emphasizing human wickedness and unworthiness have produced considerable numbers of miserable people who behave worse than they otherwise would because they feel so wretched. When they gain an improved self-image, they are not only happier but behave better towards others. Again, there is truth here, truth and perhaps also a lesson that may be reinforced by Heim's observation that Jesus did not go around inducing guilt or trying to

---

20. See *Who We Are*, pp. 418-45; see also Maurice Hogan, *The Biblical Vision of the Human Person*, European University Studies: Series 23, Theology, vol. 504 (Frankfurt am Main: Peter Lang, 1994).

make those who thought themselves well feel sick.[21] But there is also a lie, tacitly acknowledged by *The Fall*'s protagonist when he reflects, "I admitted only superiorities in me and this explained my good will and serenity."[22] Such a state of falsely generated well-being does not hold under pressure, as the novel is at pains to show. We suspect that in our day this frantic effort to make those who know themselves to be sick to feel well, covering over the symptoms of deadly disease with bromides, is a far greater danger than inducing scrupulosity and neurotic guilt. And in any case, we tend to sympathize with e. e. cummings's conclusion: "Half a century of time and several continents of space in addition to a healthily developed curiosity, haven't enabled me to locate a single peripherally situated ego."[23] To assert that our egos rightfully *belong* in the center sounds like a line borrowed from the Serpent, whose assurances we ought by now to have learned not to trust.

But even if too exalted a sense of self is a pervasive problem, is it true that *women* need to be cautioned against pride and willfulness? Is not this whole exposition based on the predispositions of only half of the human family? May not women compromise their full humanity more by self-abnegation, by failing to take proper initiatives and responsibility, and by frittering away their lives? If so, telling women that they must aspire to more humility and obedience may simply drive them deeper into their own particular sins. Self-sacrifice, to be legitimate, must be a free act coming from a measure of strength: one must first *have* a self in order to sacrifice oneself.[24]

21. Heim, *Jesus the World's Perfecter,* p. 41.

22. Camus, *The Fall,* p. 48.

23. Quoted by Niebuhr, *The Self and the Dramas of History,* p. 134.

24. This theme has been taken up by considerable numbers of feminist theologians, who argue explicitly from "women's experience" rather than from Scripture — understandably enough, given the premise that Scripture itself, as well as the deliverances of male theologians, fails to take that experience into account. See, for example, the seminal early work by Valerie Saiving Goldstein, "The Human Situation: A Feminine Viewpoint," in Simon Doniger, ed., *The Nature of Man in Theological and Psychological Perspective* (New York: Harper & Brothers, 1962), pp. 151-70; also Judith Plaskow, *Sex, Sin and Grace: Women's Experience and the Theologies of Reinhold Niebuhr and Paul Tillich* (Washington, D.C.: University Press of America, 1980). For helpful appropriation of such insights while guarding against any implication that men and women belong virtually to different species, see William J. Cahoy, "One Species or Two? Kierkegaard's Anthropology and the Feminist Critique of the Concept of Sin," *Modern Theology* 11:4 (October 1995): 429-54.

Given the indisputable fact that men and women differ — however hard it may be to specify the differences in a way that holds up across cultures and wide individual variation — it is certainly plausible that their besetting temptations and sins may also differ. Surely recent analyses have provided some striking new insights in this regard. And no one who takes radical depravity seriously[25] will be surprised that self-sacrifice and self-abnegation can be self-serving. It is at least worth observing, though, that the tendencies labeled in our day as particular problems for women appear in the narrative itself as a result of the Fall (Gen. 3:16) rather than as due to the intrinsic nature of woman — a rather remarkable bit of self-transcendence for the biblical writer, who apparently did *not* blithely assume that the traditional place of women is part of the very structure of creation (a point that can thus be seen in the second creation narrative as well as in the first). In the narrative, it is to Eve, not to Adam, that the Serpent holds out the prospect of becoming like God. And it is Adam who followed Eve's example and is often semi-exonerated on the grounds that he must have acted as he did because he wanted her fellowship and refused to abandon her — behaviors and attitudes supposedly typical of women. (This seeming reversal of expected gender roles prior to the Fall has not escaped the notice of traditionalists, who have sometimes claimed that if Adam and Eve had kept to their proper stations, the Fall would have been averted. Such an argument seems to us wrong-headed. Not only does it turn a post-Fall judgment involving women's subordination into a creation ordinance, but it makes the "real" problem to be role reversal — the breach of a supposed command never stated; instead of eating the forbidden fruit — breach of the command that was clearly stated. Surely something is seriously amiss in such thinking.) Disobedience may be a simple enough fact, but how and why someone disobeys is often complex. One also sometimes hears what sounds like a prideful undertone in denials that women's prevailing sin is pride, or sees evidence suggesting that the denier has failed to take sin generally with sufficient moral seriousness, or has redefined it to strip it of its moral content. All of this is not to gainsay the significant observations of feminist theologians. It is simply to insist that both the fall narrative and our human experience are too richly textured, and our sins too convoluted, to lend themselves

25. See the treatment below, pp. 160-67.

to entirely tidy categorization along gender lines. (See further below, pp. 155-58.) Nietzsche, we might recall, despised Christianity as a whole because he saw it, in its advocacy of self-sacrifice, as a revenge taken by the weak against the strong; and surely in speaking thus, he had in mind men more than women.

Roman Catholicism and the *Donum Superadditum*

Whereas in Protestant theology, particularly in the Reformed tradition, the Fall has been seen as a moral change radically altering human-kind's essential relationship to God; in traditional Roman Catholic theology it constitutes a kind of structural or ontological change within humankind. We have spoken above of original righteousness as the positive orientation toward God with which humankind were cre-ated. We have implied that it was intrinsic to their nature as human, which leads to the further implication that its loss affects the human person as a whole, compromising the divine image in which she is cre-ated.[26] By contrast, Roman Catholic theology has construed original righteousness not as integral to the divine image but as a "superadded gift" *(donum superadditum)* which can be, and has been, lost without changing the essential image.[27]

According to the Roman Catholic view, the two distinct elements constituting humankind — body and soul, material and immaterial — were originally so related that the lower, bodily impulses and desires were tempered by the higher faculties of reason, conscience, and will; and the reason was subject to God.[28] This state, in which the passions of the flesh were subject to the higher, spiritual faculties, could be called

---

26. See *Who We Are*, pp. 53-59, on relics or remnants of the image and on the com-plexities attached to the way the biblical writers speak of the image — whether as if nothing fundamental had been changed by the Fall, e.g., Gen. 9:6; 1 Cor. 11:7; James 3:9; or in terms of the radical newness of what is restored in Christ, e.g., Rom. 8:29; Eph. 4:24; Col. 3:10.

27. For the exegetically problematic distinction between "image" and "likeness" in Genesis 1:26 which undergirds this approach, see *Who We Are*, pp. 56-57.

28. See Thomas Aquinas, *Summa Theologica*, Part 1, Q. 95, art. 1. See also George Vandervelde, *Original Sin: Two Major Trends in Contemporary Roman Catholic Reinterpreta-tion* [Amsterdam: Rodopi N.V., 1975], pp. 28-30.

natural justice (justitia naturalis). In this state there was no sin precisely because the bodily desires were properly subdued. There was, however, a
tendency to sin that would become actuality should the fleshly appetites break through their restraints. This tendency, traditionally called
concupiscence, while itself natural and blameless, thus still provided fuel
for sin *(fomes peccati)* or a certain propensity for sin.[29] Therefore, to help
secure humankind in their original integrity, God gave them a special
gift, a "golden bridle": original righteousness over and above the divine
image. When humankind fell, they lost this special gift; the balance of
lower and higher impulses was upset so that the lower self gained ascendancy; and the propensity to sin became sin in reality.

We should caution that this view of the Fall does not necessarily entail the belief that our first parents fell *because* the lower impulses
gained ascendancy (even though it may often be interpreted that way),
but only that the Fall *gave* these impulses ascendancy. Augustine, for instance, who had a great deal to say about concupiscence, also said
plainly that, "it was not the corruptible flesh that made the soul sinful,
but the sinful soul that made the flesh corruptible. . . . It is not by having flesh, which the devil has not, but by living according to himself —
that is, according to man — that man became like the devil."[30] Nonetheless, Protestant theologians have resisted the implication that there
is a kind of inherent evil in matter, or that there is an inherent tension,
if not incompatibility, between body and spirit.[31] They have conceived
sin not as resulting from a conflict within the person, but as a conflict
between the person on the one hand and God and God's will on the
other. The whole person revolts against God, and this revolt is an act of

29. In a modern interpretation, Rahner and Vorgrimler caution that concupiscence
should not be thought to reside in the body alone, noting that the biblical σάρξ (flesh)
encompasses more than the body. They define concupiscence as, "A desire which directs
human freedom towards a partial good antecedently to any decision taken by that freedom and not altogether subject to such decision" ("Concupiscence," in *Theological Dictionary,* ed. Cornelius Ernst, O.P., trans. Richard Strachan [New York: Herder and Herder,
1965], p. 93).

30. Augustine, *City of God* 14.3; see also 1.16, 18.

31. "Inherent" is the operative word here, meaning intrinsic to the creation. One can
hardly read the New Testament and miss the conflict between flesh and spirit that results from sin (though again, "flesh" does not equal "body" *simpliciter*). Further, 2 Pet. 1:4
speaks of "the corruption that is in the world because of lust [ἐπιθυμία]"; and 1 John 2:17
says, "the world and its desires [ἐπιθυμία] are passing away."

the spirit or transcendent self. Like Augustine, they view the body as indeed implicated in the sinful, alienated life, but involved only as the instrument which manifests sin at the empirical level. This alteration of the relationship between God and humankind is the meaning of judicial and spiritual death; it is not that the constituent elements in humankind or the relationship of these elements within humankind has been changed.

4

Consequences of the Fall

Humankind's Attitude toward God

Not only does the Fall *consist in* a fundamentally changed relationship of humankind to God — a change from a positive orientation of free obedience to one manifesting unbelief and pride; it also *produces* a changed relationship to God as one of its enduring consequences. The narrative in Genesis depicts this profound change by saying that when, as a result of eating the fruit, the man's and woman's eyes were opened, they became aware of themselves as naked and made loincloths for themselves (Gen. 3:7), in stark contrast to their earlier state of being naked and unashamed (Gen. 2:25). And then they proceeded to hide from God (Gen. 3:8). The story thus intimates that, although the man and woman are obviously aware of themselves and their difference from one another in each other's presence, nonetheless their sense of nakedness and exposure terminates primarily upon God. It is from God that they hide, knowing that no fig leaves would help when they stood before him.[1]

The story is subtle and allusive. While sexual overtones can hardly be denied, the shame of the fallen pair goes beyond an anxious awareness of their bodies, just as their earlier lack of shame went beyond unself-consciousness about sex. In fact, the root used for shame in Genesis 2:25

---

1. Dubarle notes how frequently in Scripture (post-Fall, of course) hiding is the reaction to a divine manifestation; see *Biblical Doctrine of Original Sin* (London: Geoffrey Chapman, 1964), p. 71 n. 1.

(בוש) is not oriented toward sexual shame but toward the overthrowing of a former position of respect and importance (in Gen. 2:25, that is, the couple as *unashamed* were still secure in their position).[2] We might also note that while the couple themselves made loincloths, suggesting sexual content, God provided them with tunics (Gen. 3:21); while seeing a historical progression in use of clothing here is certainly possible,[3] we are somewhat inclined to the view of Charles Williams, that God is not so sex-conscious as some of the commentators.[4] Or, perhaps better, God's concerns are less narrowly focused than ours have tended to be. Adam and Eve had lost more than just sexual innocence.

It is fascinating to see how closely a modern secular psychologist's description of the phenomenon of shame (written, it would appear, innocent of conscious reflection on the biblical account, though one suspects some influence from the author's Jewish identity) parallels the biblical dynamic:

> To feel shame is to feel *seen* in a painfully diminished sense. The self feels exposed both to itself and to anyone else present. It is this sudden, unexpected feeling of exposure and accompanying self-consciousness that characterize the essential nature of the affect of shame. Contained in the experience of shame is the piercing awareness of ourselves as fundamentally deficient in some vital way as a human being. To live with shame is to experience the very essence or heart of the self as wanting. Shame is an impotence-making experience because *it feels as though* there is no way to relieve the matter, no way to restore the balance of things. One has simply failed as a human being.

However, whereas the theologian responds, "Exactly; this is in fact the human situation before God," many psychologists consider such a response "unhealthy" and recommend overthrowing the tyranny of the one (or One) who has so wounded the human self by inducing shame.[5]

---

2. See Horst Seebass, "בוש," in G. Johannes Botterweck and Helmer Ringgren, eds., *Theological Dictionary of the Old Testament*, rev. ed., trans. John T. Willis (Grand Rapids: Eerdmans, 1974-), 2:52.

3. E.g., Westermann, *Genesis 1–11*, pp. 251-52.

4. Williams, *He Came Down from Heaven*, p. 20.

5. Gershen Kaufman, *Shame: The Power of Caring*, 3rd ed. [Rochester, VT: Schenkman,

It is an interesting point that the early chapters of Genesis say so little of *love* between God and humankind or between the man and the woman but instead seem simply to imply the perfect naturalness and confidence attending these relationships: perhaps a reason might be that love as we know it always involves a kind of anguish absent from the pristine world. And so we read here not directly of lost love but of a new fear and sense of being uncovered leading to a hiding among the trees — a reflex at the conscious level of the reality of guilt. Fear of physical nakedness is a sort of parable of a deeper fear of full disclosure of one's fault, even as the curious phenomenon of blushing manifests shame at being discovered.[6] The thought at the beginning of the Bible thus parallels that at the end, where the wicked cry to the mountains and to the hills to fall upon them and cover them from the face of him who sits upon the throne and from the wrath of the Lamb: they cannot bear to look into his face (Rev. 6:16). They would rather be buried under the rocks than confront their Maker. In between the beginning and the end of human history, some hide so determinedly that they forget there is a God from whom they are hiding; pious parents try to control rebellious children by the threat — and it is a threat, not a reassurance — that God is always watching them, no matter how hidden they think their misbehaviors may be; and theology students admit that the doctrine of the divine omniscience makes them anxious. The easy fellowship is gone. It no longer seems a good thing that God should know everything about us, and we no longer walk freely before him.

We will deal further below with sex and sin.[7] However, we must at this point at least register the puzzling question of why our sense of shame and exposure at the physical level should concentrate upon the sex organs — why, when the act of disobedience was eating, a fig leaf should be the symbol of the result. (Thus Swift makes the Houyhn-

---

1992], pp. 8-9. For the reference and the general observation about psychologists, we are indebted to colleague Nancy Thurston. Kaufman is less extreme than many, but still presses the need to establish *within oneself* the power to determine how one feels about oneself and to disassociate oneself from shame-inducing influences — a curiously solipsistic model for one who emphasizes interpersonal relationships; see especially chap. 5.

6. One recalls Mark Twain's famous remark: "Man is the only animal that blushes. Or needs to" (heading of chap. 27 of *Following the Equator*).

7. Pp. 146-49.

hnms to be exceedingly puzzled at Gulliver's attempts at modesty: they could not understand "why nature should teach us to conceal what nature had given.")[8] After all, the sexual polarity of the race is a creation ordinance, antecedent to the Fall; and so is the command to be fruitful and multiply. We read not that Adam and Eve were naked and did not know it, like children (an idea Augustine attributed to the Pelagians);[9] we read that they were naked and not ashamed. Not sexual awareness as such but shame came with sin. As we have just sought to emphasize, the account of the Fall as a whole should surely be read as having a larger concern than just sexuality.

One suggestion originating with Augustine (as does so much in theology) has to do with the striking recalcitrance of the sex organs, especially obvious to and in the male: unlike a hand or a foot, they cannot be confidently commanded to respond, whether in the service of virtue or of vice, but exhibit "a certain independent autocracy" which Augustine was confident that they did not exhibit before the Fall and which makes nakedness shameful. By their disobedience, they witness to human disobedience.[10] While we might not think about it in quite such concrete terms as Augustine did, most of us do have an awareness of the power and stubborn refractoriness of our sexual impulses. They are a problem to us in a way that many of our other impulses are not (which is not to say that these other impulses may not constitute or lead to even more serious sins than does our sexuality, but to speak only in terms of our consciousness of difficulty).

Moreover, it is by the sexual act that a sinful progeny is brought into being[11] — a point that we may grant even if we do not believe that the transmission of original sin is by physical inheritance, as did Augustine. According to the Old Testament law, men who have had an emission of semen (and any women with whom they have lain) are unclean for a day (Lev. 15:16-18; see also 1 Sam. 21:5, where Ahimelech asks, before giving them the holy bread, if David and his men have at least kept themselves from women); women who have given birth are unclean for a much longer period and must offer a sin offering at its con-

---

8. Jonathan Swift, *Gulliver's Travels, Great Books,* vol. 36 (Chicago: Encyclopaedia Britannica, 1952), p. 145.

9. Augustine, *On Marriage and Concupiscence,* 6.

10. Augustine, *City of God,* 14.17, cf. 14.19-24; *Forgiveness of Sins, and Baptism,* 2.36.

11. E.g., *City of God,* 14:20.

clusion (Lev. 12). One may associate with these cultic regulations the psalmist's confession at the moral level, "Behold, I was brought forth in iniquity, and in sin did my mother conceive me" (51:5 RSV), by which we surely cannot suppose that the psalmist meant his birth was illicit, any more than that a mother's sin offering implied that her child was conceived out of wedlock. It is the confluence of all these ideas, however, that is suggestive; for, taken one by one, they are beset by myriad complications, from theories about the meanings of bodily emissions of all sorts; to observations of the primitive, widespread, and pre-ethical anxiety about sexuality and its defiling character; to the point that Leviticus 12 suggests nothing about the newborn child being itself impure — but contrast Job 14:1-4; Psalm 58:3; Isaiah 48:8, for the idea of uncleanness from birth.[12] Nonetheless, surely we cannot fail to recognize the elemental unease associated with our way of being in the world and, hence, with the way entrance into the world came about. (Ricoeur puts the relationship the other way around.)

To go at it yet another way, although, as we have noted above, the early Genesis narratives say little about love, yet our overall understanding of humankind is that they were made for a loving relationship with God and others. Once they are fallen, love is, so to speak, broken, not only with respect to God but also with respect to an uncomplicated expression in the sexual relationship, so that it takes the form of "eros" with all of its unsatisfied longing.[13] Thus the Genesis narrative with its fig leaves points in a symbolically profound way to matters which can hardly be explicated logically.

Excursus: Clothing, Modesty, and Nudity in Art

Given the depth and complexity of the impulse to protect oneself from exposure by donning clothing — an impulse we have interpreted as a parable at the physical level of a deeper spiritual issue — we surely can-

12. See, e.g., Mary Douglas, *Purity and Danger: An Analysis of Concepts of Pollution and Taboo* (London: Routledge & Kegan Paul, 1966); Ricouer, *Symbolism of Evil* (Boston: Beacon Press, 1967), p. 28; David P. Wright and Richard N. Jones, "Discharge," *Anchor Bible Dictionary*, 6 vols., ed. David Noel Freedman (New York: Doubleday, 1992), 2:204-7.

13. See Brunner, *Man in Revolt*, p. 198; also Milton, *Paradise Lost* 9.1011-16, where the opening of the eyes is interpreted as engaging in carnal looks.

not consider sufficient a naturalistic explanation of clothing as simply determined by the environment and culture: saying that one wears a fur coat, for instance, because it is cold; and that apart from purely practical considerations, being clothed or unclothed is an indifferent cultural variation. Stone Age people even in very cold environments wherein the practical need was simply for warmth still used necklaces and so on to adorn their bodies: the drive to present oneself in an attractive way is very primitive and suggests a certain self-consciousness, a certain sense that something is not ideally "right" about who one is (very likely with specific reference to one's attractiveness to the opposite sex), as does also the need for modesty. The fittingness of the idea that the good should also be beautiful and the bad, ugly, can also be seen in the depiction of characters in classical literature (e.g., respectively, in the words of Menelaus to Telemachus and the son of Nestor in the *Odyssey;* and in the description of Thersites in the *Iliad*).[14] These matters are not neutral but reflect need and anxiety.

However, the problem of a proper modesty cannot be solved by a certain judicious quantity of clothing, as the sorry history of the "missionary barrel" evidences. We cringe today when reading of missionaries doling out clothes from the barrel to people in whose setting these clothes can only be seen as grotesquely inappropriate. The procedure seems hopelessly wrongheaded and naïve. But the deeper naïveté is on the part of those who see the underlying issues as morally insignificant. Though criteria of modesty cannot be established by objective rules, persons in cultures we may call "primitive" are well aware of the difference between the modest and the immodest (as are members of nudist camps, who generally function under very strict rules of modesty);[15] and some missionaries have reported that they move much more easily amongst unclothed people in the jungle than they do on a typical beach in the United States. We can admit that standards of propriety are cultural and ought not to be imposed imperialistically on others, without denying that immodesty — exposure

14. Homer, *The Iliad* and *The Odyssey,* trans. Samuel Butler, *Great Books* vol. 4 (Chicago: Encyclopaedia Britannica, 1952), pp. 199 and 12, respectively.

15. See, e.g., Martin S. Weinberg, "Sexual Modesty, Social Meanings, and the Nudist Camp," in *Sociology and Everyday Life,* ed. Marcello Truzzi (New York: Prentice-Hall, 1968), pp. 212-20.

for the sake of exposure or for the sake of titillation of self or others
— is the Devil's work.[16]

Unfortunately, the matter is further complicated on the other side
in that we use clothes — presumably the result of our shame — as instruments of pride and lust. One recalls Isaac Watts's stanza:

> Why should our garments, made to hide
> Our parents' shame, provoke our pride?
> The art of dress did ne'er begin,
> Till Eve, our mother, learn'd to sin.[17]

And clothes also play a significant social function in symbolizing place
and role in society — a function that may if anything have been even
more pronounced in ancient Israel.[18] Thus there is theological meaning in the modern revolt against elaborate clothing. Yet attraction to
the plain or sloppy may be as much driven by fashion (and hence pride)
as insistence upon the costly or elaborate. In short, shame and pride,
hiding and display, alike are driven by the new self-consciousness
brought about by the Fall: without self-consciousness, neither is possible. Cloaking and adornment are different manifestations of the same
reflex of inadequacy. They evidence a certain shrinking of the person as
she contracts upon herself: by craving to be more, she has become
less.[19]

In any case, the Fall cannot be undone by dispensing with the fig
leaves — a point as important in morals as it is in dress. As Bonhoeffer
remarks, "covering is necessary because it keeps awake shame, . . . a necessary sign of the actual situation of disunion."[20] Paul speaks of it be-

---

16. Yet another cultural difference is pointed out by Thorlief Boman, who remarks
that Hebrew candor is auditive: sexual members could be spoken of but not shown. By
contrast, Greek candor is visual: sexual members could be shown but not spoken of ro-
bustly (*Hebrew Thought Compared with Greek,* pp. 77-84). Hence the Song of Solomon
freely uses figures of a (to us) embarrassing frankness.

17. From his *Songs Divine and Moral, for the Use of Children* (London: Charles Tilt, 1832),
p. 305; see also Shakespeare's Sonnet #146.

18. See Edgar Haulotte, "Vêtement," in Xavier Léon-Dufour, ed., *Vocabulaire de
Théologie Biblique* (Paris: Les Éditions du Cerf, 1962), pp. 1098-1103.

19. Augustine, *City of God* 14.13.

20. Dietrich Bonhoeffer, *Ethics,* trans. Neville Horton Smith (New York: Macmillan,
1955), p. 21; see also p. 372 on exposure as being cynical under conditions of the Fall.

ing shameful even to mention what certain people do in private (Eph. 5:12). Pascal reflects, "It is not enough . . . to tell nothing but the truth; we must not always tell everything that is true; we should publish only those things which it is useful to disclose, and not those which can only hurt, without doing any good."[21] Thus, the general rule becomes that one ought to avoid what is unedifying and in every case refuse to lay a snare for anyone either by speech, by dress, or by behavior: modesty "is a grace of God that moderates the overactiveness and curiosity of the minde, and orders the passions of the body, and external actions, and is directly opposed to *Curiosity,* to *Boldnesse,* to *Undecency.*"[22] In the New Testament, the symbol of healing is not a new nakedness but a "putting on" of Christ (Rom. 13:14), a being clothed in righteousness (Eph. 4:24; 6:14) or with "the new self, which is being renewed in knowledge according to the image of its creator" (Col. 3:10); and the saints in glory are garbed in bright, pure robes (Rev. 19:8). The fallen creature may not go back, but provision is made that she may go forward.

What, then, about the matter of nudity in art, and the variable number of fig leaves superimposed on art objects in the Vatican, depending on the sensitivities of successive popes? Surely there is a difference between the lascivious and the artistic, a difference the young artist in a Potok novel movingly struggles to convey to his Orthodox Jewish father — who thought such things surely were not fit to be discussed on the Sabbath — as he tries to articulate the difference between painting "naked women" and "nudes" (after his teacher had sought somewhat more successfully to convince the young man that painting "beautiful pictures of a beautiful girl" was no cause of defilement.)[23] We might initially smile at the decision of the Nashville, Tennessee, judge, who once decreed that a picture the vice squad had seized in a bar was in that setting obscene, but as art it was not; and he hoped some gallery would take it before it had to be destroyed.[24] On further reflection, though, we must acknowledge that the judge had put his finger on something: to the pure all things are pure, but to the corrupt

21. Pascal, *Provincial Letters,* #11.

22. Jeremy Taylor, *Holy Living and Holy Dying,* ed. P. G. Stanwood (Oxford: Clarendon Press, 1989), 1:99; see pp. 99-105.

23. Chaim Potok, *My Name Is Asher Lev* (New York: Fawcett Crest, 1972), pp. 288-89, 221.

24. *Life* magazine clipping, date unknown.

nothing is pure (Tit. 1:15). Some have charged that certain stories in the Bible are obscene, and indeed they would be if edited by Hollywood for a modern production.

God's Attitude toward Humankind

The broken relationship sin occasions is not solely on the part of humankind. It is not just that the man and woman *feel* guilty, alienated, and estranged, and need a bit of professional help to get them to perceive their situation — which, of course, could not really be that bad — more realistically; no, they do indeed stand condemned, according to the biblical witness. God is now the God who is angry with them. This change in God's attitude is not, as we have observed elsewhere, in any way incompatible with the divine immutability.[25] Because God is a personal God, we do not understand immutability in terms of abstract and static sameness, but rather in terms of God's faithfulness to his own nature: "I am who I am" (Exod. 3:14). Therefore, the rupture between God and humankind cannot be one-sided. God, being who he is, cannot possibly relate to sinful humankind the way he related to them before the Fall. So now, instead of the former tone of harmony, favor, peace, and approbation, we hear the note of reproof and picture the displeasure in God's countenance. God puts the accusing question, "Who told you that you were naked? Have you eaten from the tree of which I commanded you not to eat?" (Gen. 3:11). Then comes the word of retribution, of condemnation and curse: "To the woman he said, 'I will greatly increase your pangs in childbearing; in pain you shall bring forth children, yet your desire shall be for your husband, and he shall rule over you.' And to the man he said, 'Because you have listened to the voice of your wife, and have eaten of the tree about which I commanded you, "You shall not eat of it," cursed is the ground because of you; in toil you shall eat of it all the days of your life; thorns and thistles it shall bring forth for you; and you shall eat the plants of the field. By the sweat of your face you shall eat bread until you return to the ground, for out of it you were taken; you are dust, and to dust you shall return'" (Gen. 3:16-19). Notice here how the curse

25. See *God, Creation, and Revelation,* pp. 401-3.

involves the very things which were the particular gifts and glory of
the man and the woman. These gifts are not taken away, but they now
become bitter. The man and woman do not just know good and evil;
they now know good only as contaminated with evil. The woman will
still be "the mother of all living" (Gen. 3:20), but motherhood will be
accompanied by threat and pain.[26] She will still be the partner of the
man, but the relationship will be distorted by the man's dominance
and tyranny.[27] And as for the man, the good earth will no longer be a
garden of delight to him. Rather, his dominion over it will entail bitter
struggle.

Work, as we have said before,[28] is a creation ordinance, and a proper
dominion over the creation is the Creator's intent for both men and
women. Little is worse than having nothing to do, as the forgotten frail
elderly, and also the very rich who go from one party to another, often
testify. It is not work, which is our calling, but work under the curse
that we long to have terminated — not our task but its toil. Even with
the most advanced technology, work is still toilsome. And even labor
that takes place far from the soil or the expenditure of muscular energy
is likewise toilsome. Adolf von Harnack, for instance, remarked that
study as a scholar was always hard and laborious for him. (Perhaps that
is why so many people aspire to be students but never get read the
books they intend to read, never get the courses taken or the degrees
accomplished.) Similarly with a great talent like Caruso, whose widow
wrote of how rigorously disciplined and strenuous his practice sessions
were. One easily imagines that if one were gifted with such a golden
voice as that of the incomparable Enrico Caruso, all one would have to
do, aside from, perhaps, singing a few scales now and then, would be

26. Cotton Mather once preached to pregnant women, "For you ought to know,
your death has entered into you, and you may have conceived that which determines but
about nine months, at most, for you to live in the world. Preparation for death is that
most reasonable and most seasonable thing, to which you must now apply yourself"
(quoted by Margaret Hammer, "Birthing: Perspectives for Theology and Ministry," *Word
and World* 4:4 [Fall 1984]: 397). Jesus himself connected marriage and procreation to
death in Luke 20:35-36.

27. We may note that the word for the woman's "desire" for the man (תשוקה) is used
but rarely in the Hebrew OT, the other locations being Song of Solomon 7:10, where "desire" in the sexual sense clearly seems appropriate; but also Genesis 4:7, where the meaning is much more enigmatic and seemingly hostile.

28. *Who We Are,* pp. 411-14.

simply to open one's mouth and sing. But such was not the case. Just as he was always nervous and tense before a performance, so between performances he worked relentlessly, straining to perfect his art. Those tempted to move from one job to another under the illusion that surely the "right" job would be free from strain, have forgotten that they live and work under conditions of the Fall.

Devastating as is the curse and the confrontation for the first time with God as a judge who condemns humankind, yet curse and condemnation do not exhaust God's response to humankind's failure. Instead, in his gesture of providing coats of skins for the man and woman, we see his mercy. In place of our first parents' inadequate attempts to cover themselves, God gives them a more adequate covering as a token and symbol of his grace and forgiveness; indeed, we might see these coats as the first sacrament of grace. And besides that, we find in Genesis 3:15 not only a curse on Adam and Eve's enemy the serpent, but a curse that implies deliverance for them: "I will put enmity between you [the serpent] and the woman, and between your offspring and hers; he will strike your head, and you will strike his heel." Thus, even in the midst of his wrath, God does not abandon the guilty sinners but speaks out to them, and speaks out to them in such a way that they may yet have hope.

Humankind's Environment

The Fall, of course, is a spiritual and ethical matter, being, as we have argued, an act of pride and unbelief arising in the spirit of humankind against God. It entails a doubting of the divine goodness and a revolt against the divine authority, producing a profound disruption of the personal relationship between God and humankind. However, humankind are not only spirit but also dust (Gen. 2:7; 3:19); they are a part of nature as well as transcending mere nature. And the Scriptures reflect the idea that the whole scene of human life, the whole larger order of nature in which human beings participate, shares in the judgment on humankind.[29] The very ground is cursed for their

29. George Whitefield preached, "I have often thought, when I was abroad, that if there were no other argument to prove original sin, the rising of wolves and tigers

sake (Gen. 3:17). The whole creation was subjected to futility, not of its own will but by the will of the one who subjected it in hope (Rom. 8:20). That is to say, the creation as such is not fallen; the lower orders of creation are incapable of falling. But they suffer for humanity's sake, who are fallen; and they groan while waiting for God's final act of redemption and salvation, the coming of the freedom of the glory of the children of God (Rom. 8:19-23). In that day, the ground will no longer be cursed with thorns and thistles, but all the orders of nature will be at peace with one another, with humankind, and with God. This is the time when none shall hurt or destroy in all God's holy mountain, when the child shall play at the hole of the asp and the wolf and lamb lie down together, and the lion shall eat straw like the ox (Isa. 11:7; 65:25).

From this description of a golden age of peace and tranquility, free of struggle, warfare, disease, and death (and from the biblical data referring to an original vegetarianism, as well as mental pictures of Adam naming a parade of docile and friendly beasts), theologians have traditionally inferred that before the Fall and the entrance of sin into the world, all of life must likewise have lived in harmony, with no intrusion of noxious weeds, carnivorous animals, or death; and the Fall worked a catastrophic change. With this supposition the empirical facts as we know them simply cannot be made to mesh. Indeed, we cannot conceive how this world could long endure apart from death. We reintroduce wolves into Yellowstone Park not maliciously but to restore a balance of nature whose loss, seemingly paradoxically, threatens the health of the very creatures on whom the wolves will prey. Efforts to preserve crops by eliminating birds that eat them results in a still greater loss of crops to the insects that the birds would also have eaten, and so on.[30] The delicacy of the balance and the fact that we live in a limited environment strongly suggest that things have always func-

---

against man, nay, the barking of a dog against us, is proof of original sin. . . . When the creatures rise up against us, it is as much as to say, You have sinned against God, and we take up our Master's quarrel" ("The Method of Grace," in *Select Sermons of George Whitefield* [London: Banner of Truth Trust, 1958], pp. 51-52). Contemporary scientific scenarios envision the whole of earth eventually cold and dead, when the sun finally burns itself out. However, nature shares with humankind in praise as well as being affected by the curse: see, e.g., Ps. 98:7-8; 148; Isa. 42:10-11.

30. See *Who We Are,* pp. 399-402.

tioned in principle the way they do now. And this suspicion is confirmed by the fossil record, which shows, for instance, the perforated shells of creatures that died as prey of other creatures, as well as skeletal remains introducing us to whole species of animals that lived for a time and then became extinct and disappeared, all long before humankind appeared on the scene. The evidence virtually compels assent to the assumption that death and the suffering that goes with it have been a reality since the beginning of the drama of life in this world. Nature has always been red in tooth and claw — sometimes in fantastically brutal ways that mock the very thought of a loving or even benign divine hand designing it thus.[31]

What might be said to all of this? For one thing, a close look at the Genesis narrative reveals little which might imply that plant or animal life were at the beginning fundamentally any different than they are now — no denial that the leaves of the trees wilted and dropped, that the fruit rotted, or, for that matter, that the animals behaved the same way they do now (apart from the suggestion of Gen. 9:2 that their fear of people is post-Fall). Indeed, the psalmist celebrates the picture of the young lion roaring after his prey, along with the rest of nature, as part of God's manifold works for which he is to be praised (Ps. 104:21).[32] He does not appear to be torn by thinking of the suffering of the prey, and so it is in the Old Testament as a whole. It is the death of humankind, and especially their violent death at the hands of a murderous assassin, that is the great evil, for they are the image of God (Gen. 9:6). Thus, it may be quite improper (however natural) to extrapolate back from the prophetic pictures of the golden age of the Messiah to the primal history and suppose them to be similar states. The Bible seems rather to indicate that the new creation in Christ is more than simply a restoration; it goes beyond the original. God makes all things new, both heavens and earth (Rev. 21:1, 5). Indeed, having looked closely at evolutionary data, John Haught thinks we do better to interpret nature as a sort

31. See, for various examples, Annie Dillard, *Pilgrim at Tinker Creek* (New York: Harper & Row, 1974), passim, and esp. chap. 13.

32. If we assume that such Psalms come from approximately the same period and setting as does the first creation narrative, as many do assume, then it may be a misreading of Genesis 1 to suppose that its affirmation of the goodness of creation excludes an order where lions devour prey.

of promise of God, from which we may rightly expect future fulfillment but not perfection or lack of ambiguity now.[33]

However, no matter what we may affirm of the superiority of the final state to the first and of the importance of keeping in mind God's work as Redeemer even as we view his work as Creator, we must also acknowledge that the Genesis narrative does join the presence of thorns and thistles and death to humankind's fall. Paul likewise counts death as the wages of sin (Rom. 6:23). So something still needs to be said about an empirical record that seems to show uniformity, when the biblical record would lead us to expect a significant measure of discontinuity. None of the suggestions of which we are aware is entirely satisfactory, though some are surely less satisfactory than others. Prominent among the latter would be the early hypothesis of an anxious church that fossils do not reflect any real record of life and death on earth prior to the Fall but were simply created by God in the rocks (for whatever purposes of challenge or testing of faith one may speculate to one's heart's content). Only a little better is the thesis that thorns and thistles and other characteristics of nature that bring to mind human sin and alienation were greatly accentuated after the Fall, perhaps on the model of the plagues of Egypt: the plagues could virtually all be construed as heightened instances of familiar-enough nuisances — flies, frogs, lice, and so on — that under particular circumstances threatened life in that ancient land. But to argue that the Fall produced a shift of this kind in the natural order of things, symbolized by the prominence of thorns and thistles, would seem to require the presence of a sort of permanent negative miracle and hence strains credulity.

A very different approach is taken by those who want to affirm that there is meaning in the opening chapter of Genesis' repeated affirmation of the goodness of creation, but who also affirm that "the way things are" in the natural world manifests God's original intention — not, surely, his final intention; but nonetheless his original, albeit provisional, one. Thus, Hendrikus Berkhof argues that not only death, which is necessary to the balance of nature, but even something that would initially seem more closely connected to sin like human aggressiveness, can be construed as good because of its characteristic of being

33. He made these remarks in an interview for *Research News and Opportunities in Theology*, March/April 2001, quoted by Martin Marty in *Context* 33:15 (Aug. 15, 2001): 7.

a stimulus to the development of life. Goodness should not be seen as static perfection but as suitability to its purpose; and that purpose is not to be seen realized in the First Adam of dust but moves toward the Last Adam, a life-giving spirit (1 Cor. 15:45). Because, though, Berkhof stoutly resists attributing the current state of the created order to sin, he not only finds evil a mystery (as does every serious thinker, one way or another), but also says that God "evidently wants his creation to go through a history of resistance and struggle, of suffering and dying"[34] — surely not quite what the Scriptures say.

Barth, too, speaks in terms of what might be called a provisional quality of this present world, a world that must be seen in the context of its fulfillment in Christ (to which latter point we have agreed). Even now, though, he affirms it to be good because it is what God has made and thus must be regarded as well pleasing to him. Barth avers that we human beings cannot fully know either the exultation or the misery of our own being; and while we should by no means evade the latter, and so evade our dependence upon God, neither should we allow it to darken our assent to the world's goodness. When Christ returns, we shall know that light and shadow alike have always been God's perfect creation.[35] Thus he removes the vicissitudes and sufferings of our natural life from the realm of "nothingness" (the category under which he treats of evil, which is *not* God's good creation). There is something enormously refreshing about the humility and faith manifest in Barth's exposition, something that preserves both the dignity of our humanity in its struggles and the full glory of God. Yet it seems (no doubt because of Barth's supralapsarian commitments along with his attention to the biblical record) to waver between an affirmation of the present state of things and a "nonetheless, in the beginning it was not so."[36]

---

34. Hendrikus Berkhof, *Christian Faith: An Introduction to the Study of the Faith*, trans. Sierd Woudstra (Grand Rapids: Eerdmans, 1979), p. 170; see pp. 169-72. Much earlier, Origen construed the world as created by God for the instruction and purification of humans, whose fall was prehistorical, having taken place in a spiritual arena (see the brief discussion in Bengt Häglund, *History of Theology*, 3rd ed., trans. Gene J. Lund [St. Louis: Concordia, 1968], p. 66).

35. Barth, *Church Dogmatics*, III/1: 366-76; III/3: 295-302.

36. Contrast, for instance, Barth, *Church Dogmatics*, III/1: 208-12, with the passages cited above.

We ought not, of course, identify the whole pre-Fall creation with Eden.[37] It is easy to forget that the image of the "garden" of Eden *distinguishes* this spot from the rest of the world, as does the image of Adam and Eve being driven from it after the Fall. If we struggle to make anything more than metaphorical sense of such a place, we might at least use as an analogy our understanding of prayer and the providence of God, if we affirm that being rightly related to God in prayer may make certain differences in our concrete circumstances even now, in a world vitiated by sin. And even now, animals may be uncharacteristically docile with certain people who love them. Insofar as the most fundamental characteristic of the Garden was that our first parents were still in harmony with God and their surroundings, we can imagine that that could surely have had consequences for the functioning of the whole little sphere in which they lived.

Another sort of suggestion — perhaps as plausible as any, though lacking specific biblical warrant and hence to be held lightly — is that the natural world indeed continues as it always has, but that is because God created it as he did, not as a positive ideal and not as if he had to wait to see how humankind would turn out, but as the appropriate setting for the fallen, alienated, sinful human history he knew full well would eventuate.[38] That is to say, he tied the lower orders of the terres-

---

37. Though, as a matter of fact, such identification was popular with medieval theologians; see Jean Delumeau, *History of Paradise,* pp. 150-51.

38. Various intimations of this position go back at least to the time of Gregory of Nyssa (recall his belief that the two sexes were created in anticipation of the Fall) and Augustine: the latter affirmed that God ordered his own purposes according to his foreknowledge of the sin of the first humans (*Enchiridion* 104). Delitzsch wrote, seemingly plainly, "the whole of the six days' creation is, so to speak, supralapsarian, *i.e.* so constituted that the consequences of the foreseen fall of man were taken into account, and that there should be no need of remodelling of creation" (Franz Julius Delitzsch, *A New Commentary on Genesis,* 2 vols., trans. Sophia Taylor [Edinburgh: T&T Clark, 1899], 1:103); yet he intended here to refer only to humans' being physiologically constituted for eating meat. He had insisted just before, "The subsequent order of the world is not the original; at the beginning peace prevailed between man and the beasts, and among the beasts towards each other" (p. 102). Brunner takes up the full-blown thought, though very tentatively: "If then God knew beforehand that the Fall of man would take place, should not His creation of the world have taken *this* sort of man into account? . . . Is not a world in which, from the very beginning, from the first emergence of living creatures, there has been the struggle for existence, with all its suffering and its 'cruelty,' an arena suitable for sinful man?" (Brunner, *Christian Doctrine of Creation and Redemption,* p. 131). This idea, that is, has long been found in some sense attractive and yet fraught with uncertainty.

trial creation with the destiny and lot of humankind, the crown of the creation. The lower orders were subjected to vanity (Rom. 8:20) by an act of God, in a way that would confront humankind as sinners with the fact of the curse.

Death, though it was on this view part of the original creation as physical fact, is a curse to humankind because they are fallen (see 1 Cor. 15:56). Adam and Eve, as well as the animals and plants, would have died in any case, but they would have experienced death simply as a transition to the next life rather than as an enemy to be feared. It would have been no more dreadful than being born, no more terrible than closing one's eyes at one moment and opening them again in another world.[39]

As a sort of an aside, we might note the possibility that certain of the cultic acts and laws of the Old Testament should be attributed to this linking of nature with the fate of humankind as sinners. For example, Exodus 21:28 teaches that an ox which gores a man or woman to death shall be stoned: surely, unless one supposes — as people did in the Middle Ages — that animals are guilty of sins and crimes, one must see this law as teaching the children of Israel the value of human life, not teaching them that animals commit murder as such. An animal used for bestiality is to be killed (Lev. 20:15). Animals may be forced to fast and to wear sackcloth (Jon. 3:7-8). Again, involving animals in these ways is irrational in itself. Such ceremonial acts are to be seen as reflections of deeper spiritual truths; and some of them do seem to bind other creatures to humankind in their punishment and their guilt before God. (A widespread identification of the creation with humankind on the side of blessing may also be found.)

We have, of course, already taken a frankly anthropocentric view of creation and have further agreed that its ultimate purpose is eschatological.[40] We have also admitted certain problems with this anthropocentric view, not least being the danger of blinking the inscrutability of suffering in the animal world — not quite the same as human suffering, to be sure, but nonetheless real suffering, as can be seen in animals' caution and fearfulness in the face of danger: such suffering we cannot

---

39. For extended treatment of death as we fallen creatures actually experience it, see Appendix 1, "Physical Death as Existential Reality," pp. 230-62.

40. See *God, Creation, and Revelation*, pp. 492-501.

rationally reconcile with the goodness of the creation. And we have heard the concern of environmentalists that pervasive Christian anthropocentrism threatens the very survival of the creation by robbing it of its own proper worth and dignity.[41] Theologians from other cultures bring further insights. For instance, Andrew Sung Park complains that the whole traditional treatment of sin has a sort of self-centeredness about it, focusing on the sinner rather than on the victim. He emphasizes the Asian idea of *han,* the result of sin, which is something that nature also suffers; and he notes Cyprian's treating of the results of original sin as wounds. (Park, however, denies the universality of *han,* which is essential to the matter at hand.)[42] In short, the whole matter is riddled with difficulties, which may in itself be a manifestation of the confounding nature of sin.

We should note, in any case, that taking the position that God made a world fit for a fallen humanity involves making a distinction between giving a reason for an event and supplying it with a causal explanation, and arguing that Romans 6:23 ("the wages of sin is death") gives a theological reason for and not a causal explanation of death (a distinction that would not be made in a prescientific age, wherein it would simply be assumed that there must be a chronological sequence of sin and death).[43] Causes but not reasons must precede the relevant event: the *reason* I go to the store is to get a book, but neither getting the book nor thinking about getting the book *causes* me to go to the store — that is, moves me from here to there. Similarly, we can say that the *reason* for the universal reign of death is human sin without saying that human sin came first. That is not to deny that sin may in certain cases actually cause death: a person may drink herself to death, for instance. But if my grandfather dies *because* of cancer, that does not change the fact that at a deeper level he dies because he is a descendent of Adam's sinful race; and that is also the reason we all die. Similarly, the Resurrection of Jesus is the reason that there will in the age to come be no more sin and death, neither for those of his own who died before he lived, nor for us who now believe, nor for others yet to be born.

41. See *Who We Are,* pp. 351-57.

42. See Andrew Sung Park, *The Wounded Heart of God: The Asian Concept of Han and the Christian Doctrine of Sin* (Nashville: Abingdon, 1993).

43. For the distinction, see, for instance, Michael Polanyi, *Personal Knowledge,* pp. 331-32.

Of course we make no pretense that a view of this kind neatly resolves the felt discrepancy between the language of the creation narratives (the symbolic nature of which we have granted) and our understanding of the actual history of our earth. Every time the problem of evil enters in, our powers of conceptualization break down. And we are continually chastened by Charles Williams's blast against those who overreach themselves, to the effect, "Any fool can invent theories of the Fall, and when fools were interested in theology they frequently did."[44] Still, if one were faced with the question, What use is an account of an idyllic world if it never actually existed?, one might at least respond that only an account of that kind can truly reveal the kind of God with whom we are dealing and rightly indicate our own responsibility. It makes a moral affirmation, as well as an affirmation about God's creative power. One might also — by admittedly distant analogy — ask, What use is the commandment not to covet if everything we know about ourselves leads us to believe that this commandment will be virtually universally violated? But in this case, it is obvious that the failure of the command to prevail does not destroy its claim.

Fallen Human History

In contemplating the biblical narratives, we tend to think a good deal about salvation history *(Heilsgeschichte),* the ongoing revelation of what God has done on our behalf; and it is good that we should focus in this way. And yet, there is also a more somber strand of revelation, a death history *(Todesgeschichte),* that record of the unfolding of the effects of the Fall in human history. The representative character of our first parents' act is underscored in that the effects of their disobedience were visited not just on them but on their posterity as well: death came upon all; none could return to the Garden. What is more, the primal history sets a sort of trajectory of evil that leaves us little room for surprise at human wickedness — unlike the fictional king of Brobdingnag, who "was perfectly astonished with the historical account [Gulliver] gave him of our affairs during the last century; protesting it was only a

---

44. Charles Williams, *Forgiveness of Sins* (1942; Grand Rapids: Eerdmans, 1984), p. 3.

heap of conspiracies, rebellions, murders, massacres, revolutions, banishments; the very worst effects that avarice, faction, hypocrisy, perfidiousness, cruelty, rage, madness, hatred, envy, lust, malice, and ambition could produce."[45] One of the most striking things about human history is the staggering "monotony of the pride in which man has obviously always lived to his own detriment and to that of his neighbour."[46] As Barth summarized Schopenhauer's pessimistic view:

> In great things as in small, life offers itself to us as perpetual deception. It does not keep its promises except to show how little desirable was that which we desired. If it gave it was only to take. . . . Life is merely death delayed and restrained — the death which must finally conquer. . . . "The best of all possible worlds?" On the contrary, the world is as bad as it possibly can be if it is to be at all. . . . There is indeed an eternal justice, but it consists only in the fact that on the whole the misery of man is not greater than his unworthiness.[47]

In the Genesis account, Adam and Eve first refuse responsibility for their own actions and seek to pass the blame (Gen. 3:12-13), compromising their solidarity with one another. Then envy, malice, and anger lead to murder, Cain rising to slay his own brother (Gen. 4:8); yet he still has enough reverence for the right to evade admitting it (Gen. 4:9). But let a few generations pass,[48] and we find Lamech not only murdering but boasting of murder to his wives: "I have killed a man for wounding me, a young man for striking me. If Cain is avenged sevenfold, truly Lamech seventy-sevenfold" (Gen. 4:23). We also see with Lamech the first record of bigamy, violation of the marriage ordinance of a single man and woman given to one another. By the time of the Flood, "The LORD saw that the wickedness of humankind was great in the earth, and that every inclination of the thoughts of their hearts was only evil continually" (Gen. 6:5) — one of the most emphatic statements about radical human depravity found anywhere in Scripture. This violent and

45. Jonathan Swift, *Gulliver's Travels*, p. 76.
46. Barth, *Church Dogmatics*, IV/1: 507.
47. Barth, *Church Dogmatics*, III/1: 336.
48. We have granted, of course, that the whole primal history is compressed on the timeline. See above, p. 4; *Who We Are*, p. 357.

universal corruption (Gen. 6:11-12) provides the theological setting for the Flood narrative, which serves as a sequel to that of the Fall and shows that sin leads at last to judgment.[49]

With remarkable theological acuity, James Weldon Johnson, in his sermon in verse, "Noah Built the Ark," tied the Flood first to the Fall and then to God's final judgment. The concluding lines of the sermon read:

> God hung out his rainbow cross the sky,
> And he said to Noah: That's my sign!
> No more will I judge the world by flood —
> Next time I'll rain down fire.[50]

He rightly captured the central point that the Flood serves as a sort of parable or type of the final judgment of the wicked world, like the fall of Babylon in Revelation 18-19. (It does not accomplish redemption from sin; sin continues after the Deluge, just as sin continues in hell.)[51]

The effect of the disruption that has occurred can be seen in the post-Flood dictum that God will require a reckoning for human life, of each person for the blood of another (Gen. 9:5). That the thing needed to be said — could be said — at all shows the state to which humankind had come. No longer are relationships only positively constitutive of our humanity, but they are now sources of pain and disorder from the most intimate to the most global levels.[52] We inescapably hurt and are

---

49. We might also note that life span progressively declines from the antediluvians, through the patriarchs, until, after Exodus, it reaches approximately today's length — suggestive, again, of deterioration that impinges on later descendants (see Dubarle, *Biblical Doctrine of Original Sin*, pp. 84-85), and illustrative of the association of sin and death. Calvin devotes several sections to demonstrating that the blessing of the patriarchs was not earthly, but rather they were subject to many miseries (*Institutes* 2.10.10-12, 17).

50. James Weldon Johnson, *God's Trombones*, p. 37.

51. It therefore misses the real import of the narrative to inquire in a scientific manner about the universal scope of the Flood: universal language is frequently used in Scripture in a way that cannot be pressed literally (e.g., Dan. 2:38; Luke 2:1; John 12:19; Acts 2:5; 17:6). Furthermore, the story itself presupposes natural phenomena: rain, and the later retreat of the waters. A devastating local flood of the type not unknown in the Tigris-Euphrates Valley would suffice to illustrate the grim reality of judgment.

52. Bonhoeffer notes that medieval visual symbolism for the Fall puts a tree with a serpent coiled around it between the man and the woman, separating them from one

hurt by those closest to us, as well as those half a world away. Our efficiency in doing the latter increases with our power, whether in the use of weapons of mass destruction, the global effects of pollution, or the ravages of self-interested but interdependent economies. The principle of interrelatedness, however, remains the same: no one has ever rightly been able to argue that her behavior affected none but herself. And once evil has entered in, the necessary efforts to restrain the disorder — all the impositions of law and investigations of ethics — will themselves give opportunity to sin as well as contain it, as the apostle Paul made so plain in his deliverances on the impotence of the Law.[53] Hence the sovereignty of the divine covenant, the Lord's promise that he will not, in spite of everything, reject his people forever, forsake them, or abandon his heritage (Lam. 3:31; Ps. 94:14), takes on new significance.

---

another (*The Communion of Saints*, trans. R. Gregor Smith [New York: Harper & Row, 1963], p. 42).

53. One source of the impotence of law and ethics may be seen in Charles Williams's striking observation that Adam and Eve in their shame "fled from facts" (*He Came Down from Heaven*, p. 116): the knowledge of good and evil they had gained did not produce in them either the desire or the ability to face the truth. This lack of any necessary relationship between knowledge and truthfulness is particularly significant in an age like ours, in which knowledge accumulates so quickly (and is a different point from the also necessary distinction of knowledge from wisdom).

5

The Divine Purpose and Moral Evil

Our reflections on the problem of evil at the practical level must await our treatments of providence and of salvation, where we will consider, respectively, what God is doing and what God has done for our salvation. At this point, we will touch only upon the general, theoretical problem of theodicy: if God is omniscient, omnipotent, and perfectly good, whence evil? How is such a thing as the Fall even possible? (We will focus on moral evil here, leaving natural evil — for which we have said moral evil is ultimately the reason — for later. This side of Auschwitz, the focus in discussion of the problem of evil has in any case been on moral evil; whereas earlier, natural disasters such as the Lisbon earthquake of 1755, which took somewhere between ten and sixty thousand lives, held center stage.)

We must acknowledge straightway that the theodicy question is dangerous both intellectually and morally.[1] It is dangerous intellectually because it obscures the great gulf fixed between the creature and the Creator and suggests that the creature's mind can penetrate or somehow "get behind" the divine mind. It supposes that the creature can judge what is or is not "possible" for God, or what God's purposes for a world like this one must be.[2] But surely, of matters of this kind, we

---

1. See, for example, Terrence W. Tilly, *The Evils of Theodicy* (Washington, D.C.: Georgetown University Press, 1991). While he makes many helpful points, it should be noted that he is working with a much narrower and more technical understanding of the "theodicy" enterprise than we are using here.

2. We are not speaking here of logical possibility and impossibility within the created order as we know it: as we have said, to affirm that God cannot make a stick with

know only what God has chosen to reveal to us; and one of the things he has revealed to us is that it is not to our good that we should know everything (Exod. 33:18-20). The psalmist implies that it is possible for us to occupy ourselves "with things too great and marvelous" for us (Ps. 131:1). Let us candidly confess, then, that we do not know what we are talking about when we attribute "necessity" to some action of God's. Yet, God has given human beings the kind of intelligence that will insist upon wrestling with such problems; so one doubtless does well to counsel humility in facing them rather than futilely advise disengagement from them.

The kind of humility required is not merely intellectual, though. The desire to justify God in the face of suffering quickly degenerates into the desire to justify suffering, with all the consequent loss of personal, empathic engagement with the particularity of human agony. Talking about evil in the abstract, that is, can insulate one from both feeling and action on behalf of the afflicted. Furthermore, insofar as one posits suffering as inevitable or, worse, as "necessary" either to the individual's growth or to some larger plan, it reduces motivation to alleviate the suffering. Ironically, then, the studied defense of God's goodness can lessen acts expressive of ordinary human goodness. Thus, while both the intellectual and the moral danger attending the enterprise of theodicy are serious, the moral danger is the more important: intellectual hubris finally makes us only silly, but moral hubris can make us monsters.

Divine Sovereignty

It is thus with great caution that we would venture remarks at the theoretical level, knowing that we can see, if at all, but "through a glass darkly."[3] These remarks make no pretense of carving new inroads into

---

one end has to do with the definition of "stick" in the world God has actually made (see *God, Creation, and Revelation,* pp. 353-55); and such an affirmation is legitimate. But to seek to get behind the creation to speculative possibilities and impossibilities is to overreach ourselves — like trying to force curved space to obey the axioms of Euclidean geometry, to use an earthly analogy.

3. While Milton boldly set it as the purpose of his great poem to "assert Eternal Providence,/And justifie the wayes of God to men" (*Paradise Lost,* 1.25-26); A. E. Housman later

the problem but attempt only a laying out what we would take to be important parameters of the discussion, in light of biblical revelation. The first of these is reaffirmation of the divine sovereignty. If God is the God "who accomplishes all things according to his counsel and will" (Eph. 1:11); the one who declares "the end from the beginning and from ancient times things not yet done, saying, 'My purpose shall stand, and I will fulfill my intention'" (Isa. 46:10); who "has made everything for its purpose, even the wicked for the day of trouble" (Prov. 16:4; see also Job 12:16); then we must somehow understand the Fall from the standpoint of God's eternal purpose.[4] Not that we can fully discern what God's purpose in the Fall is; we rather affirm by faith that even though the Fall is evil, God wills to use it for his good end. We cannot speak of the Fall as if it were an accident, through which history slipped somehow out of God's control.

Our confidence in making this affirmation is buttressed by the astonishing conviction with which the early Christians asserted God's governance even in the wicked actions of evil people. Note, for instance, this prayer:

> "Sovereign Lord, who made the heaven and the earth, the sea, and everything in them, it is you who said by the Holy Spirit through our ancestor David, your servant: 'Why did the Gentiles rage, and the peoples imagine vain things? The kings of the earth took their stand, and the rulers have gathered together against the Lord and against his Messiah.' For in this city, in fact, both Herod and Pontius Pilate, with the Gentiles and the peoples of Israel, gathered together against your holy servant Jesus, whom you anointed, to do whatever your hand and your plan had predestined to take place. And now, Lord, look at their threats, and grant to your servants to speak your word with all boldness, while you stretch out your hand to heal, and signs and wonders are performed through the name of your holy servant Jesus." (Acts 4:24-30)

---

wrote cynically, "malt does more than Milton can/To justify God's ways to man" (from "Terence, This Is Stupid Stuff," in *Mentor Book of Major British Poets*, ed. Oscar Williams [New York: New American Library, 1963], p. 407). The greatest of efforts does not prevail in the face of actual human misery, which is more easily deadened than reasoned away.

4. See also Acts 15:18: a well-attested reading is, "Known to God from of old are all his works."

Or take this line in Peter's Pentecost sermon — one that many of us would have softened, had he shown us his manuscript in advance: "This man, handed over to you according to the definite plan and foreknowledge of God, you crucified and killed by the hands of those outside the law" (Acts 2:23). Now, if such texts are saying anything, surely they are saying that Calvary fulfills the will of God, even though, *at the same time*, it manifests the culmination of human revolt against God's will, that revolt that began with the Fall.

Is God Responsible for Sin?

The immediate objection to the position that we have here taken, putting emphasis on the divine sovereignty, is that it makes God the author of sin, an idea that most theologians have considered inadmissible.[5] We concur with this majority judgment. Sin is rebellion against God, and God cannot rebel against himself. Furthermore, committing sin means that one is a responsible creature, one who can be called to account for her actions; but God is by definition not responsible to the creature: "no one . . . can stay his hand or say to him, 'What are you doing?'" (Dan. 4:35). The "author of sin," therefore, must be the one in whose mind the first sinful act of rebellion against God is conceived — Satan, as far as we know; and, in the case of humankind, our first parents. Nonetheless, one might retort, God surely seems to be responsible for sin if he causes people to do what they do. But we have been rather careful to avoid the language of causality, taken in the sense of determinism.

---

5. Schleiermacher, however, frankly affirmed that God was the Author of sin, though he quickly qualified this affirmation by saying that he is such only as sin is related to redemption (and he also differentiated between God's commanding and his efficient will). See *The Christian Faith*, ed. H. R. Mackintosh and J. S. Stewart (Edinburgh: T&T Clark, 1928), pp. 325-38. The problem can arise at the level of each new birth, if one is a creationist (as opposed to a traducianist) with respect to the soul and if one affirms original sin. Faced with this dilemma, twelfth-century theologian Odo of Tournai simply asserted, making analogy to Adam, "the soul is the work of God and . . . sin is the work of man" (*On Original Sin* and *A Disputation with the Jew, Leo, Concerning the Advent of Christ, the Son of God*, trans. Irven M. Resnick [Philadelphia: University of Pennsylvania Press, 1994], p. 59).

The Scriptures sometimes do speak in what we might interpret as causal terms of the divine efficacy, even with regard to sinful acts. For instance, the hiphil verb tense in Hebrew, which is understood to mean that one "caused" thus and such to occur, is frequently used of God as well as of humans; and we also find such bald and disconcerting statements as "the LORD hardened the heart of Pharaoh" (Exod. 9:12; see also Rom. 11:32, "For God has imprisoned all in disobedience so that he may be merciful to all"), which surely sound as if God actively produced the effect. However, it is important to recall that the Scriptures were written before the rise of modern science and our consequent scientific and philosophical notions of causality. It is therefore anachronistic to interpret such texts in the light of these notions.

We really do not know how God works to bring about his own purposes in and through the free and responsible acts of people. But we must seek to say how he does *not* work, namely, in such a way that human decisions for good or evil are determined by an external force or power, as is a stone rolling down hill or water seeking its own level.[6] God does not, that is, determine a person's choices or the decisions of her heart in the way the motion of material objects is determined by the law of gravity. Nor is a human being a sinner in the way that a fox is a fox: God does not give humans their being in the same way that he gives being to the lower creatures, but gives it in such a way that the gift is also a responsibility. Thus, all we can say is that human beings never finally frustrate God's design, and God never violates human freedom. That is why the Scriptures can assert in the same chapter both that the LORD hardened Pharaoh's heart and, a few verses later, that Pharaoh hardened his own heart (Exod. 9:12, 34). This paradox of the complete divine sovereignty and the responsible freedom of people is deeply em-

---

6. It is true that Proverbs 21:1 uses the analogy of water in speaking of God's dealings with people — "The king's heart is a stream of water in the hand of the LORD; he turns it wherever he will" — but surely the univocal element of the analogy should not be construed to be at the level of causality. We reject, therefore, the conclusion of Ahab in Moby Dick: "Is Ahab, Ahab? Is it I, God, or who, that lifts this arm? But if the great sun move not of himself; but is as an errand-boy in heaven; nor one single star can revolve, but by some invisible power; how then can this one small heart beat; this one small brain think thoughts; unless God does that beating, does that thinking, does that living, *and not I*" (Herman Melville, *Moby-Dick; or, The Whale, Great Books,* vol. 48 [Chicago: Encyclopaedia Britannica, 1952], p. 396, emphasis added).

bedded in Scripture and is a mystery that must be preserved rather than dissolved.

Therefore, even while we hold that the Fall does not frustrate God's purpose, we do not consider it an occasion for singing the "Doxology," in the tradition of those who speak of it as a "happy guilt" *(felix culpa),* since it leads finally to the redemption in Christ that we could not otherwise have known.[7] This idea, however, has a long history. The Roman mass for the night before Easter (which may go back to the fifth century) contains in the *Exultet* the line, "O happy guilt, which merited such and so great a Redeemer!" Similarly, the fourteenth- or fifteenth-century English carol "Adam Lay Ybounden" says:

Ne had the apple taken been,
The apple taken been,
Ne had never our lady
A-been heavene queen.

Blessed be the time
That apple taken was.
Therefore we moun singen
Deo Gracias!

And by the twelfth book of *Paradise Lost,* the initially distraught Adam can ask:

Whether I should repent me now of sin
By mee done and occasioned, or rejoyce
Much more, that much more good thereof shall spring,
To God more glory, more good will to Men
From God, and over wrauth grace shall abound. (ll. 474-78)

Such affirmations are not made without biblical reason. Consider, for instance, Paul's remark that God has shut up all to unbelief *in order that* (ἵνα) he might have mercy upon all (Rom. 11:32). However — and, to us, more hauntingly, and truer overall to the biblical ethos as it bears on our own responsibilities (as typified by Paul's horror at the idea that we

---

7. It can also be linked to the immaturity theory of the Fall (a theory we have rejected): the Fall proved fortunate because it provided our first parents with a learning experience.

should sin in order that grace might abound, Rom. 6:1-2) — modern poet W. H. Auden, having reflected on all the poetic inspiration his somewhat dissipated life had brought him, pondered the possibility that,

> God may reduce you
> on Judgment Day
> to tears of shame,
> reciting by heart
> the poems you would
> have written, had
> your life been good.[8]

It is improper for the creature to celebrate what she can only rightly mourn, corrupting for the sinner to justify evil. Better, rather, simply to confess that God's ways are beyond us.

Is Evil Necessary for Good?

For all of its affirmation of the divine sovereignty, Scripture never speaks quite in terms that suggest evil to be a *necessary* condition for good. While it can boldly affirm that evil, including moral evil, will redound to the ultimate glory of God; it also presents to us the picture of the angels who, without having fallen, enjoy the beatific vision of God, and that of Jesus Christ, who supremely fulfilled our humanity, yet realized his full potential without sin.

Thus, though we have already rejected the idea of tragedy as an adequate category to interpret our condition, neither can we confidently go the route of Leibniz (who coined the term "theodicy") and say that this is "the best of all possible worlds" — a maximally rich and varied world in which the most positive possible balance of good and evil obtains. It is, of course, true that certain virtues are developed in seeking to combat pain and evil — courage, heroism, self-sacrifice, and so on. Scripture itself affirms positive outcomes from suffering (e.g., 2 Cor. 1:3-7; Heb. 2:10; 5:8; 1 Pet. 4:1). It is also true that our experience of many goods is

---

8. From "Thanksgiving for a Habitat," in W. H. Auden, *Collected Poems*, p. 525.

sharpened by contrast with a corresponding evil: we get little pleasure from food if we are not hungry, feel little joy at deliverance if we are not sensible of danger, cannot make many a beautiful painting without dark tones.[9] And, in a finite world as we know it, the existence of separate individuals and assorted limits means that there will be irresolvable conflicts of needs and interests: often, whatever choice or decision is made will hurt someone. However, to speak of shadows in a painting, or even the unfortunate fact that if Jill gets the promotion, Jack will not (but Jack gets to benefit from a chance to learn generosity and humility), is not quite the same thing as contemplating so much as a child torturing an animal, not to mention such indescribable horrors as Hiroshima or Auschwitz. Surely the unfathomable depth and scope of actual moral evil should teach us, if we are capable of instruction at all, that it is improper — indeed, impious and dangerous — to imagine that God could purpose good and evil *in the same sense.* That God can redeem evil and make it serve him, we affirm by faith; that he wills moral evil as a positive means to his larger ends (or that he "needs" the reprobate in order fully to display his glory), we deny as a moral impossibility.[10]

Keble's poem for the twelfth Sunday after Trinity depicts even Jesus as sighing at the weight of evil, as he engaged in his acts of healing (with reference to Mark 7:34): how, then, can the sinner blithely fit evil into her tidy schemes?[11] Indeed, the moral offense caused by the idea that innocent suffering could somehow be essential to a larger harmony generates the powerful sort of "protest atheism" exemplified by Ivan Karamazov: "'Tell me yourself, I challenge you — answer. Imagine that you are creating a fabric of human destiny with the object of making men happy in the end, giving them peace and rest at last, but that it was essential and inevitable to torture to death only one tiny creature

---

9. See Augustine's reflections on these matters in the *Confessions,* 8.7. Barth, too, takes up this idea: "God's supreme and truest good for creation . . . is revealed in its full splendour only when its obedience and blessedness are not simply its nature . . . but when they are salvation from the edge of an abyss" (*Church Dogmatics,* II/1: 595). But if contrast with its opposite is essential to the experience of the good, whence the joys of Eden, or of heaven?

10. Let us make explicit our rejection of the idea that this world is optimal for "soul-making": set this theory alongside the humanly instigated monstrosities of the twentieth century and it condemns itself.

11. John Keble, *The Christian Year* (New York: Frederick A. Stokes, c. 1827), pp. 137-39.

... and to found that edifice on its unavenged tears, would you consent to be the architect on those conditions? Tell me, and tell the truth.'"[12] The Cross is a special case; but we have said that God both does and does not will the actions that brought it to pass.

The most widely accepted alternative or supplementary view is that in choosing to make human beings and angels truly free, God risked that they would misuse their freedom; and they did (as God foreknew they would).[13] The whole spiraling history of evil is but the unfolding of free but sinful choices, first by fallen angels and then on the part of humankind. Well, yes; in one sense we must agree. We have refused to deny the reality of human (or, by reasonable extension, angelic) freedom in the interests of any sort of determinism; we have insisted on human responsibility. However, unless one is a metaphysical dualist and grants Satan equal status with God, or at least truly independent status (which Christians do not), one must take Luther's point that even the Devil himself is God's Devil.[14] For all his destructiveness and railing, he cannot win in the end. And we have already quoted scriptural evidence that God uses the free but sinful acts of people to his own ends. If we affirm that God has power to bring history to the end he has purposed, we must also grant that in some sense he has evil on a leash. Why, then — we may ask with many others before us — such a long leash?

In an interesting paragraph, Kierkegaard argued that only an omnipotent being has the power so to "take itself back" as to make another being truly free. Since freedom is the greatest good that can be granted, granting it is also a manifestation of God's goodness.[15] By

---

12. Fyodor Dostoyevsky, *The Brothers Karamazov,* trans. Constance Garnett (New York: Modern Library, 1950), p. 291.

13. Those in the Augustinian tradition naturally speak more strongly of the divine initiative. In Augustine's words, "the God and Lord of all things, who in His strength created all things good, and foreknew that evil things would arise out of good, and knew that it pertained to His most omnipotent goodness even to do good out of evil things rather than not to allow evil things to be at all, so ordained the life of angels and men that in it He might first of all show what their free will was capable of, and then what the kindness of His grace and the judgment of His righteousness was capable of" (*On Rebuke and Grace,* chap. 27).

14. Similarly, by contrast to Zoroastrianism, the dualism of light and darkness in Scripture is not metaphysical but moral.

15. Søren Kierkegaard, *Journals,* trans. Alexander Dru (London: Oxford University Press, 1938), pp. 180-81.

contrast, Bayle protested that no true benefactor will bestow a gift that he knows will be so abused as to bring about the ruin of the one upon whom it is bestowed; nor will he fail to act to prevent harm, even if such action impinges on another's freedom.[16] Besides, the impetus to misuse freedom, or even to choose a lower over a higher good (to draw in an aspect of the Platonic and Augustinian view of evil as manifesting deficit or lack rather than having positive substance) must come from somewhere; and calling its source a "deficient" instead of an "efficient" cause would not seem to throw much light on the matter (as Augustine admits even while making this very distinction).[17] Calvin candidly refuses the supposed distinction between God's will and his permission as incompatible with the divine sovereignty.[18]

Much, then, remains hidden to us.[19] We do best to ground our faith in God's power to transform evil to good in the Cross and Resurrection, where he was both Victim and Victor on our behalf. There, the "you meant it for evil, but God meant it for good" (the words of Joseph to his brothers in Gen. 50:20), the ability of God to ensure that all things will work together for good for those who love him and are called according to his purpose (Rom. 8:28), take on their fullest meaning and deepest promise. It is only because we know that this is the kind of God with whom we have to do that we can trust him to be neither malevolent nor indifferent to our suffering, whatever the realities of human existence might otherwise lead us to believe. Only on such grounds can we even contemplate Augustine's insistence that "if it were not a good that evil should exist, its existence would not be permitted by the omnipotent God."[20] But, again, this is a statement of faith in the face of inscrutable mystery; it must never be turned into a rational justification of evil.

We take very seriously the agonized caveat of Robert McAfee Brown in his book on Elie Wiesel: "if we could understand it would be worse. . . . If one could understand a universe in which the Holocaust made sense, or develop a concept of God in relation to whom the Holocaust could be 'justified,' that would be a universe in which the judge

16. *Historical and Critical Dictionary,* ed. Richard H. Popkin (Indianapolis: Bobbs-Merrill, 1965), p. 177-78.

17. Augustine, *City of God,* 12:7.

18. Calvin, *Institutes,* 3.23.7-8.

19. See our remarks on God's hiddenness in *God, Creation, and Revelation,* pp. 85-88.

20. Augustine, *Enchiridion,* 96.

would not care to live, that would be a God in whom he would not want to believe."[21] We would take the dual perspective of the book of Job, in which the wager of God with Satan set up at the beginning remains unknown to Job (and seems to have an entirely different tone than the unfolding of the story), to be a sort of parable of our circumstances: it is not, surely, to be taken as teaching that God is toying with us, nor simply that a "happy ending" will finally make up for everything, but that we must act without knowing the cosmic background of our situation. And somehow, as Karl Heim reminds us, this background involves battle with an enemy: we must face the paradox that while in the end we have to do only with God alone and our own fault before him, yet in the meantime the struggle against satanic evil is real.[22] Thus, we must not at all costs imagine ourselves free to model ourselves upon a supposed divine example and do a little evil that good may come: it was the serpent who sought to get behind God's commands to his alleged motives and so led our first parents astray. We would also counsel a certain measure of caution with respect to the experiences reported by many Christians in times of trial (and, especially, by mystics of all traditions), of God making his presence and love so powerfully known to them that they are certain "everything will be all right" — no matter what happens. While we celebrate such experiences for the comfort they may be to individuals, if they so dissolve the distinction between good and evil that they make persons less motivated to identify and fight evil, evil may gain wider scope. (Isaiah 5:20 warns against those who call evil good and good evil.)

Thus, while we may acknowledge particular instances in which, say, suffering brings a depth and nobility to a person that she never had before, as a kind of hint of what God can make of evil, it is only a hint and not a justification for suffering. We must attribute the good to God, not to the evil (which, even in its lesser forms, as readily destroys as builds up).[23] And, while we hold firm to an eschatological hope of the

21. Robert McAfee Brown, *Elie Wiesel: Messenger to All Humanity* (Notre Dame: University of Notre Dame Press, 1983), p. 143.

22. Karl Heim, *Jesus the Lord* (Philadelphia: Muhlenberg, 1961), pp. 103-110, 129-35.

23. Barth makes a similar point: "If our share in the misery of life has the power to bind us to God, and thus to assure us of the justification of being, that is not due to the power of creaturely existence itself, and therefore to our own power, but to the independent power of divine revelation which transcends all creaturely power" (*Church Dogmatics,* III/1: 375).

day when tears, death, mourning, and pain will be no more (Rev. 21:4); we cannot — for the sake of the neighbor Scripture relentlessly commends to our care — act or think as if heaven makes earth of no account.[24]

Our response therefore bows before God's answer to Job from the whirlwind: God answers; but he answers not with reasons and justifications but with questions, questions designed to demonstrate the impossibility that a human should comprehend God (Job 38-41; see also Ps. 139:6; Isa. 55:8-9; Rom. 11:33-34). Job got neither solutions nor comfort, but God did address him, which is not nothing. Said G. K. Chesterton, "He has been told nothing, but he feels the terrible and tingling atmosphere of something too good to be told. The riddles of God are more satisfying than the solutions of man."[25] Doubly so when human solutions are as impossible and even offensive as those to the problem of evil inevitably are.

Of the too-muchness of evil for the human heart and mind, the Christian Charles Williams wrote that God "neither forbore to create because we were about to sin nor ceased to sustain when we had begun to sin. It is the choice of a God, not of a man; we should have been less harsh. We should not have created because we could not have endured; we could not have willed; we could not have loved. It is the choice of a

24. It is true, of course, that Scripture often uses the hope of heaven to relativize the troubles of earth: e.g., "the sufferings of this present time are not worth comparing with the glory about to be revealed to us" (Rom. 8:18); "this slight momentary affliction is preparing us for an eternal weight of glory beyond all measure" (2 Cor. 4:17); or, quite baldly, "if we endure [υπομενω, which has the sense of enduring difficulty or suffering], we will also reign with him" (2 Tim. 2:12). Note, however, that such texts are addressed to those needing to manage their own suffering before God, not offered as an attitude recommended toward the suffering of others, or toward evil in general.

25. Quoted by Untermeyer, *A Treasury of Great Poems* (New York: Simon & Schuster, 1955), p. 21. Rudolf Otto's conclusion is similar: Job, and we, are not given something that can be rendered in simply rational categories; "that of which we are conscious is rather an *intrinsic value* in the incomprehensible — a value inexpressible, positive, and 'fascinating.' This is incommensurable with thoughts of rational human teleology and is not assimilated to them: it remains in all its mystery. But it is as it becomes felt in consciousness that Elohim is justified and at the same time Job's soul brought to peace" (*The Idea of the Holy*, trans. John W. Harvey [London: Oxford University Press, 1926], p. 83; see also pp. 80-82). Likewise Martin Buber, who came "to sense in the nameable torment the nameless grace" (quoted in Paul Emen, "Isaac Singer at Jabbok's Ford," *Christian Century* 96:18 [May 16, 1979]: 549).

God, not of a man."[26] And the Jew Elie Wiesel described a strange trial, inside the kingdom of night, in which "three rabbis — all erudite and pious men — decided one winter evening to indict God for allowing His children to be massacred." They found him guilty as charged. Then, after the trial, one of them looked at the watch he had somehow managed to retain and said, "Oy! It's time for prayers." And the three rabbis, all erudite and pious men, bowed their heads and prayed.[27] Only by faith can we say that this mysterious God is the good Lord, "just in all his ways, and kind in all his doings" (Ps. 145:17; see also Ezek. 14:23). Only by faith can we continue to believe in and seek "the everlasting fountain of the waters of joy that our sorrow uses for tears."[28]

---

26. Charles Williams, *Forgiveness of Sins,* p. 100.

27. Brown, *Elie Wiesel,* p. 154.

28. Auden, "For the Time Being," in *Collected Poems,* p. 274. Beethoven repudiated his "Ode to Joy," but Christians incorporate it in their hymn books in spite of everything.

Part II

The Doctrine of Sin

What a chimera then is man! What a novelty! What a monster, what a chaos, what a contradiction, what a prodigy! Judge of all things, imbecile worm of the earth; depositary of truth, a sink of uncertainty and error; the pride and refuse of the universe!

Blaise Pascal, *Pensées*

From such crooked wood as a man is made of, nothing perfectly straight can be built.

Immanuel Kant, *Idea for a Universal History
from a Cosmopolitan Point of View*

6

The Nature of Sin

The doctrine of the Fall, as we have noted, has come upon rather hard times, and not without a measure of scholarly cause. But the Fall — whatever its existential reverberations in individual lives — we can at least picture as being safely remote in time and place. Discussions of sin, on the other hand, come with a disconcerting and intrusive immediacy that late twentieth- and early twenty-first-century society seems determined to hold at bay, as intimated in the Ziggy cartoon in which a bearded prophet carries a bold "SINNERS REPENT" sign whose message is moderated by a parenthetical "nothing personal." Or take the prayer of "confession" printed in a church bulletin during Advent of 2001 (presumably a season for serious self-examination and repentance in preparation for the coming of the Lord):

> God of grace, as followers of your Son, we are always on a journey. On our pilgrimage there is no time when we can afford to stop growing in love, in strength, and in our knowledge of you. So it is that when we gather to worship we would confess those places in which we need to grow. In preparation for the coming of the Christ, hear us as we confess our need for growth, in silence prompted by your Spirit.[1]

1. The bulletin credits Ruth C. Duck, ed., *Bread for the Journey* (New York: Pilgrim Press, 1985), for the prayer.

Again, "nothing personal," or even especially culpable. Just a few imma-
ture spots that can be cured by a bit of "growth." Other parts of the service of worship are not exempt from this trend. Certain contemporary
hymnals recommend that we no longer sing,

> Amazing grace! (how sweet the sound!)
> That saved a wretch like me!

but rather,

> Amazing grace! How sweet the sound!
> That saved and strengthened me![2]

An analysis of sermons on the parable of the Prodigal Son shows that
Southern Baptist and Presbyterian preachers alike manifest a marked
squeamishness about confronting hearers with the possibility that
they themselves are addressed as real sinners by the parable.[3] Or, moving to the frankly secular arena, attention to the popular media brings
the judgment that for all their depiction of horrendous evil, the very
outrageousness of the evil allows audiences to keep it "out there," distinct from the ordinary behaviors of normal human beings. Mass mur-
derers, bombers of public buildings, child molesters, terrorists: these
are the sources of serious evil, who can be caught and punished, thus
exorcising the problem from society (and even then, the perpetrators
will likely be seen not just as monsters but as victims of society and of
their past, or of their biological makeup — anything to escape the religious category of sin).[4]

2. Brian Abel Ragen, "A Wretch Like Who?" *America* 162 (January 29, 1994): 8-11. After
further comment, the author concludes, "while the 18th-century slaver [the hymn's author John Newton] may have been a wretch, the singers of the new version are not: They
are good people. The only question left is why they need to be saved" (p. 9).

3. Marsha G. Witten, *All Is Forgiven: The Secular Message in American Protestantism*
(Princeton: Princeton University Press, 1993).

4. See Quentin J. Schultze, "Civil Sin: Evil and Purgation in the Media," *Theology Today* 50:2 (July 1993): 229-42. One recalls psychiatrist Karl Menninger's work, *Whatever Became of Sin?* (New York: Hawthorne, 1973), in which he criticizes the abdication of theologians in favor of those offering medical and psychological categories in which to
describe human malaise. This tendency to medicalize and psychologize appears to have
replaced the earlier optimism that progress and education would successfully mitigate
human evil: the essays in the opening volume of the Britannica *Great Books* series (*The*

Not, of course, that we should lose sight of the labors and insights of those who have sensitized us to the devastating effects of structural and systemic evils, including oppression and discrimination in their myriad forms. Sin is not just a matter of small-scale personal nastiness. Nor would we deny that genetic and biochemical factors give some persons predispositions and vulnerabilities from which others are free.[5] Nonetheless, loss of the category of sin at the individual level more surely robs us of dignity and of hope than does the most punishing "miserable sinner" theology of another age. After all, "miserable sinners" retain the status of those who have responsibility for their behavior and the prospects of a Savior who can deliver them. Those who are only victims of governments, cultures, psychology, or biology are shut up to whatever help compassion for their state may (or may not) evoke, whatever healing a new technology may provide, or whatever transformations the latest public reform efforts or private bootstrap operations may produce — a set of options that should not cheer the clear-eyed observer of human history. These efforts to protest individual innocence, that is, come at an extremely high — not to mention unbiblical — price.

To insist that the doctrine of sin is an essential protection of human dignity is certainly not to deny that sin is, first and most basically, an evil. Now that latter affirmation is hardly, one might protest, an insight one needs a volume of theology to gain; yet it remains a necessary caution in a day when some would seek to make sin a necessary step in human development and self-realization, an "adult" breaking away from dependence and oppressive authority, or a vital and interesting component of a not-too-rigid character structure, and thus a good when seen in the context of a larger whole (or else a reference to something delectable and chocolate interdicted by the body beautiful police).[6] Scripture does not speak

---

Great Conversation, published in 1952), for instance, never refer to sin, although the topic does constitute one of the chapters in the volumes entitled *The Great Ideas* (it appears in vol. 3); and the volume containing works of Kant never mentions his views on radical evil (nor does the *Encyclopaedia Britannica* itself; indeed a search of the entire Britannica 2001 DVD-ROM [Encyclopaedia Britannica, Inc., 1994-2001], which contains the whole text of the encyclopedia, reveals not a single reference to radical evil anywhere).

5. See below, pp. 117-27, on sin and sickness.

6. All of this (and especially that which bears on evolutionary arguments) brings with it denial that sin is "natural": as Augustine put it, "if sin be natural, it is not sin at all" (*City of God,* 11.15; see also 11.17).

in this way.[7] Humankind were good before they sinned, and sin perverts that good. Sin does not enable but destroys the truly human. Furthermore, sin is a positive evil — positive in the sense that it is not mere lack, limitation, or privation of the good (an idea of Plato's taken up by Augustine, and followed in his own way by Barth). Even the turning from a higher to a lower good that generates evil is not just a negation but an act.[8] Third, sin is a moral evil, an evil that belongs to the realm of "ought" and "ought not."[9] And finally, sin is that which ought not to be *before God*, with reference to the order God has established (see Ps. 51:4, which can be read as accusing the sinner of transgressing the First Commandment;[10] also Lev. 20:1-3; 2 Sam. 12:13: in each case the sin against the human beings involved is subsumed under the sin against God).

Sin as Act

Sin and the Divine Law

Sin is a positive moral evil that violates God's order. *Sin as act* is any behavior lacking conformity to the law of God — including sins both of commission and of omission.[11] Putting matters this way differentiates

---

7. See Appendix 2 for a summary of the biblical vocabulary related to sin.

8. Characterization of sin as a power points in the same direction. Bromiley rightly cautions, however, that the idea of sin as a positive reality must not be pressed too far, in the sense that sin has no part in the positive will of God (see his "Sin," *International Standard Bible Encyclopedia*, fully revised, 4 vols., ed. G. W. Bromiley [Grand Rapids: Eerdmans, 1979-88], 4:519). We have already refused sin an independent place over against God. See also Brunner, *The Christian Doctrine of the Church, Faith, and the Consummation*, trans. David Cairns (Philadelphia: Westminster, 1962), p. 435.

9. We have acknowledged above (pp. 71-79) that there is a connection between moral and natural evil: the fall of humankind had consequences for their total environment, and natural evil comes upon humankind because of their moral evil. This is not the place to probe this interrelationship; for now the point is to contrast, say, a terrorist attack with an earthquake: that the same number of people may have perished as the result of each in a particular case does not make them equivalent events in other respects.

10. Hans-Joachim Kraus, *Psalms 1-59*, trans. Hilton C. Oswald (Minneapolis: Fortress, 1993), p. 503.

11. Note the definition of the Westminster Shorter Catechism, answer to question 14: "Sin is any want of conformity unto, or transgression of, the law of God" (with reference given to 1 John 3:4; James 4:17; Rom. 3:23).

sin from violation of scruples arising from one's neuroses or of mandates imposed by one's society; and it also differentiates the commandment from a demand which one's "higher self" imposes on one's "lower self," after the manner of Kant's categorical imperative. The standard comes from outside of oneself and from beyond cultural or political strictures.

To make this differentiation is not to deny, of course, that in any given case, one's scruples or society or "higher self" may be in actual conformity with God's law, but simply to deny that these are identical. It is also true that one may sin by violating one's conscience before God or injuring the conscience of one's neighbor even if one's act is in itself indifferent (Rom. 14:23; 1 Cor. 8:13). And the "powers that be" do not have to be perfect to give one a prima facie duty to obey them (Rom. 13:1-7). As to a "categorical imperative," wholly apart from the question of whether a particular formulation is correct or not, its weakness comes in that the imperative is self-imposed rather than confronting one from the outside with absolute sovereignty. Consider, for instance, the different situations faced by a spare-rib-loving dieter convinced she ought to quit eating pork in the interests of her diet, and a Muslim whose religion forbids that she eat pork. It is not hard to guess which is more likely still to be abstaining a year from now.

When we speak of God's law, we understand that the sovereignty of the Lawgiver stands behind it, and the law is the way that the will of God confronts us. The law, therefore, is not simply a set of abstract, absolute, and perhaps disparate rules, but rather the revelation of the One who addresses us, speaks to us, demands that we do certain things and refrain from doing other things. Thus, in giving the Ten Commandments, God does not say, "It is wrong to steal"; rather, "You shall not steal" (Exod. 20:15) — in the form not of abstract principle but of personal engagement. Furthermore, the obedience demanded is set in the context of God's work as Redeemer: "I am the LORD your God, who brought you out of the land of Egypt, out of the house of slavery" (Exod. 20:2). Everything else follows from the fact that it is the God who has kept his covenant promises who obligates his people to do his will.

Because persons with various needs and impulses confront a world presenting them with various obligations — religious, social, interpersonal, environmental, and so on — it might seem as if only endlessly multiplied laws could encompass humankind's duties; and indeed, assorted ever-expanding systems of regulations, not to mention ever-increasing collections of case law, have reinforced this view. Fundamentally, however, this view is a mistake. There is really only one basic commandment, "You shall love the Lord your God with all your heart, and with all your soul, and with all your mind"; and a second that is like it, "You shall love your neighbor as yourself" (Matt. 22:37-39; Mark 12:30-31; cf. Luke 10:27). Correspondingly, to break any part of the law is to be guilty of breaking the whole of it (James 2:10). That is to say that the law has its unity in the will of the Lawgiver, and breach of any aspect of the law shows one to be wrongly related to him.[12] Failure to heed this point promotes a kind of obsessive legalism that, however sincerely motivated initially, quickly leads to disproportion and threatens to provoke self-concern instead of focus on God and neighbor (see, e.g., Matt. 23:23). Ironically, then, one who has been consumed with *keeping* the law may become guilty of the same sins of pride and unbelief that marked the fault of our first parents when they broke it — this time, pride in a sense of achievement and unbelief in the mercy of God toward both oneself and others. (The tendency of those conscious of their own virtue to become harsh and punitive, and hence to make virtue a servant of sin, is notorious.) And furthermore, precisely in focusing on the general demands of the legal code, the legalist is likely to miss God's specific requirement in the moment as well as his encompassing demand on her whole life.[13]

In any case, whether in the overt breach of God's commandments or in the subtler assumption that one can, as it were, bring their demand under one's own control (like the Rich Young Ruler, Matt. 19:20; Luke 18:21), sin as act involves a kind of bending in of one's will upon oneself, as Augustine, and Luther following him, emphasized. Disobedience means one prefers one's own way to God's. Pride means one prefers one's own glory to God's. Unbelief means one prefers one's own understanding to God's.

Self-centeredness or selfishness is sometimes counted, by develop-

12. In saying this, we do not mean to imply that there are no distinctions in the seriousness of sins (see below, pp. 137-43), but only that, because sin is before God and not just against some arbitrary code, it always involves one's relationship to God.

13. See Heinrich Ott, *Theology and Preaching*, trans. Harold Knight (London: Lutterworth Press, 1965), pp. 70-74. Milton makes "A mind not to be chang'd by Place or Time" a characteristic of Satan (*Paradise Lost* 1.253).

mental psychologists and others, an inevitable concomitant of the way
one enters into the world, needy and helpless, and the fact that one can
never experience the bodily and emotional states of others with quite
the full-orbed immediacy with which one experiences one's own. (Part
of the loneliness of all states of pain is that they are opaque to others.)
However, whatever the strictures of our created existence in these regards, to be human is to know that we have a duty given by God in our
powers of self-transcendence not to be shut up in these "natural" impulses.[14] Thus, few of us would hesitate to pass judgment on the noble
of former days who might beat a slave who was late in bringing him his
warm water, while merely observing that he was a worthless fellow if he
committed a willful murder.[15] We feel dismayed that the suffering of
African Americans has not made many of them eschew discrimination
against women, and that the suffering of Jews has not inoculated them
against every impulse to persecute Palestinians. These failures of mutuality strike us as wrong. To be human is to be related to God and others; the more we are confined in ourselves, the more we have lost our
humanity — which, of course, is what sin brings about. Thus, selfish
"self-expression" will not enhance us as human beings, as we tend to
suppose, but will diminish us. Conversely, it is when most diminished
in their capacity to act as responsible people — before the age of discre-
tion, say; or when they have been reduced by starvation to frantic concern for nothing but bread — that ordinary humans will be most im-
pulsively selfish. That these drives are in some sense natural does not
mean that we pass no judgment on them. Indeed, as Hocking mildly
put it, we cannot move from the proposition that to err is human, to
the proposition that error is not error; or again, "As nobody can do
anything that cannot with equal reason be referred to nature, this reasoning [that whatever is natural is right and whatever is impulsive is
natural] would at a stroke abolish the category of sin"[16] — an outcome
that, where it has been welcomed, has not noticeably enhanced the human quality of life.

14. See, for instance, Pannenberg, *Anthropology in Theological Perspective* (Philadelphia:
Westminster, 1985), pp. 107-9.

15. Edward Gibbon, *The Decline and Fall of the Roman Empire, Great Books,* vol. 40 (Chicago: Encyclopaedia Britannica, 1952) p. 500.

16. W. E. Hocking, *Human Nature and Its Remaking,* rev. ed. (New Haven: Yale University Press, 1923), pp. 133-34.

Sensuality is a kind of self-centeredness in which the bending in of the will upon the self is particularly evident: it is concentrated on one's own bodily pleasure. The reason sensuality is such a powerful and persistent sort of sin is not that there is anything intrinsically wrong in the God-given pleasures of the flesh, but that when they become goals in themselves, they have such a curious power to obscure others from view. (Also, since they cannot finally satisfy humans, who were made for more than sensual enjoyment, they tend to lead to jadedness and thence to excesses and frank, even frantic, perversion; and the worse the excess, the more God and the neighbor disappear from consideration. In themselves — when they are not being made to serve a purpose they cannot finally fulfill — they are self-limiting. I need only so much food to satisfy a strictly physical hunger. But no amount of food will fill a spiritual emptiness.) Thus the term "flesh" (σάρξ) frequently has an ethical meaning in the New Testament, referring not to the body as bad in itself, but to impulses drawing us away from God, tempting us to break his law (e.g., Rom. 7:14-24). Luther is famous for his remark that one cannot pray in the marriage bed — an observation that does not prove marital relations somehow illicit, but that does flag a potential danger. In a fascinating footnote Hocking wrote, "If pleasure is used in such wise as to blur or banish the holiness, or dignity, or beauty, or infinitude of the conscious horizon, it is false to *that* meaning. From this side, *sin is secularization.*"[17] Even at the level of comforts, most people are remarkably selfish, deeply unwilling to use fewer resources in the interests of the good of others: their bodily desires for ease are simply compelling and trump all environmentalist pleas to adjust thermostats, curtail driving, and eat less meat. Note that it is not necessary that the person acting out of sensuality *intend* to ignore or misuse God, other persons, or the environment: it just happens. Thus, the essentially sinful thing about it is its intrinsic self-centeredness, the way it wrongly directs attention (violating the Great Commandment).

It would be quite false, however, to imply that self-centeredness must come out of primitive drives and involve sensuality or self-indulgence of the physical kind. Take, for instance, the case of Goethe, a man consumed with intellectual self-development. His efforts and his achievements were astonishing. Yet, by at least one evaluation,

---

17. Hocking, *Human Nature and Its Remaking,* p. 149; emphasis his.

for all purposes of inspiring moral and spiritual enthusiasm he is practically useless. His selfishness, however high its kind, accomplished its work and left him cold, unapproachable, isolated. . . . No one who has not warmth from other sources pouring in upon him can have much communion with Goethe without losing vitality, and in his presence the Divine passion of self-sacrificing love looks out of place, or even slightly absurd. His power is fascinating, but it freezes all the sources of the nobler spiritual emotions, and ultimately must tend to the impoverishing of human nature and the lowering of the level of human life.[18]

Or take the observations of St. Francis de Sales on how self-love and competitiveness enter in even in our religious efforts to do good: he concludes that self-love is ever alive in us, and even when for a time it "sleeps like a crafty fox," it will later dash out once again.[19] In such descriptions, the fundamental relationship of self-centeredness to pride is obvious (whereas in discussions of sensuality, the felt "neediness" of the self may obscure the pride involved in giving one's desires center stage).

Finally, however, despite the dangers of self-centeredness, it does not follow that all desire in itself is wrong. Christians do not, like Buddhists, find perfection in lack of desire. Nor, like the Greeks, do they despise desire because it is irrational, productive of passion against which reason is impotent.[20] Ἐπιθυμία ("desire") is wrong precisely insofar as it involves disobedience to the command of God.[21] Thus, while ἐπιθυμία most often has a negative connotation, it does not always: it may be simply natural (e.g., Luke 16:21) or for something good (e.g., 1 Tim. 3:1; Heb. 6:11). Furthermore, imagery in Old Testament and New of the Promised Land or the Kingdom of God suggests the fulfilling rather than the annihilation of normal human desires. The trouble is

---

18. Andrew Harper, *The Book of Deuteronomy, The Expositor's Bible,* ed. W. R. Nicoll, vols. 5-6 (New York: A. C. Armstrong and Son, 1903), pp. 113-14.

19. Francis de Sales, "To a Religious, a Letter on Self-Love, 1615," in *A History of Christianity: Readings in the History of the Church from the Reformation to the Present,* ed. Clyde L. Manschreck (Englewood Cliffs, NJ: Prentice-Hall, 1964), p. 155.

20. See E. R. Dodds, *The Greeks and the Irrational* (Berkeley and Los Angeles: University of California Press, 1959), pp. 186-87, 256n.11.

21. Büchsel, "θύμος, κτλ," *TDNT,* 3:170-71.

that, unlike the desires of animals, human desires have a boundless quality that is a function of human self-transcendence and imagination and that leads people continually to aggrandize themselves and encroach on the rights of others.[22] In this way desire and sin are closely related.

Observe, again, that when one's right relationship to God has been destroyed, almost anything goes because one has lost the proper ordering dynamic of one's life. In Berkhof's phrase, "the vacuum created by . . . doubt [unbelief] is then filled by the combination of pride and desire."[23] From this unsound center flow all sorts of disobedience.

We must now make explicit what has thus far been largely implicit, namely, that one transgresses God's law as surely by culpable omissions, or by silence in the face of evil, as by blatant commissions. One can kill with a ballot denying essential resources as well as with a bullet; one shows self-centeredness in one's distracted obliviousness to another's need as well as in obsessive preoccupation with one's own. It is sin that makes us insensitive to the less dramatic, less visible evils: we would rise up in horror if jumbo jets, each loaded with 350 children, crashed every fourteen minutes, killing all aboard, and no one did anything; but starvation silently and relentlessly produces the same end result.[24] For the conventional, law-abiding, mind-her-own-business-and-stay-out-of-trouble sort of citizen, the most unnerving part of the New Testament may be Jesus' story of the sheep and the goats, in which the goats are condemned not for what they did but for what they failed to do; not even for what they willfully refused to do but for what they did not even notice was their duty (Matt. 25:31-46; see also Prov. 24:11-12: "If you hold back from rescuing those taken away to death, those who go staggering to the slaughter; if you say, 'Look, we did not know this' — does not he who weighs the heart perceive it? Does not he who keeps watch over your soul know it? And will he not repay all according to their deeds?"). God's law, that is, is positive and not only negative in its demands; it does not grant immunity to those who always color within the lines (the

22. See Reinhold Niebuhr, *Moral Man and Immoral Society* (New York: Scribners, 1960), *passim*.

23. Hendrikus Berkhof, *Christian Faith* (Grand Rapids: Eerdmans, 1979), p. 192.

24. Jim Wallis, *The Soul of Politics* (San Diego: Harcourt Brace & Co., 1995), p. 71. Wallis comments that the origin of this frequently used analogy is unknown, though based on reliable computations.

steward who tried only to play it safe was likewise condemned, Matt.
25:14-30; Luke 19:11-27). The law cannot be kept without trust in the Lawgiver as well as love for him and the neighbor, love that is not mere senti- ✗
ment but is expressed in action. Critical omissions argue a critical lack
of love. As Drummond put it at the end of his famous sermon, "the
withholding of love is the negation of the spirit of Christ, the proof that
we never knew Him, that for us He lived in vain. It means that He suggested nothing in all our thoughts, that He inspired nothing in all our
lives, that we were not once near enough to Him to be seized with the
spell of His compassion for the world."[25] (This recognition of the vital
importance of what we omit to do is one of the significant virtues of
Barth's emphasis on sloth as a major aspect of sin.)[26]

However, the fact that we argue for the essential unity of the law as
expressive of God's personal will, and that we insist on the necessity of
love if the law is to be fulfilled — indeed, that anything not motivated
by love of God and neighbor is sin — should not be taken to mean that
we put love in place of the law, much less that we put it in opposition to
the law (differentiating the law itself from the legalism we have
critiqued above). The Decalogue is not abrogated by the law of love.
Nor can love operate autonomously. Rather, love fulfills the law (Rom.
13:8-10).[27] And love needs the law to show it the shape it must have in a
world like ours — indeed, to show it what it must look like in order even
to qualify as love. In an ideal, unfallen world, perhaps undefined love
would be enough; but in the one we face, it falls ready prey to distortion, selfishness, and sentimentality. Thus, to defend ourselves by pro-

25. Henry Drummond, *The Greatest Thing in the World* (Old Tappan, NJ: Revell, rpt., n.d.), p. 62.
26. See especially *Church Dogmatics* IV/2: 403-98. Barth's treatment of sloth is much subtler and broader than mere discussion of omissions, however: this form of sin may involve not just inactivity but putting another activity in the place of the one that is re-ally required.
27. For the complexities of Paul's attitude toward the law, along with the affirma-tion that the law is permanent, see G. E. Ladd, *A Theology of the New Testament*, rev. ed., ed. Donald A. Hagner (Grand Rapids: Eerdmans, 1993), chap. 36, esp. pp. 553-54. In particu-lar, Rom. 10:4, "For Christ is the end of the law so that there may be righteousness for everyone who believes" (τέλος γὰρ νόμου Χριστὸς εἰς δικαιοσύνην παντὶ τῷ πιστεύοντι), should probably *not* be read with the slant given it by the NRSV, but rather understood as saying that the law (which abides) is no longer the means of righteousness for believers (see ibid., p. 546).

testing that we have acted out of love will not do if we have flown in the face of the law: probably all but the most casual adulterers consider themselves moved by love. Law and love must be held together, as they are in the One who gave them. We cannot truly violate one without violating the other.

Sin and Human Law: Crime and Civil Disobedience

To define sin as act as a violation of the law of God leaves room for differentiating sins from crimes, the latter being acts that violate human laws.[28] Not everything that is a sin is a crime: it is perfectly legal to gamble away one's entire living in Las Vegas or to drink oneself into a stupor in the privacy of one's own home (provided one does not disturb the peace); but these actions are surely immoral. Injustices large and small are committed by local slumlords and international marketing experts, not to mention police and the military: in many cases, no tribunal could or would call the perpetrators to account, but that does not prove that no sins have been committed.[29] Conversely, not everything that is a crime is a sin: it was illegal, but profoundly moral, to shelter Jews from the Nazis during World War II, or to invite black South Africans to share white facilities during the long era of apartheid. The whole plot of Sophocles' *Antigone* rests on the conflict between the laws of heaven and those of the state, and the choice to follow heaven's laws at all costs.[30]

   While the propriety of certain judgments in such matters seems ob-

28. Both sins and crimes must also be differentiated from sickness; see below, pp. 117-27.

29. William F. May claims, "The vast majority of killings in the twentieth century have been committed not by lawbreakers who lived explicitly beyond the pale of the law, but, terrifyingly enough, by those who were officers of the law performing their duties to the state" (*Catalogue of Sins,* p. 188). Barth says of war that it "allows and commands almost everything that God has forbidden" (*Church Dogmatics* IV/2: 436).

30. Antigone insisted in the opening scene of the play, when speaking to her sister of her plan illegally to bury her brother, "I shall rest, a loved one with him whom I have loved, sinless in my crime; for I owe a longer allegiance to the dead than to the living: in that world I shall abide for ever. But if *thou* wilt, be guilty of dishonouring laws which the gods have stablished in honour" (*Great Books,* vol. 5 [Chicago: Encyclopaedia Britannica, 1952], p. 131).

vious enough, especially given a little distance, this whole problem is greatly complicated by the fact that the laws even of an imperfect state — or imperfect church; see Matt. 17:27 — do have a claim on the Christian (Matt. 22:15-22; Mark 12:13-17; Luke 20:20-26; Rom. 13:1-7; and this, even though the people's early request for a king met with cautions about the evils attendant upon the fulfilling of such a request, 1 Sam. 8). All states in a fallen world will be imperfect: human laws will never exactly reflect the divine law. Nonetheless, civil order is necessary, and even those who disagree with a government's policies derive certain benefits from whatever order prevails. That is why those who support civil disobedience of laws seen as unjust have usually agreed that those who disobey must be willing to suffer the penalty the state imposes for their actions. (Such a stricture also tends to increase the moral seriousness with which civil disobedience is contemplated and to curb frivolous expressions.) Given these caveats, it remains true, as stated in the Westminster Confession, that "God alone is Lord of the conscience, and hath left it free from the doctrines and commandments of men which are in anything contrary to his Word, or beside it in matters of faith or worship."[31] This affirmation echoes the apostles in Acts, who, when ordered not to preach, challenged their captors to judge whether it was right that they listen to men rather than to God (Acts 4:19), and later asserted, "We must obey God rather than any human authority" (Acts 5:29). And it is possible that the state may become so wholly corrupt as to be fundamentally anti-God (Rev. 13), in which case Christians have a duty to stand against it.

Despite the failings of the secular state, history has not greatly blessed the theocratic vision, the effort to make civil law and divine law identical, so that all sins are crimes. The church as institution also makes judgments corrupted by sin. Even in early Israel, a theocratic system *provoked* what might well be called sin in the judgment the more leisured, who could observe the details of the law, passed on laborers like shepherds, who could not. Little more seriously compromised Calvin's reputation than his execution of Servetus for heresy, or has made the

31. It is interesting that while the writers of the Confession seemed to have had only religion in mind, their heirs rebelled on more secular grounds in 1776, which at least suggests that de-absolutizing the state may free people to act against it in ways that would hardly be possible as long as it is held to be inviolable. On the role of conscience, see *Who We Are*, pp. 77-95.

fundamentalist Muslim world seem more threatening than its sentence of death imposed (in 1989) on novelist Salman Rushdie for alleged blasphemy. In a multicultural, multi-faith society, such efforts are even more surely futile and dangerous than they were in earlier days.

The secular state, by contrast, does not concern itself with sins as such. But where the line should be drawn between sin and crime is not always easy to discern. Usually, we consider crimes those behaviors that directly threaten the property, rights, or well-being of others (as in the case of the drunk who gets behind the wheel of a car instead of staying in his room), and we advocate leaving alone matters of opinion and private piety or the lack thereof.[32] However, certain things we consider intrinsically dangerous or corrupting and ban absolutely, like the use of cocaine (or, in times so recent that only a 2003 Supreme Court ruling may have brought them to a close, the practice of homosexuality). Experiments of a quarter-century ago in simply letting people do what they want provided they were not violent — such as one in Boston in which pornography was given free rein in a portion of the city — in fact led to spiraling violence; and there is no reason to suppose that legalizing drugs would have a happier outcome.[33] Sins, that is, are linked together as sin; one cannot safely assume that ones that are not immediately violent do not count. And because sin violates God's good order for the world he made and disrupts relationships within it, we should not be surprised at the broad overlap between what civil law and God's law ban, or at the complexity of deciding what should and what should not be regulated by the state.

---

32. Even here matters get complicated, though: may Native Americans smoke peyote, a hallucinogenic plant, in their religious rituals? May adherents of Santería sacrifice live animals? What about the local merchants' claim that the disciples' preaching was disturbing not just the peace, but also the local economy (Acts 16:16-24; 19:23-27)?

33. See *Los Angeles Times,* May 31, 1977, pt. 1, p. 18, for discussion of Boston's "Combat Zone"; also May 30, 1977, pt. 1, p. 1, for the linkage of violence and sex in Hollywood. Homosexuality is a particularly vexing question in this regard. For our broad sympathy with homosexual persons, see the extended treatment in *Who We Are,* pp. 290-350. Homosexual persons have every right to argue that the great majority of sex crimes are perpetrated by non-homosexuals; and we simply do not have data that make it clear whether open acceptance of homosexual relationships between consenting adults is a fatally "slippery slope" on the level of civil law.

Sin as Condition

Sin as the Culpable Moral Perversion of Human Nature

Sin is first of all act, behavior not motivated by love of God and neighbor. Indeed human sin, as we have said, enters the world with the act of disobedience by our first parents. But our present human lack of conformity to God's will runs deeper than any overt behavior. It involves what we might call a moral state of being.[34] We are not actively sinning while we are asleep in bed, but we do not for that reason cease to be sinners (as our dreams often reveal). As condition, then, sin involves our natures as depraved — polluted or perverted in the moral sense of our having a bent or inclination in the direction of evil, particularly evil characterized as self-interestedness.[35] Thus, our understanding is darkened and our hearts are hardened (Eph. 4:18), with the result that we consider the gospel to be foolishness and do not really see evil for what it is. Our wills are enslaved to evil (Rom. 6:17, 19); not that our capacity for choice is rendered inoperative, but that it is radically inclined in the wrong direction, to the point that we cannot in and of ourselves love God with all our hearts and our neighbors as ourselves. Our affections or passions have become vile (Rom. 1:26), so that we become inflamed with wrong desires. Even our consciences fail to do their proper work but become seared by our sin (1 Tim. 4:2). In short, we are in a state of hostility or enmity with God (Rom. 8:7), possessed of hearts that are devious and perverse (Jer. 17:9; "deceitful above all things and desperately wicked," in the words of the KJV). And it is critical to observe that this enmity characterizes the whole of us, in our best and highest human attributes and not just in our presumably "animal" appetites. We

---

34. We will take up this issue further below, in our discussion of original sin and the extent of sin, pp. 159-71.

35. We speak of a *moral* bent in distinction to the condemned views of Flacius, who believed that the change worked in humankind by their sin affected their very substance as human. We are not sinners as a fox *is* a fox; rather, we remain actively responsible for our sin. To decline to put things as Flacius did, however, is not to suggest that this bent of human nature is intermittent or other than universal. Brunner used the interesting figure of a chessboard that has been shaken: the pieces are themselves unbroken, yet their relationships are hopelessly distorted (Brunner, *Man in Revolt*, p. 137).

have no solid place to stand from which we could by our own power remedy the situation.[36]

Perhaps one of the most striking evidences of the truth of the dismal picture we have just painted is provided not by the horrendousness of specific actions, which we could argue are isolated aberrations (always a danger, were we to view sin as act alone), but by the lengths to which we go to deceive ourselves about the quality of our day-to-day behaviors and inclinations and to imply that what we do is not really so bad after all. There is a pervasive underlying readiness, that is, to obscure the truth (note Paul's observation that ignorance results from sin, not the reverse, Rom. 1:21). Particular efforts may be rationalizations that pick up a positive component of one's behavior and ignore its essential wrongness, as when a student defends stealing an exam ahead of time as something that really contributed to her education, since she learned more than she otherwise would have; or when another justifies taking an exam on a fellow student's behalf because that person was failing and badly needed help; or when a manager decides skimming some funds just gives him the raise he should have gotten anyway. Or they may show a stunning refusal (masquerading as innocence) of common standards of morality, as when a senator defended having mailed advertisements for his car dealership at taxpayer expense by saying, "I don't know every damned thing in that ethics law."[37] While one suspects (trusts?) that the senator at some level knew better, one likewise suspects that then-President Reagan supposed himself to be telling the simple truth when he said of his cuts in social services, "My program hasn't hurt anybody"; and of the environment, "There is today in the United States as much forest as there was when Washing-

---

36. Superior powers of intelligence will not help us here. Like all our powers, our reason is corrupt and readily pressed into the service of evil. A series of articles published in a local Mensa newsletter, for instance, argued seriously that not only the mentally defective and the old but also most of the homeless are useless to society and "should be humanely done away with, like abandoned kittens"; and that Hitler's greatest offense was that "his actions prevent a rational discussion of the creation of the master race" (quoted in Nora Zamichow, "Newsletter Articles Stir Furor in High-IQ Group," *Los Angeles Times,* Jan. 10, 1995, p. B1). Similarly, but if possible worse, Princeton University ethicist Peter Singer is noted for denying the human rights and dignity of those deemed in various ways "defective."

37. "No Comment Department," *Christian Century* 111:21 (July 13-20, 1994): 674.

ton was at Valley Forge."[38] In such examples one sees something resembling what Dante called the loss of the good of the intellect,[39] the loss of veridical perception — along with a desire to justify oneself that demonstrates the speaker has not in fact lost all powers of moral discrimination but has rather corrupted them. It has been commonly observed that the person who is blind to her own culpability often sees her fault with especial clarity when it appears in others.[40] One does not wish to be seen as a wrongdoer, no matter what one has done; indeed, let every standard against which one could be judged guilty fall, if only one can thus preserve one's own innocence and the legitimacy of one's own inclinations.[41] This self-justification, this refusal to see oneself as a sinner, Luther believed to be the final form of sin.[42]

38. Quoted, along with other examples of distorted perception, in an advertisement for *The Nation*, no date. One wonders, similarly, whether donors or solicitors are more the object of the (self?)deception involved in CBN fund-raising letters, at the bottom of which appears the statement, "All funds are used for designated projects and for the world-wide ministry of CBN in accordance with Ezra 7:17-18." Ezra 7:18 reads, "Whatever seems good to you and your colleagues to do with the rest of the silver and gold, you may do, according to the will of your God." (See "The Expanding CBN Empire," *Christian Century* 111:22 [July 27-Aug. 3, 1994]: 712.)

39. Dante, *Hell*, 3.18.

40. Simone Weil put matters charitably in saying, "When we do evil we do not know it, because evil flies from the light" (*Gravity and Grace*, quoted by Ratzinger, *In the Beginning* [Grand Rapids: Eerdmans, 1995], p. 63). It is not always easy to tell when discrepancies between words and deeds are merely cynical; when the words reflect values one genuinely holds and aspires to, even if without adequate performance; and when one is consciously unaware of one's own failings. Such ambiguities are part of the deceptiveness of sin as well as the complexities of individual psychology. But that the discrepancies may have appalling consequences can be seen, to take just one instance, in the large rise in the late twentieth century in the use of torture by nations which have signed the United Nations Declaration of Human Rights, which explicitly bans it.

41. "Each of us insists on being innocent at all cost, even if he has to accuse the whole human race and heaven itself. . . . As I told you, it's a matter of dodging judgment" (Camus, *The Fall*, pp. 81-81). Or again, "to perceive somehow our own complicity with evil is a horror not to be borne. [It is] much more reassuring to see the world in terms of totally innocent victims and totally evil instigators of the monstrous violence we see all about. At all costs, never disturb our innocence" (Arthur Miller, from "With Respect for Her Agony — but with Love," quoted in Rollo May, *Power and Innocence* [New York: Delta, 1972], p. 47).

42. Noted by Niebuhr, *Nature and Destiny of Man* (New York: Scribners, 1941), 1:200. He quotes Luther from his *Works*, WE, vol. 3, p. 288.

Corruption of language, by both euphemism and obfuscation, provides a particularly pervasive means of hiding from ourselves and others what we are doing. For example, the Pentagon has exhibited impressive skills in this regard: back in 1977, it won the annual "Doublespeak Award" of the National Council of Teachers of English for referring to the neutron bomb as a "radiation enhancement weapon";[43] but the ongoing habit of calling civilian deaths "collateral damage" is in the same league, and describing a nuclear accident as a "normal aberration" simply defies appropriate response — and that, of course, is the reason for speaking this way.[44] Reclassify catsup as a vegetable and you can save on school lunch costs (never mind that tomatoes are botanically fruit anyway). Refuse to deal with the realities of aging: old people are "chronologically gifted" or "senior citizens." If you want your state's lottery to succeed, never use the word "gambling": the California lottery spent twenty-two million dollars on advertising in its first year to convince people that they were not gambling but just having fun.[45] No matter if we are a little imprecise, since, after all, nothing is sure in the end but negative patient care outcome and revenue enhancement. But, actually, precision matters a great deal. No one would bother to corrupt language if she did not intend thereby to alter reactions and behavior. And when the tools one uses for conceiving and choosing have become distorted, the capacity for discerning how best to respond is severely reduced. Yet it is a rare person indeed who will not describe her own behavior in a way designed with the anticipated response as well as the facts of the situation in view. (Obviously, we are speaking here not of the intrinsic limitations of language and the inevitable biasing effect of perspective that are a function of finitude, which make the truth of situations elusive enough; but of interested misuse of language, which is sin.)

We are not innocent. We are not only sinful but guilty for our sin — guilty and blameworthy. We may see the guilt more readily when we frankly break God's Law; but we will be more dismayed by it when we recognize that it characterizes who we *are:* we more easily suppose that we can change our seemingly-incidental actions than pull up their root.

43. *Los Angeles Times,* Nov. 25, 1977, pt. 1, p. 27.

44. See James J. Farrell, "Speaking of Nuclear War: A Semantic Defense Initiative," *Christian Century* 103:32 (Oct. 29, 1986): 939-42.

45. *Los Angeles Times,* Sept. 9, 1985, pt. 1, p. 3.

At the same time, we know deeply, even if we cannot explain how these things could be, that who we are as sinners is not a fate that makes us innocent victims, but a fact for which we bear responsibility. There is no way that we can separate our sin from our guilt.[46] Again, we know this, even if the specifics are hidden in the deeper mystery of evil. And we know it at least in part because we know that our hearts and minds contradict God's holiness and righteousness. Thus, Scripture speaks to the effect that we are not to be pitied and excused, as if our foibles were not our fault, and as if our guilt could be reduced to guilt feelings that make us mistakenly suppose that God is angry with us; but rather we really are judged and condemned by a God who, because of his nature as just, cannot and will not simply shrug off guilt (Exod. 34:7; Rom. 1:18). We recognize that judgment is just every time we recognize that, no matter what excuses or extenuating circumstances we marshal in our defense, we not only *should* but *could* have done differently. And we also know our guilt when we recognize, with whatever measure of horror and shame, malicious impulses that seem to spring up spontaneously, like relief at a competitor's misfortune or jealousy at a friend's promotion: we can neither prevent such feelings nor deny that we ought not to have them. When reflecting on another's circumstances and faults, we may conclude that "to understand everything is to forgive everything": we see that the pressures she has faced have been very great; but when honestly looking at ourselves we can more rightly say, with Arthur Koestler, that to understand everything is to forgive ourselves nothing.[47]

Sin, Finitude, and Sickness

The conclusion we have drawn about our being responsible for our sinful condition and therefore guilty before God has come under sustained attack both by those who believe in the essential goodness and positive

46. See Brunner, *The Christian Doctrine of Creation and Redemption*, p. 106.

47. Arthur Koestler, *The Ghost in the Machine* (New York: Macmillan, 1967), p. 218. Bonhoeffer wrote, altogether similarly, "The psychological motivation of sin can be analysed right up to the deed, but the deed itself is something entirely new, done in freedom, and psychologically inexplicable. All explanations whether in the psychic or the mental realm are historicisings, excuses, weakenings of the fact of sin" (*Communion of Saints*, p. 81). See likewise Niebuhr, *Nature and Destiny of Man*, 1:255.

potential of humankind, and by those who see humans as being so fundamentally determined by forces beyond their control that language suggesting blame is at best meaningless or unhelpful and at worst actively destructive. Instead of the traditional theological category of *sin,* the medical or psychological category of *sickness* takes over.[48] Depending on the context, this latter category may absorb components of everything from genetics to results of environmental influences to the limitations of finitude. Its use, that is, is most commonly premised on acknowledging undoubted influences or constraints on human behavior; and it is on such constraints that we intend to focus here.

Nonetheless, we must also at least take note of other uses or implications of substituting ideas of sickness and health for those of guilt and responsibility. For instance, it may reflect a change with respect to which of the various authorities and diagnostic vocabularies are granted status, as when a <u>couch potato</u> is labeled <u>not as engaging in gluttony and sloth</u>, but rather as practicing an unhealthful lifestyle. No longer is it God who is offended, but a sort of abstract ideal with only individual bearing and immanent claims. Or — perhaps most dangerous of all — it may be a way of dispensing with all standards except those provided by individual discomfort and failures of "adjustment" to one's surroundings (however corrupt those surroundings may be, and without recognition that lack of distress may signify not health but a seared conscience). What do we say when the American Psychiatric Association declines to count pedophilia as problematic (sickness) unless it causes subjective distress or problems in social functioning?[49] What do we say about the observation that Eichmann was untroubled by guilt, insomnia, or loss of appetite, but appeared as a "calm, 'well-balanced,' unperturbed official conscientiously going about his desk work, his administrative job which happened to be the supervision of mass murder"?[50] Those who seem perfectly sane and have perfectly

---

48. Ricoeur considers explanation of evil by the body to be basically a symbol, an etiological myth; but he goes on to say that if the explanation becomes scientific, as it has in modern times, then the ethical category "evil" disappears altogether — which, of course, is exactly what those wishing to affirm fundamental human goodness claim (see *Symbolism of Evil,* p. 336).

49. *Diagnostic and Statistical Manual,* 4th ed., 1994.

50. Thomas Merton, quoted by Karl A. Plank, "Meditating on Merton's Eichmann," *Christian Century* 102:30 (Oct. 9, 1985): 894.

good reasons for what they are doing can busy themselves building weapons that can destroy the world, without their neighbors — who in one sense know perfectly well what they are doing — ever thinking for a moment that something must be wrong somewhere. "Sanity" can no more save us than reason can. One recalls the "well" in the Gospels, who needed no physician (Matt. 9:12; Mark 2:17; Luke 5:31).

In contemplating such matters, let us first dispense with excuses based upon finitude, which must not be confused with sin, although it does provide occasion for sin. Still, in itself, it neither causes nor results from sin, but is part of creaturely reality. To say that the human Jesus learned obedience and grew in wisdom (Luke 2:52; Heb. 2:17; 5:8) is not to say that he was subject to sin (Heb. 4:15). Error — making a mistake in arithmetic, using the wrong German verb form — is not sin. Even wrong-headedness to the point of folly, like the subway sign inviting the illiterate to write for help, is still not sin. Choosing the less bad of two imperfect options is wisdom, not sin; in fact, insisting upon "perfection or nothing" may manifest the kind of refusal of finitude that *is* sin, and that certainly gives greater scope to evil by refusing to differentiate the better from the worse.[51] Not limits but the refusal of limits through pride and unbelief is characteristic of sin.

The problem of sickness is intrinsically more complicated, for sickness is related to sin even though it is not to be identified with sin. As an evil, we would see it as in principle resultant from the Fall (which is very far from saying that a particular instance of sickness necessarily results from the ill individual's wrongdoing, as we can see by considering the children of farm workers who, in various locations affected by particular pesticides, show rates of childhood cancer many times higher than the usual level: it is indeed sin, but certainly not the children's sin, that leads to such illness). A given individual's own sin may, of course, cause sickness, physical or psychological, as commonly occurs with sexually transmitted diseases or use of illegal drugs, and at least sometimes occurs when wrong behavior leads, say, to depression or obsessive guilt.[52] At least occasionally, people recover from physical

51. See James M. Wall, "Hoping for the Best at State," *Christian Century* 98:17 (May 13, 1981): 531.

52. Psychologist O. Hobart Mowrer made rather extreme claims about psychopathology being due to real guilt, claims that doubtless recaptured aspects of an impor-

illnesses once they have been relieved of a burden of conscience. Conversely, a given sickness may significantly predispose one to sin, as when a biologically grounded depression prompts suicidal despair. But the question comes precisely at the point of deciding whether or when causal language can be used in cases like the latter, or alternatively, whether the language of "sickness" should displace the language of "sin" altogether (with the consequence that one rightly regards the problem only with sympathy and healing in mind, rather than thinking in terms of the propriety of judgment, punishment, and repentance; and with the further consequence that one sees the trouble as something that can be reached from the "outside," so to speak, rather than requiring inner change of heart).[53]

When we review the biblical data, we cannot doubt that Scripture recognizes a connection between sin and sickness, though certainly not a completely straightforward one. Jewish culture did assume that sickness resulted from someone's sin — if not one's own, then one's relatives' (John 9:2; see also 1 Cor. 11:29-30; the deliverances of Job's friends, e.g., Job 18:13; and, very explicitly, Ps. 107:17: "Some were sick through their sinful ways, and because of their iniquities endured affliction"). The law of leprosy (Lev. 14) provided for making a sin offering if one was healed of the disease. The Lord promised the Israelites in the wilderness that he would put on them none of the diseases that he had put on the Egyptians, provided that they heeded his statutes and commandments (Ex. 15:26; see also Ex. 23:25). Although Jesus denied any one-to-one relationship between being sick and having sinned, at the same time he maintained the propriety of associating failure to repent with disastrous consequences (John 9:3; 5:14; Luke 13:1-5; see also Matt. 9:2-8; Mark 2:1-12; Luke 5:17-26; James 5:14-15; Gestrich emphasizes that in Mark 2, the narrative calls attention "in a whole new way" to the unity of righteousness before God and health).[54] In all of these cases, even as qualified by Jesus, the movement is clearly from sin to sickness,

---

tant reality but that did not sufficiently take into account those genetic and environmental influences for which a sufferer is not culpable.

53. See Karl Rahner, "Guilt and Its Remission: The Borderland Between Theology and Psychotherapy," in *Theological Investigations,* vol. 2, trans. Karl H. Kruger (Baltimore: Helicon, 1963), pp. 265-81.

54. Christof Gestrich, *The Return of Splendor in the World* (Grand Rapids: Eerdmans, 1997), p. 211.

not the reverse. Similarly, the Bible seems to see sin as given opportunity by the environment, as in the case of David and Bathsheba (2 Sam. 11), but does not refer to the environment as a means of alleviating or excusing the guilt of sin. About as close as one can come to moderating language is found in Matthew 26:41, where Jesus says, "the spirit indeed is willing, but the flesh is weak" (also Mark 14:38); and Hebrews 5:2, which says of the high priest that he "is able to deal gently with the ignorant and wayward, since he himself is subject to weakness"; and even here, more finitude than high-handed sin seems to be in view (or, more specifically, the "sins of ignorance" treated in Num. 15:22-31).

In any case, there surely seems to be no doubt that human beings are profoundly shaped by forces that they do not choose. Every time we remark family resemblances of personality as well as of appearance, we acknowledge the importance of genetics.[55] Every time we worry that an abused child will abuse her own children, and every time we organize activities to provide alternatives to gangs in a blighted neighborhood, we recognize the significance of environment. Every time we administer a psychotropic drug (or acknowledge that we get "high" from a long run), we admit the chemical influences upon thinking and behavior. But on the other side, even if, for instance, it should be conclusively demonstrated that an inability to drink moderately has biological determinants, some persons with alcoholic tendencies land in the gutter and some stay sober: a predisposition does not preclude options or definitively remove a behavior from the moral realm. Even though environmental influences are powerful, some children seem to be invulnerable to the most horrendous circumstances and manage to live responsible lives in spite of everything.[56] Thus, Stanford psychologist

---

55. Let doubters about genetic influence upon temperament contemplate the difference between a Labrador retriever and a pit bull — virtually any Lab (that has not been abused) and any pit bull. Or take the mutant mice so aggressive that they must be kept in solitary confinement, mice with too much serotonin in their brains and lacking a critical enzyme, like — and here is the punch line — a family of Dutch men with a remarkable history of violent criminal behavior, who also had too-high levels of several neurotransmitters, including serotonin, and lacked the same enzyme (Terence Monmaney, "Of Mice and Mayhem," *Los Angeles Times,* June 6, 1996, p. B2).

56. For instance, an article contrasts two Hispanic men, both of whom had been born in grinding poverty and both of whom grew up to be of harsh and unbending disposition; but one of them became a criminal and the other went into law enforcement (Evan Maxwell, "Prison Drug Raid: A Matter of Honor," *Los Angeles Times,* Jan. 6, 1975, pt. 1, p. 1+).

Albert Bandura comments that "our theories grossly overpredict pathology. . . . People who believe they have the power to exercise some measure of control over their lives are healthier, more effective and more successful than those who lack faith in their ability to effect changes in their lives."[57] Most kids basically make it, he says, even if they grow up in dismal settings.

Consider further that prescription drugs, like street drugs, may greatly alter one's outlook, but some people are as adamant about avoiding the legal as the illegal chemicals, wanting to preserve something that they rightly or wrongly identify as themselves. Here we think not so much of those who, out of paranoia reinforced by unpleasant side-effects, want to refuse the antipsychotics they think are poisoning them, but those who hesitate about antidepressants such as Prozac and its ilk, which some people report make them feel "better than well" (and which some would want to impose on the depressed on the grounds that only their hopelessness, which is a symptom of their disease — like the delusions of the paranoid — makes them want to refuse it). Is the depressed person who behaves slothfully without the drug a sinner while off of it, in a way that she is not while taking the drug, if it enables her to behave differently? To say that such matters are complicated is significantly to understate the problem.[58] Another factor is the sometimes unclear line between repairing and enhancing.[59] This factor bears on the problem of sin and addictions: it has been argued that many who take street drugs are trying to accomplish something of the same thing that those who have access to prescription psychiatric medications are after: a reduction in the pain of a life that has, one way or another, become unmanageable. Similarly, it has recently been discovered that the chain smoking common in many schizophrenics may relate to the fact that nicotine affects a gene that contributes to schizophrenia. Many people, that is, self-medicate, using whatever is available to them; and whether their chosen substance is approved or disap-

57. "Swimming against the Tide of Gene Pools and Helplessness," Stanford University News Service, July 1999 (http://www.stanford.edu/dept/news/pr/99/990729bandura.html).

58. See John Stapert, "Curing an Illness or Transforming the Self? The Power of Prozac," *Christian Century* 111:21 (July 13-20, 1994): 684-87.

59. This issue is broached briefly in *Who We Are,* p. 433.

proved may depend more on their social circumstances than on their virtue.

In short, every time a person can take a stance toward a potential determinant of her life, she shows that that determinant is not absolute. And one of the curious things even about sins that we hate, is that we may be profoundly afraid to give them up, for we feel as if we could hardly recognize ourselves as ourselves without them — another evidence that, deep down, we know ourselves only as sinners.

It is sobering to recall that in behavioral psychology's heyday, the impact of environment on human development was thought to be so absolute that John Broadus Watson could make his famous claim, "Give me a dozen healthy infants, well-formed, and my own specified world to bring them up in and I'll guarantee to take any one at random and train him to become any type of specialist I might select — doctor, lawyer, artist, merchant-chief and, yes, even beggar-man and thief, regardless of his talents, penchants, tendencies, abilities, vocations, and race of his ancestors."[60] By contrast, less than seventy-five years later, a newspaper headline queries, "Is There a Gene Behind Suicide?" and the article cites evidence from studies of identical twins separated at birth that suggests that, indeed, a tendency to suicide (beyond a mere tendency to depression) may be genetically transmitted.[61] Cases of schizophrenia once attributed with confidence to bad parenting are now attributed with equal conviction to bad inheritance. Such extreme swings of scientific opinion might at least counsel caution. Almost everyone agrees that complex human behaviors usually have multiple genetic determinants (not to mention other sorts of determinants as well, including most particularly environmental ones); and that even in cases where a single dominant gene may prevail, having that gene does not itself establish how strongly the trait it governs will be expressed. Also, even though we may find biological commonalities among those who succumb to certain pressures, we do not know how many have the same biological makeup but do *not* succumb: the latter group are neither identified nor tested.

It would seem that we face a situation much like that which we con-

---

60. Quoted from John Broadus Watson's book *Behaviorism,* in Edna Heidbreder, *Seven Psychologies* (New York: Appleton-Century-Crofts, 1933), p. 248.

61. Shari Roan, *Los Angeles Times,* Aug. 22, 1996, p. E1.

fronted when we spoke earlier of temptation and brainwashing: constraints upon one's behavior — say in the case of a rapidly encroaching
brain tumor — may be so great that one is destroyed as a moral agent;
but short of that state, it remains appropriate to speak of sin.[62] Of
course there are degrees of constraint and many other complexly inter-
twined factors here: we can both be guilty and need healing at the same
time and for the same act. But even when Paul spoke so forcefully of sin
as a power that he could say that not he, but sin that dwelt within him,
did those actions that he hated (Rom. 7:17, 20), he was not finally denying his own agency (Rom. 7:15); he was rather reflecting back upon behavior admittedly his that he could not explain to himself. We do not
come into the world, much less reach years of moral accountability, as
blank slates; but even our bent dispositions are still our own and must
be acknowledged as such.

Lest such matters remain abstract, consider their bearing on crime
(or, for that matter, on discipline within the family). While we have refused above to identify sin and crime, the issue of what is to be treated
as sickness and what is to be judged and punished comes into sharp focus in the stance the state takes to criminals. If persons cannot be held
responsible for their behavior, whether sinful or criminal, then indeed
the imposition of punishment for misbehavior is nothing but medieval
anachronism or sheer sadism. Wrong-doers should not be incarcerated

---

62. See above, pp. 38-40. In a particularly telling conclusion to an article arguing
(on the much debated and debatable grounds of sociobiological theory) that a tendency to adultery is genetically programmed into the human male, the author solemnly intones, "The danger is that people will . . . react to the new knowledge by surrendering to 'natural' impulses, as if what's 'in our genes' were beyond reach of self-
control" (Robert Wright, "Our Cheating Hearts," *Time* 144:7 [Aug. 15, 1994]: 43-52).
Indeed; but surely this is a sentiment one would think more likely to be embraced by
an utterly unchastened voluntarist. It can be an instructive diversion to track the reg-
ularity with which assorted determinists beg us to take some particular posture toward determinism (an obviously unnecessary effort were determinism anything like
the whole story). Consider as sophisticated a theorist as Evelyn Fox Keller, who writes,
"the very possibility of choice depends on a residual domain of agency that can remain free only to the extent that it remains unexamined": are we, then, free either to
examine or not to examine it? ("Nature, Nurture, and the Human Genome Project," in
The Code of Codes: Scientific and Social Issues in the Human Genome Project, ed. Daniel J.
Kevles and Leroy Hood [Cambridge and London: Harvard University Press, 1992],
p. 299).

but hospitalized, medicated, operated upon, or somehow restored to "normalcy." But it is not without reason that reference to hospitals, drugs, and surgery for criminals raises specters of the totalitarian state and fears about what, precisely, someone in power will decide needs to be "cured." At least the effort to mete out fitting and just retribution leaves the criminal as a person with rights and choices, who can argue about justice and injustice, serve her sentence, and having met her obligation, return to a society in which she is fundamentally like others in being guilty of wrongdoing (a category every reasonable person understands and can apply to herself) rather then fundamentally unlike them because she is a psychopathological "case."[63] Everyone knows about temptations to do wrong, and everyone knows something about succumbing. As Milton's Samson said,

> if weakness may excuse
> What Murtherer, what Traytor, Parricide,
> Incestuous, Sacrilegious, but may plead it?
> All wickedness is weakness.[64]

Note that even advocating use of a pragmatic criterion like employing punishment when it can deter crime, and attributing guilt to acts that can at least theoretically be deterred by foreseeable punishment, assumes basic personal responsibility, along with the conviction that responsibility is reduced or abrogated under conditions of insanity or of actions whose ill effects were unintended and unforeseeable.[65]

We consider it significant that the legal code will typically explicitly exclude persons with "antisocial personalities" from using the insanity defense, if their only evidence of mental illness is repeated criminal

63. See M. Eugene Osterhaven, "Anselm and the Modern Mind," in *Perspectives on Christology*, ed. Marguerite Shuster and Richard A. Muller (Grand Rapids: Zondervan, 1991), pp. 243-52, for discussion of criminology in its relation to atonement theory; also Mark Horst, "Sin, Psychopathology and Father Brown," *Christian Century* 104:2 (Jan. 21, 1987): 46-47, for the argument that the concepts of sin and psychopathology lead to fundamentally different views of the criminal.

64. John Milton, "Samson Agonistes," *Great Books*, vol. 32 (Chicago: Encyclopaedia Britannica, 1952), p. 357. For ridicule of the insanity defense, see Dostoyevski, *Brothers Karamazov*, pp. 702-3.

65. See John Staddon, "On Responsibility and Punishment," *Atlantic Monthly* 275:2 (Feb. 1995): 88-94.

acts; and it also excludes those who allegedly acted out of uncontrollable or irresistible impulse; but it does *not* exclude those who are affected by alcohol or drugs.[66] Antisocial personality disorder is a recognized and highly recalcitrant syndrome characterized not so much by
not knowing the difference between right and wrong as by not caring.
The intoxicated, by contrast, may not at the crucial moment have
known the difference, but they were responsible for getting intoxicated
in the first place and in some cases have considerably better prospects
for change than the person with a personality disorder. What if the
"not caring" is strongly genetically predisposed? Do we then still go on
the basis of the effectiveness of punishment to deter (and consequences do tend to make a difference to these people)? But consider
that punishment can also work with persons who are obviously mentally incompetent due to very low IQ, whom many would wish to treat
differently. Obviously, we face a morass here.[67]

The upshot is that we must insist once again that sin is inexplicable.
Every time a causal explanation fully succeeds, we are no longer dealing
with sin. Even when she pleads extenuating circumstances, the self
making the argument gravely risks deceiving herself about the abso-

---

66. E.g., *California Jury Instructions Criminal,* 5th ed., vol. 1, ed. Arnold Levin (St. Paul,
MN: West Publishing Co., 1988), pp. 142, 146, 149; while this is the current (2001) state of
affairs, there has been a long history of change in this arena, with levels of tolerance
waxing and waning.

67. That we have taken the position that justice has an appropriate penal element
should not be understood to imply that it therefore does not matter if prisons are abusive, or that efforts to provide for the rehabilitation of incarcerated criminals are inappropriate. Let us repeat that we do not deny the significance of environment or of biology; all we deny is that, in most cases, they leave a person with no meaningful choices
or personal responsibility. Prisons are, no doubt, schools of crime; but not every criminal uses her time in prison to hone her criminal skills. As Dorothy Sayers put it — perhaps a little too categorically, and yet with truth — "If a man is once convinced of his
own guilt, and that he is sentenced by a just tribunal, all punishment of whatever kind
is remedial, since it lies with him to make it so; if he is not so convinced, then all punishment, however enlightened, remains merely vindictive, since he sees it so and will
not make it otherwise" (in her "Introduction" to Dante's *Purgatory* [Baltimore: Penguin, 1955], pp. 15-16). Contrariwise, all the crime-fighting technology science can devise will not root out all of those determined to profit from crime, as efforts to win the
drug war demonstrate (Douglas Jehl, "The Science of Fighting a Drug War," *Los Angeles
Times,* Nov. 6, 1989, pt. 1, p. 1+; similarly Peter White, "The Poppy," *National Geographic*
167:2 (Feb. 1985): 142-89).

luteness of the external or biological constraints upon her. In fact, should she believe very strongly in her helplessness, she will be very likely to behave less well than she otherwise would.[68] But even those who know themselves to be responsible continue to be sinners and to sin.

68. Hence psychiatrist Karl Menninger's popular book *Whatever Became of Sin* argues that if we surrender a sense that some things are wrong and that we should not do them, period, we have not only lost our bearings but also the resource that taking responsibility gives. (From our point of view, the proper argument is not that we should not believe in our helplessness because it has a bad outcome, but rather that the excuses we use for our bad behavior are not true, or not sufficiently true.) Menninger, however, for all of his desire to recapture the idea of sin, appears to lack a clear sense of grace and of a power outside ourselves that can help us in the face of the real power of sin. Hence, the book ends with an expression of bafflement about the human condition.

Sin

A Sermon Preached by Marguerite Shuster
at the Whitworth Institute of Ministry, Spokane, Washington
July 23, 1998

In the spring of the year, the time when kings go out to battle, David sent Joab with his officers and all Israel with him; they ravaged the Ammonites, and besieged Rabbah. But David remained at Jerusalem. It happened, late one afternoon, when David rose from his couch and was walking about on the roof of the king's house, that he saw from the roof a woman bathing; the woman was very beautiful. David sent someone to inquire about the woman. It was reported, "This is Bathsheba daughter of Eliam, the wife of Uriah the Hittite." So David sent messengers to get her, and she came to him, and he lay with her. (Now she was purifying herself after her period.) Then she returned to her house. The woman conceived; and she sent and told David, "I am pregnant." So David sent word to Joab, "Send me Uriah the Hittite." And Joab sent Uriah to David. When Uriah came to him, David asked how Joab and the people fared, and how the war was going. Then David said to Uriah, "Go down to your house, and wash your feet." Uriah went out of the king's house, and there followed him a present from the king. But Uriah slept at the entrance of the king's house with all the servants of his lord, and did not go down to his house. When they told David, "Uriah did not go down to his house," David said to Uriah, "You have just come from a journey. Why did you not go down to your house?" Uriah said to David, "The ark and Israel and Judah remain in booths; and my lord Joab and the servants of my lord are camping in the open field; shall I then go to my house, to eat and to drink, and to lie with my wife? As you live, and as your soul lives, I will not do such a thing." Then David said to Uriah, "Remain here today also, and tomorrow I will send you back." So Uriah remained in Jerusalem that day. On the next day, David invited him to eat and drink in his presence and made him drunk; and in the evening he went out to lie on his couch with the servants of his lord, but he did not go down to his house. In the morning David wrote a letter to Joab, and

128

sent it by the hand of Uriah. In the letter he wrote, "Set Uriah in the fore-front of the hardest fighting, and then draw back from him, so that he may be struck down and die."

2 SAM. 11:1-15 (NRSV)

A cartoon shows an elderly clergyman discoursing with a portly, worried-looking parishioner over coffee. He says firmly, "Oh, I'm still opposed to sin — I'm just no longer sure what qualifies." It's a common-enough problem. A while ago I was attending a lecture by a noted Christian psychologist, who in the course of his remarks had a few things to say about sin, things he said in such a way as to make plain that he simply assumed that "sin," as the term has traditionally been used, is indeed a meaningful category. Another psychologist, who should, in my view, have known better, immediately jumped in to ask if the lecturer didn't think the term was imprecise and unhelpful. After all, people have bad genes, poor environments, controlling parents, un-reasonable bosses, incredible economic pressures, multitudinous per-fectly natural feelings and impulses that they don't understand very well and hence can't control, and so on. Isn't it mainly ignorance and lack of power that make people do bad things, he wanted to know?

What, then, does count as sin? Have our analyses — and our desires to excuse ourselves — so modified our perceptions that we can no lon-ger recognize sin when we see it?

Contrast my text for this evening. I don't think it is, fundamentally, "about" lust or covetousness or deception or murder, though these are the forms that sin takes in the story. Basically, I think the story is sim-ply about *sin* in all its starkness. And I would suggest that we have no fine-spun difficulties identifying the sin when we read this account.

You know the plot perfectly well. King David was loitering at home when, perhaps, he should have been out with his troops. He sees a beautiful woman, who just happens, inconveniently, to be married. He desires her. He takes her. She inconveniently gets pregnant. He sends for her husband, allegedly to ask for news of the war, but actually as-suming that he will behave like a normal soldier on leave. He inconve-niently doesn't, not even when David keeps him an extra day and tries to deaden his sensibilities and arouse his desire with alcohol. So David sends a note to his military chief to make sure that the man, conveniently, gets killed in battle. End of this part of the story.

The whole thing is austerely, unremittingly, unrelentingly blatant. Nowhere do we find a word of explanation, much less of excuse, for David's behavior. Presumably it needed no explaining and could bear no excusing. He sinned. Period.

I'm reminded of a satire Garrison Keillor wrote for the *New Yorker* some years ago, entitled, "The Current Crisis in Remorse." He describes "remorse" as a new area in social work:

> We in remorse are in a radical minority within the social work community. We believe that not every wrong in our society is the result of complex factors such as poor early-learning environment and resultative dissocialized communication. Some wrong is the result of badness. We believe that some people act like jerks, and that when dealing with jerks one doesn't waste too much time on sympathy. They're jerks. They do bad things. They should feel sorry for what they did and stop doing it.[1]

Badness — *sin* — that was David's problem.

I'm fascinated, by contrast, with how many commentators try somehow to get David at least partially off the hook. Surely Bathsheba shouldn't have been bathing where she could, by any stretch of the neck or the imagination, have been seen. Surely she must have been flirting. Surely she shouldn't have just *come* when David sent for her. And so on. But the commentators seem unaccountably blind to the fact that should be perfectly obvious: this isn't Bathsheba's story. It's David's story. The writer is manifestly uninterested in Bathsheba's behavior. Her behavior, whether absolutely decorous or patently scandalous, obviously does not bear on what the writer is communicating here. Only what David does is at issue. No excuses.

Note, too, that the story says nothing of David's feelings, by way of either arousing sympathy for him or condemning him. Passion, boredom, fear, anxiety about "the good of the kingdom" — none of these is even mentioned. We can read them in, of course; and perhaps we can safely assume that they were there. Our writer, however, obviously does

1. Quoted in *Context* 16:18 (Oct. 15, 1984): 5.

not consider the usual human emotions to be relevant, either. Nothing enters in to ameliorate David's sin. Karl Barth puts it well:

> In the affair in which David becomes a transgressor there is no element of human greatness even in the tragic sense. It is primitive and undignified and brutal, especially in the stratagem by which David tries to maintain his honor. . . . At every point . . . it is . . . petty and repulsive.[2]

"Petty and repulsive" — a good description of sin. Sin insists upon self at the expense of one's duty to God and at the expense of one's duty to others and at the expense of whatever one knows about what is right and good and true. Sin is willful and, as the way the story is told makes plain, sin is inexcusable.

Now let's look at the story from another angle. Sin is not only inexcusable, but it will be manifested with most devastating effect by the powerful. Stop for a moment and take that in — that sin will be manifested with most devastating effect by the powerful — because that claim goes flatly against all of our hopes of making enough social progress finally to eliminate it. That claim implies that eliminating poverty and bad parenting and inadequate education will *not* reduce the proclivity of humankind to do evil, but may even increase the means to do evil, just as it is precisely the scientific *progress* we have made that puts our entire world at risk of extinction. (Let me make perfectly clear that by making such a strong statement, I am *certainly* not suggesting that we should refrain from doing all we rightly can to reduce human suffering of every kind. I am just saying that doing so will not solve the problem of sin.)

Consider David. Here was a man who had everything. He had wealth. He had religion. Presumably he had education. He certainly had culture. And he had more than enough wives. Trying to attribute his behavior to sexual frustration, ignorance, or the lack of concern for the future manifested by those buried in hopeless poverty simply won't fly. No, he just wanted what he wanted, and wanted it now. Because he was king, he could have it.

No ordinary citizen of the age for military service could decide

---

2. Barth, *Church Dogmatics*, IV/2: 465-66.

when he would go out to battle and when he would stay home. No ordinary citizen could send messengers to summon a neighbor's wife — any neighbor's wife, known or unknown — and be just about one hundred percent sure that she would come, or be brought, if she would not come. No ordinary citizen could ask that a man be sent home from battle, or that a way be found that he be killed in battle (no matter if a few others be lost at the same time); only the commander-in-chief of the armed forces could do that. No ordinary citizen had it within his power to sin quite as spectacularly as David sinned.

Because sin stems from corruption of the will and not from weakness, increasing power and freedom increase possibilities for evil.[3] Having "everything" gives one all sorts of opportunities to sin, all sorts of temptations, all sorts of illusions (which, alas, in this world too often prove not to be illusions after all) that one is immune from normal consequences of one's behavior, or normal sanctions for misbehavior. A powerful person can get away with all sorts of things that a less powerful person wouldn't even dare think of trying. And power is intoxicating: the more one has, the more one wants; and the more justified one feels in exercising it. David was neither the first nor the last government official, neither the first nor the last wealthy person, neither the first nor the last military hero, who thought he could do as he pleased. People around him, for the most part, seem to have winked at it all, even as they wink today.

Now let's take one more look, this time at ourselves. Sin is not only inexcusable, and perfectly easily recognizable, at least in ourselves, when we strip away the rationalizations. Sin is not only manifested most horrendously in those with power, so that we may *not* assume that if we were only mightier, we would also be more virtuous. Sin is just as much present, and just as culpable, in those lacking opportunities or too weak or too frightened to act it out. Hannah More, a remarkable eighteenth-century woman much admired for her learning and piety, commented sharply on the tendency of persons to be critical of those whose particular sins they lacked the ability to commit. She said,

3. See R. M. Brown, ed., *The Essential Reinhold Niebuhr* (New Haven: Yale University Press, 1986), p. 94.

She who is as vain, as dissipated and as extravagant as existing circumstances allow would surely be as vain, dissipated and extravagant as the most flamboyant objects of her invective if she could
change places with them. It is not merely by what we do that we
can be sure the spirit of the world has no dominion over us, but
by fairly considering what we would probably do if more were in
our power.[4]

Ah, yes; what *would* we do if more were in our power? What would we do
if we were King David?

The open opportunities before us make a difference, too. Even old
and battle-worn psychological tests from a more optimistic day have
fewer illusions about our virtue in the face of specific temptations than
most of us do. Let me take an example from one instrument, recast so
as not to violate professional standards about revealing the content of
standardized tests. Suppose you had a chance to walk into a ballpark
without being seen, and without having purchased a ticket: would you
do it? If you say No, that particular instrument is scored on the assumption that you are lying. The test-makers are fairly certain that almost everyone *would* do it. Examine yourself. Maybe you are one of the
rare ones who would in fact buy a ticket even if you didn't have to; but
you see the point anyway. Human beings will most often try to get away
with something, particularly if they figure that it's a perfectly safe bet
and it doesn't hurt anyone, anyway (and in some moods, we also tend
not to be very perceptive of what hurt is likely to be done).

Or, suppose that one has both the ability and the opportunity to
sin, but refrains out of fear? That fear spares others, and is of use on
that account; but what does it say about the state of one's own soul?
Hear the remark of Charles Spurgeon:

If the heart *would,* but the hand *dares not,* the person will be
judged by what he desires rather than by his actions. We are before
God what in our hearts we wish to be. The raven is not a dove so
long as it longs for carrion, even though it may sit in a cage, and
act like the gentlest of birds. Christ did not come to scare us from

4. D. L. Jeffrey, ed., *A Burning and a Shining Light* (Grand Rapids: Eerdmans, 1987),
p. 488.

sin, but to save us from it. Even if there were no hell, true saints would hate sin, and strive after holiness.[5]

Let us, again, examine ourselves. Insofar as we *wish* we were free to sin, or even to commit one particular sin, we are, most surely, sinners.

Sin is inexcusable (and easily enough recognized when stripped of all the excuses). Power won't fix it. Weakness won't prevent it. So now what?

We won't be finished with the story of David and Bathsheba to-night, so there's more to come. But let me draw just a couple of conclusions at this rather odd stopping point, this point where all we have in hand — all Uriah has in hand — is that incredibly cold-blooded note to Joab reading, "Set Uriah in the forefront of the hardest fighting, and then draw back from him, so that he may be struck down and die." What shall we say?

First, we must say that the work of God is not accomplished by blameless persons, but is accomplished by God in spite of sinful ones. We need endless reminders of that fact. The work remains God's work, in his control; and he will not be defeated simply because his creatures do wicked things. Sin is not mightier than God.

Second, if the first point is true; and if sin is inexcusable and power won't fix it and weakness won't prevent it; then it's high time that we stopped hiding from God and from ourselves, and stopped scrambling to find some new technology or technique to make it go away, and stopped pleading the meagerness of our resources as a reason that we couldn't really do anything very bad. It's high time we were simply straight with ourselves and with God about the evil we willingly do and the evil we would do if we could. It's high time we took sin as seriously as God does, in sending Jesus Christ to die for us and save us from it. It's high time we asked God's mercy — in faith, in gratitude for his gift of Jesus, in thanksgiving that he does continue to use even such sinners as David was, and as we are.

---

5. Charles Spurgeon, *Illustrations and Meditations* (Passmore & Alabaster, 1883), p. 173.

7

Sin and Sins

In considering the nature of sin, it is important to insist both upon its
initial and ongoing form as particular expressions of rebellion against
God (sins), and upon the peculiar and recalcitrant unity of its underlying reality (sin).[1] To concentrate too exclusively on the former easily
leads to the illusion that if only we could weed out *this* manifestation of
evil, we might at last be whole and happy, and leaves us baffled that evil
actually appears more like a Hydra that grows more heads for each one
whacked off. To concentrate too exclusively on the latter can make it
seem too much like an impersonal fate or ontological "given" in which
we personally are only incidentally concerned.

All sin makes us guilty before God: it is not as if we can rebel or dis-
believe or be prideful and self-centered "just a little," too little actually
to incur guilt; for guilt comes with turning in the wrong direction,
however small the following step (Matt. 5:19; James 2:10). Nor is it as if
we can rebel and then take back our action and thus wipe out our guilt.
Part of the harsh reality of guilt is that human beings cannot undo the
past. We have been warned against the "try it; you'll like it" come-on,
on the grounds that once we have tried it, it will not matter whether we

---

1. In an amazing figure, Milton makes the myriad particular sins to be born of the
rape of Sin by her offspring Death (*Paradise Lost* 2.790-97). Says Roland Frye, "This rape
too is inevitable because Sin, personifying the finite assertion of infinity, exerts upon
Death, the personification of inescapable finitude, a violent attraction . . ." (*Perspective
on Man: Literature and the Christian Tradition* [Philadelphia: Westminster, 1961], p. 49).
Thus understood, the poem shows strikingly "modern" psychological insight.

like it; the act will have already begun to generate its own consequences.[2] And the quality of sin as a power, with its demonic cast,
which the apostle Paul bemoans, may be traced all the way back to the
Garden and the blandishments of the serpent: there is a sort of unity in
the kingdom of evil. This unity means that sin tends strongly to lead to
sin — indeed, to deeper and deeper sin, even as a fly caught in a spider's
web gets more deeply entangled while seeking to escape. One does not
have to intend such a result: the young seducer does not intend that his
victim end up as a whore; white Americans did not consciously intend
that segregated schools be unequal; even the procrastinator with respect to some critical good act does not intend that opportunity to
perform it will be lost forever, with devastating consequences.[3] It may
be that the critical turn comes by an act committed in mere absence of
mind, as one wanders down the wrong road with the wrong compan-
ions. It may come, as Buber notes, out of failure to decide upon a
clearly defined good, which failure leaves one subject to poorly governed impulses.[4] However it happens, individuals and groups do get
caught up and are swept along, as can be seen in the train of events surrounding Calvary: we could not be satisfied with questioning Jesus but
must dispute; we could not stop with disputing but must mock, spit in
his face, crucify him, bury him, seal up the tomb, put up a guard, make
it as "secure" as we can; and had there been any more we could have
done, including sending up a rocket to pull down God's throne, we
would have done it. We always think that we can break off at the critical point, only to find that, somehow and in some way beyond our ken,
we have lost that power.[5]

2. See Robin W. Lovin, "Beyond Tidying Up the Iron Cage," *Christian Century* 108:3
(Jan. 23, 1991): 80-81.

3. One may, however, intend it: Thielicke makes the intriguing suggestion that one
reason sin leads to sin, and indeed to recruitment of others to sin, is because sin makes
us lonely and thus makes us want to find, or create, company that is like us (Helmut
Thielicke, *How the World Began*, trans. John W. Doberstein [Philadelphia: Fortress, 1961],
pp. 159-60).

4. See Malcolm L. Diamond, *Martin Buber: Jewish Existentialist* (New York: Oxford
University Press, 1960), pp. 142-44.

5. The problem of the spiraling of sin in both personal and international relations
may be illustrated graphically by the problem of revenge. Today, we tend to see the *lex
talionis* ("an eye for an eye and a tooth for a tooth," Exod. 21:24; Lev. 24:20) as primitive
and brutal; it was intended, however, not to condone inhumanity but to *limit* the cycle of

To fail to acknowledge the interlinked and spiraling character of sin is to fail to see it aright. To make that point is not to deny, however, that we can speak of degrees of sin and of culpability; though we must admit that Scripture says remarkably little about differences in the weightiness of sins.[6] And it can also be useful to consider varying characteristics of different types of sin.

Degrees of Sin and of Culpability

To affirm that sin is sin, that no one can herself atone for her own sin, and that the ground is level at the foot of the Cross, with all standing equally in need of the grace of God to be saved, is both true and potentially dangerous, given the "less and more" of historical circumstances.[7] The affirmation is essential if certain categories of "respectable" sinners are not to think of themselves as in no real danger, or at least in no real danger that they cannot with due diligence escape. It is dangerous if it leads to fatalism ("since it's all the same in the end, I might just as well lie rather than be embarrassed") or to concentration only on effects on oneself and not on the neighbor (it may in some sense be all the same for the sinner whether he lusts after a neighbor or goes to bed with her [Matt. 5:27-28; see also 1 John 3:15], but it makes a considerable

---

revenge: one may not exact more from one's enemy than one has suffered. Wars of this decade in Africa, in the Balkans, and in particular between Israel and Palestine surely show that we have not yet reached the Old Testament standard, much less gone beyond it. The return of this much more mortar fire for that most recent suicide bomber is never-ending. Nor is the United States immune from this temptation to excess: following the attacks on the World Trade Center, a *Los Angeles Times* front-page subhead read, "Bush Vows Full Assault, says 'Good Will Prevail'" — without even a hint of irony (Sept. 13, 2001, p. A1). There is nothing more effective than the self-righteousness of victims to blind them to the evil they are planning.

6. Even Calvin was willing to make distinctions in the seriousness of sins, but he did so specifically in the context of church discipline (*Institutes* 4.12.3, 4, 6). Augustine, however, insisted that only God could judge which sins are heinous and which trivial (*Enchiridion* 78). He continued, "there are some sins which would be considered very trifling, if the Scriptures did not show that they are really very serious" (ibid., 79); and he cited Matt. 5:22, 23.

7. It would also go against those passages of Scripture that do seem to speak of degrees of sin, e.g., Ezek. 5:6; 8:15; John 19:11.

difference to his wife and to the neighbor and her family). And it is likewise dangerous if it leads to the morbid scrupulosity that, in an infinite regress, repents <u>obsessively of the sin of thinking of sin</u>.[8]

Christianity has tended to measure culpability with a view to relative freedom from compulsion (of which there are many types),[9] knowledge (including what one is responsible for knowing),[10] and, generally, cold-blooded calculation (as contrasted with sins of passion; or, especially, crimes committed without forethought or enmity — note the provision made for unintentional slayers, Num. 35). Other circumstances also bear, as in the case of David and Bathsheba: the point of Nathan's accusatory parable was that David, a rich man with many wives, took the only wife of Uriah the Hittite (2 Sam. 11-12). These circumstances (apart from those that destroy one's moral agency altogether — we have spoken already of the principle that absolute compulsion removes an action from the realm of sin) do not determine whether or not a thing is sinful: that is determined by its failure to conform to the law of God; but they may aggravate or alleviate guilt.

In thinking of the less and more of actual sins, we might propose that it may be just possible that a sense in which we are all equally sinners has to do with the less and more of our hereditary and environmental circumstances. That is to say, most of us, if we think deeply, would hesitate to assert with too much certainty what we could or could not be guilty of in exactly the wrong circumstances. And insofar

8. See, for instance, reflections on a Roman Catholic upbringing that refused any distinction in seriousness between thought and act, and the moral crises such teaching can provoke in young people, especially at moments of dawning sexual awareness (Emmett McLoughlin, *People's Padre* [Boston: Beacon Press, 1954], pp. 88-89).

9. Recall, again, that relative freedom from compulsion is not the same thing as direct intentionality: we have noted above the (quite proper) knowledge of our deep sinfulness that we can gain from unworthy feelings that simply spring up in us unbidden; we could just as well speak of the failure to have sentiments that are proper, such as gratitude. These are culpable defects. (See, for helpful discussion of this whole issue, Robert M. Adams, "Involuntary Sins," *Philosophical Review* 94:1 [Jan. 1985]: 3-31.)

10. Hence Keble's poem for Good Friday:

Oh! shame beyond the bitterest thought
    That evil spirit ever framed,
That sinners know what Jesus wrought
    Yet feel their haughty hearts untamed.
        (*The Christian Year* [New York: Frederick A. Stokes, c. 1827], p. 79)

as we have it in us to resist particular temptations, this strength may well be attributable to certain unknown (even to us) "aids" to our virtue, whether stemming from nature or from grace.

With respect to analysts of the seriousness of sin, the criterion of knowledge is at once obvious and complex, since we have said that sin has the characteristic of hiding from us what we need to know (note Ps. 19:12-13; Rom. 1:21). Furthermore, this criterion would seem to make "sins of ignorance" impossible (e.g., Lev. 4:2, 13, 27; 5:15; Num. 15:24-29; Ezek. 45:20). There is, however, such a thing as culpable ignorance of one's obligations, including culpable ignorance of the ceremonial law. (The traffic officer who stops us for an unwitting violation is justified in proclaiming, "Ignorance of the law is no excuse." Pascal brutally mocks ignorance and a clean conscience as an excuse in his *Provincial Letters*, #4.) That does not appear to be the whole story, though. Pharaoh and his house were afflicted with plagues when he quite innocently took Abram's wife to be his wife, in the belief that she was Abram's sister, as Abram had claimed (Gen. 12:10-20). Here, apparently only the objective breach of the law counted. Also, we find in the Old Testament a very physicalistic view of pollution as incurring guilt, to which knowledge and intention are simply irrelevant. That this aspect of guilt due to unintentional physical defilement is not carried over to the New Testament (with the possible exception of Heb. 10:26; Heb. 9:7 refers to the old cultus) can be seen in Paul's attitude to meat offered to idols: eating it does not in itself pollute; the issue is one of conscience (Rom. 14:13-23; 1 Cor. 8; but cf. Acts 15:20); similarly Jesus on that which defiles as coming from within rather than without (Matt. 15:11, 18-20; Mark 7:14-23).

In any case, ignorance is suggested as a mitigating factor (Luke 23:34; Acts 17:30; 1 Tim. 1:13). It does not follow that sin is not sin and will not have consequences, but just that punishment allotted will take degree of knowledge into account — not only less for those with less knowledge (Luke 12:47-48), but also more for those who slip back from a knowledge they once had (2 Pet. 2:20).

The question of calculation and sustained malice versus sudden passion is similarly both obvious and complex in the way it is played out. On the one hand, planned-out and intended sin clearly suggests a deeper corruption of character than does a sudden and impulsive act. The kind of protracted planning and preparation, with clear thoughts of doing the maximum possible harm, that marked the terrorist strikes against the World Trade Center and the Pentagon in September 2001 arouse a particular horror. However, the church has tended to see sexual sin (which is often impulsive) as especially serious, as we will see below. Furthermore, we generally react more strongly to and condemn more vehemently the person who bombs a single bank than the slumlord who persists in subjecting dozens of tenants to vermin-infested apartments — and this, despite the fact that we would also hold, in theory, that people should be weighed more heavily than property in our calculations. Something about violent crime with immediate and dramatic effects arouses moral outrage, while we easily shut our eyes to other types of sin.[11] Perhaps illustrating a similar principle, we tend to be remarkably tolerant of white-collar crime, despite its horrendous economic consequences — at least until assorted swindles deprive large numbers of older citizens of their life's savings. Evidence abounds that deep-rooted corruption marks everything from Defense Department contracts to the reporting of scientific findings bearing on ecological concerns (which findings, of course, have economic consequences for those who want them to read in a particular way).[12] One wonders whether the public mainly takes an "out of sight, out of mind" approach, or whether people sense their own temptations sufficiently close at hand that they brush these sins off. In any case, such sins are surely both calculated and widely harmful, yet they do not evoke a proportionate response by church or society. Thus, it is clear that our reactions to actual sins do not correspond precisely to the criteria of culpability we might theoretically offer.

Another way that our calculations may get thrown off is by the heroic element we sometimes perceive in wickedness (not to mention the

11. One wonders, then, about our deep attraction to violence in the media, an attraction so pervasive that one magazine reportedly titled its account of the aforementioned terrorist attacks, "This Is Not the Movie"; and rentals of terrorist-themed videos actually increased after the attacks. What we condemn and what draws us are frighteningly closely related.

12. For just a single example documenting specific cases — and examples could be multiplied almost endlessly — see the tenth anniversary issue of *Common Cause Magazine* (Nov.-Dec. 1990). Corporate crime probably totals some $200 billion per year, three times organized crime; fraud and embezzlement by individuals cost ten times the sum of all theft, burglary, and robbery; and criminals perpetrating these crimes are rarely prosecuted ("Crime and Punishment," *Britannica 2001* DVD-ROM).

romantic tradition of "honor among thieves"). For instance, in William Rose Benét's poem "Jesse James," we find the Robin Hood-like lines,

> Jesse raked in the di'mon' rings,
> The big gold watches an' the yuther things;
> Jesse divvied' em then an' thar'
> With a cryin' child had lost her mar.[13]

And a contemporary newspaper reports a party in honor of the twenty-fifth anniversary of the disappearance of what it calls a "jet age Jesse James," the hijacker D. B. Cooper, who was admired for the technical skill of his exploit, even as James was admired for his powers as a marksman.[14] Such examples provide a sobering reminder both that certain positive aspects of character and ability are not proof against corruption, and that great gifts corrupted can do more damage than lesser ones equally corrupted. (Pascal remarked that "an extraordinary greatness of soul" is necessary to attain to certain kinds of evil [*Pensées*, #408]). Like a parasitic plant, sin cannot wholly destroy the virtue of its host without finally destroying itself. It does not follow, however, that "down deep" such criminals are good people, but only that the mystery of iniquity is very profound.

In a related thought, reflecting on the dreary but unremitting banality of most evil, George Bernard Shaw wondered if the spectacular villain might in the end do less harm to society than the ordinary person:

> We see the able villain, Mephistopheles-like, doing a huge amount of good in order to win the power to do a little daring evil, out of which he is as likely as not to be cheated in the end; whilst your normal respectable man will countenance, connive at, and grovel his way through all sorts of meanness, baseness, servility, and cruel indifference to suffering in order to enjoy a miserable tuppence worth of social position, piety, comfort, and domestic affection, of which he, too, is often ironically defrauded by Fate.[15]

---

13. *Treasury of Great Poems,* ed. Louis Untermeyer (New York: Simon & Schuster, 1955), p. 1133.

14. Richard E. Meyer, "The Legend of a Jet Age Jesse James," *Los Angeles Times,* Dec. 6, 1996, p. A1+.

15. Quoted in *Elbert Hubbard's Scrap Book* (New York: Wm. H. Wise & Co., 1923), p. 9.

Whatever the inaccuracy and inconsistency in the application of our standards, though, and whatever the practical and psychological necessity of nevertheless making some rough distinctions in the level of seriousness of sins, such distinctions have misfired if they lead anyone to try to figure out just how far she can go without being in real trouble: such an attitude already shows in itself, prior to any further activity, the relative freedom from coercion, high level of awareness, and cold-blooded calculation that mark the most serious kind of sin.

On quite the other end of the spectrum is the person tormented by the thought that she has already committed "the unforgivable sin" — perhaps by some youthful serious misdeed — and hence is beyond hope. The usual pastoral response is to suggest that the concern the person is expressing is itself evidence against the validity of the fear, since a sinner concerned about her condition would appear not to be hardened past all prospect of repentance. We concur with that argument. It must of course be admitted that allusions to "the unforgivable sin" in Scripture are anything but specific and leave a good deal of room for the scrupulous conscience to brood (as well as room for exegetes to debate the relationships among the relevant texts; see Matt. 12:31; Mark 3:29; Luke 12:10; Heb. 6:4-6; 10:26-27; 1 John 5:16 [this last text the Roman Catholic church has related not to the "unforgivable sin" but to its distinction between mortal and venial sins]).

Note that the "unforgivable sin" is not to be confused with the "mortal sin" of Roman Catholic theology. "Mortal sins" are presumed to be forgivable; else the Roman Catholic sacrament of confession and penance[16] would be meaningless. A "mortal sin" is one characterized by "clear knowledge, free consent and grave matter," by which the sinner rejects the Creator's will for the basic structure of his creation and thus contradicts her own nature and the purpose of her freedom, which is to love God.[17] Such sins must be confessed and pardoned or God's grace is believed to be lost. Venial sins (those where knowledge or freedom is compromised or which are less serious in their substance), by contrast, do not automatically lead to a loss of grace. It does not follow, however, that venial sins are not sins or are unimportant: they not only disrupt

---

16. Now called the sacrament of reconciliation.

17. Rahner and Vorgrimler, "Sin," *Theological Dictionary* (New York: Herder and Herder, 1965), p. 436; see Aquinas, *Summa Theologica*, II/I, Q. 88.

relationships but also may predispose the sinner to mortal sin. Protestants have not used this distinction, though they have, as we have indicated, been willing to talk about certain gradations in the seriousness of sin. The major reason is their emphasis on sin — any sin, all sin — as an act of the whole person who has turned in the wrong direction. Sin has a depth that cannot be read off of the surface of the act. Therefore the wages of any sin is death (Rom. 6:23). God's mercy does not so much calculate the weight of the sin as capture the heart of the sinner. All sinners must repent and be forgiven if they are to be saved.

The very lack of specificity in Scripture's references to "the unforgiveable sin," however, suggests that this sin is not a particular forbidden act, like that of partaking of the forbidden Tree in the Garden. Rather, it is rejection of the gospel by one who knows the power of the gospel and turns away anyway. It is not ignorant rejection but willful apostasy; it is not even apostasy out of a moment's terrible weakness, but apostasy by one commanding her full powers — one who, knowing the truth, yet refuses it. One cannot, therefore, commit this sin as it were by accident. It has something of the character of Milton's Satan, saying, while (very significantly) bidding farewell to hope and fear and remorse, "Evil be thou my Good."[18] Hope or fear or remorse — perhaps especially hope in the Lord's mercy — would have made all the difference. But part of the terrible mystery of iniquity is that it is possible freely to reject the truth that one knows, in a way that therefore puts one beyond the reach, so to speak, of that truth.

Categories of Sins

The New Testament contains various vice lists (e.g., among many others, Rom. 1:29-31; 1 Cor. 6:9-10; Gal. 5:19-21; 1 Tim. 1:9-10; Rev. 9:20-21; these are characteristic of literature of that period) but no catalogue of sins. One might suppose that the reason is twofold. First, except in particular instances like food laws, it affirms rather than rejects the substance of the law of the Old Testament (e.g., Matt. 5:17-20; Rom. 7:12; with the proviso, of course, that affirming the substance of the Law is not the same thing as making it the way of salvation). Jesus even increased its rigor in some

18. John Milton, *Paradise Lost*, 4.108.

instances by emphasizing inward attitude and not just outward act (e.g., Matt. 5:22, 28). Second, as we have repeatedly emphasized, it speaks of sin in a way that does not allow reduction of sin to concrete acts alone, apart from the whole disposition of the sinner. The Rich Young Ruler was mistaken in supposing that he could keep the law's requirement by obeying discrete commands while failing to yield his whole heart to God (Matt. 19:20; Luke 18:21).[19] Thus, discussion of particular failings serves an illustrative purpose; we find no suggestion that if only we could avoid some five — or some five thousand — faults, all would be well.

Nonetheless, the church has been intrigued with analysis of types of sins, from the "Seven Deadly Sins" of the Middle Ages to the various books on vices and virtues written in the late twentieth century. A series of forums on the seven deadly sins offered at Stanford University in 1987 was reportedly one of the more popular events on campus. Obviously, then, people seek an understanding of the specific characteristics of particular sins, and of their likely seriousness and effects. One suspects that this curiosity is not just morbid or in the service of titillation, but also is a way of seeking to get some kind of handle on the amorphous and pervasive evils of our day.[20] Another route to that end is to look at a few prominent occasions for sin: facts of our common life that are not in themselves bad but that seem especially prone to plague us with temptations.

The Seven Deadly Sins

The generally accepted list of deadly or capital sins was established by Aquinas and includes vainglory, envy, anger, sloth, covetousness, glut-

---

19. Thus Milton's Samson, turning away praise for his abstemiousness as regards alcohol, said, "But what avail'd this temperance, not compleat/Against another object more enticing?/What boots it at one gate to make defence/And at another to let in the foe . . . ?" ("Samson Agonistes," ll. 558-61).

20. While we doubt that human sinfulness has increased over time, we do see differences in the way it is expressed. A striking example comes from a survey of changes in the top disciplinary problems in public schools: in the 1940s, the list began with talking and proceeded to chewing gum, making noise, running in hallways, cutting in line, dressing improperly, and not putting paper in wastebaskets; in the 1980s, drug abuse was followed by alcohol abuse, pregnancy, suicide, rape, robbery, and assault (Doug Burleigh, "Good News for Tough Times," *Relationships*, April 1988, p. 2).

tony, and lust.[21] These he considered capital sins in the sense that they are the source of other sins, not in the sense of the punishment they merit;[22] thus they are not to be exactly identified with mortal as contrasted with venial sins in Roman Catholic theology (wrath, for instance, may be mortal or venial depending on the action to which it tends).[23] The list merits reflection, not least because of its striking orientation to disposition rather than to act: obviously, it seeks the root of behavior rather than simply interdicting behaviors.[24] One can even see why, say, so egregious and obvious a sin as cruelty is not on the list, since cruelty would usually be a manifestation of, or in the service of, one of the other capital sins. It is also interesting that it overlaps the Decalogue — which is act oriented — but little. In fact, such a selection does not boast direct scriptural support, which is doubtless one reason Protestants have not emphasized it. It is nonetheless sobering to consider the extent to which all of these sins have been touted in our day almost as virtues: someone remarked, for instance, that the whole advertising industry — maybe even the whole American economy — rests upon covetousness.

21. Aquinas, *Summa Theologica*, II/I, Q. 84, art. 4. The Latin terms *(superbia, invidia, ira, acedia, avaritia, gula, luxuria)* are somewhat variously translated. For a splendidly helpful and accessible treatment, see Dorothy Sayers's essay, "The Other Six Deadly Sins," in *The Whimsical Christian* (New York: Macmillan, 1978), pp. 157-79.

22. Aquinas, *Summa Theologica*, II/I, Q.84, art. 3.

23. Aquinas, *Summa Theologica*, Q. 88, art. 5.

24. As William May notes, it is based on a faculty psychology — one of the ways of talking about sins without having them proliferate endlessly. Other strategies he mentions include categorizing sins according to the divine laws disobeyed (especially the Ten Commandments); according to the divine perfections or the divine acts of self-disclosure contradicted or counterfeited; or (May's own choice) according to the environment they distort (*Catalogue of Sins* [New York: Holt, Rinehart and Winston, 1967], pp. 14-18). Bavinck adds to categories we have already mentioned, division into public and secret sins; or into sins of thought, word, and deed; or into human and diabolic sins; but he repeats the caution that while each group has its particular characteristics and temptations, all are finally interrelated (*Our Reasonable Faith*, trans. Henry Zylstra [Grand Rapids: Eerdmans, 1956], pp. 247-49).

Sex and Sin[25]

While the advertising industry may rest upon covetousness, no one can look at many ads without becoming sharply aware that that industry finds it most advantageous to arouse covetousness by means of another of the capital sins, namely lust. And that brings us to think once again about the lofty place sex has had in the church's hierarchy of sins, and the assumption embedded in common usage that if a person is dubbed "immoral," then she has committed sexual misdeeds. On the one hand, the private bedroom behavior of two consenting adults hardly seems to merit the overwhelming proportion of moral concern that has been lavished on sexuality: an act of sharply-directed viciousness seems worthier of reprobation than an act of misdirected love or even lust. But on the other hand, there *is* something peculiar about sexuality and its sometimes all-consuming quality that makes one suspect that the church's concentration upon it is not entirely without reason, however hard it is to state the reason precisely, and however disproportionate and hence harmful this focus has been.[26] Precisely because Scripture does not appear, by and large, to rate sexual sins as a kind of epitome of wickedness, one must inquire as to why they have gained this reputation.[27]

25. See the earlier treatment of this theme in *Who We Are,* pp. 262-66, where there is an interpretation of the difficult passage 1 Cor. 6:12-20, and pp. 290-350 for extended discussion of homosexuality; see also above, pp. 63-69, in our discussion of the consequences of the Fall and the issue of modesty, and p. 106, on sin as act. This matter keeps reappearing!

26. Helpful discussion — despite a certain prevalence of male-female stereotypes — may be found in Helmut Thielicke, *The Ethics of Sex,* trans. John W. Doberstein (Grand Rapids: Baker, 1964), esp. parts II and V. See also Niebuhr, *Nature and Destiny of Man* (New York: Scribners, 1941), 1:228-40: "Once sin is presupposed . . . the instincts of sex are particularly effective tools for both the assertion of the self and the flight from the self" (pp. 236-37).

27. Speaking of disproportion, Emmett McLoughlin, a Roman Catholic priest who eventually left the priesthood and married, reflects on the overwhelming preoccupation of (pre–Vatican II) Roman Catholic moral theology with sex and notes wryly the remark attributed to Alfred Kinsey (of the Kinsey reports on human sexuality), that the Vatican Library contains the largest collection in the world of books on the subject of sex. McLoughlin says:

A compendium of Roman Catholic moral theology, merely a summary of the several volumes studied in the seminary, devoted thirty-two pages of the fine print to the

Not so long ago, it was widely assumed that, given the triumphs of science over conception and disease, restraints on sexual expression could rightly be eased, with nothing but benefits resulting for the mental and physical health of all concerned. The epidemics of abortion and AIDS should write a sharp caution by that assumption (whatever the eventual outcome of efforts to curb these particular tragedies): it would appear that one way or another, unfettered sexuality has a way of bringing great sorrow and suffering with it. Victims of incest and other forms of sexual abuse find it very difficult to recover, even if they did not resist at the time; and divorce, despite its prevalence, has not ceased to be traumatic. Formal consent is not enough when sex is involved.

Furthermore, a more permissive attitude toward sexuality has obviously not reduced prostitution, sex slavery, rape, pornography (including child pornography), or frank perversion; which should put to rest the thesis that the only trouble with sex comes from repressing it.[28] None of these aberrations is new: a name particularly associated with sexual depravity is that of the Marquis de Sade (1740-1814), but histories of the Roman Caesars provide material easily in the same league.[29]

---

infinitesimal details of the multiplicity of sexual sins. In a mere twelve pages it disposes of the hierarchy's teachings on assault, suicide, murder, dueling, capital punishment, the relations among nations, and the morality of war from the stone age to the atomic age. (*People's Padre,* pp. 195-96)

One can safely say that something is wrong here.

28. Augustine berated the Cynics for their view that since intercourse between husband and wife was honorable, it should be practiced in public; he considered it a violation of natural shame rather than a promotion of virtue: "Such barefaced obscenity deserved to receive the name of dogs; and so they went by the title of 'Cynics'" [from κυνικοι, dog-like] (*On Marriage and Concupiscence,* 1.24). Luther may similarly have confused shame with modesty when he said that it betokens shame that a man steals away to his wife in the darkness of night. Nonetheless, the deep sense that even the most innocent and proper sexual behavior is not something one rightly puts on public display would seem to be confirmed by the dismal sequelae of immodesty in our day. And Matthew 5:28, condemning lustful looks, would seem clearly to apply to pornography.

29. In a fascinating passage, Arno Karlen describes de Sade's alternation in his writings of orgies involving every sort of perversion from bestiality to dismemberment and murder, with philosophical lectures attempting to justify them. The former, Karlen says, "are truly pornographic, devoid of content or significance aside from the sexual acts"; the latter "show how men cannot live without somehow justifying themselves to themselves" — in this case by arguing, in part, that "if perversion exists, then it is a fact of nature, and nature must have her due" (*Sexuality and Homosexuality* [New York: W. W.

Certain forms of access to sexual experience are new, however: the ready availability of pornography on the internet, cable and satellite television, and "dial-a-porn" services; "virtual affairs" (sometimes leading to physical affairs) carried on via online chat rooms; international "sex tourism" providing titillation at a safe (?) distance from home, while victimizing countless women and men, and especially girls and boys, in other lands. "Adult" dot-com businesses have been by far the most consistently profitable category, so much so that struggling companies have been widely tempted to expand in this direction. And one can only suppose that the ever more explicit material provided by the film media both reflects and contributes to the jadedness of appetite that is a sure sign of sexual behaviors having been severed from their proper interpersonal significance. As in the case of much sin, it may be an indication of the deepest trouble if one can seemingly indulge without psychic consequence in casual or unbridled sex; and today's implicit message from the secular world that we *should* be able to engage in merely recreational intercourse seems (given the effects of heeding the message) to go against something intrinsic to our nature.[30]

Even apart from perversion, it is dismayingly easy for sexual expression to go wrong, in terms of how or with whom it is engaged. And when it goes wrong, precisely because of the depth of interpersonal communion toward which it is properly oriented, the depth of distress it generates is far more serious than casual philanderers or armchair libertines foresee or are prone to believe. We suspect that this combination — the ease of falling into improper attachments, the consuming and rationally uncontrollable emotions aroused, and their potentially devastating effect on all involved — generates a mixture of fear and de-

---

Norton & Co., 1971], p. 156). Karlen notes that de Sade, though vicious enough in his actual behavior, was considerably worse on paper than in life; but the playing out of his most extreme fantasies was carefully documented during the Holocaust (p. 157). As to the Roman nobility, see, for instance, Gibbon, *Decline and Fall of the Roman Empire*, 40:60.

30. One hardly knows how to construe the statements of the La Habra, California, businessman who wished to open a juice bar featuring bikini-clad young women, when he defended himself by saying that he did not understand the controversy. He was simply bringing business to the city, and also providing job training "for girls to go to the hard core topless club"; besides, the club was to be smoke-free and would have a dress code prohibiting carrying long or exposed knives. One hopes the man was merely being self-interested and dishonest; the alternatives are worse (Brian Hall, "Clubbed Zeal," *La Habra Star*, June 9, 1994, pp. 1+).

sire sufficient to explain the otherwise puzzling historical preoccupation of the church and many moralists with sexual behavior. To put it
another way, it is not so much that the *heart* is more wrong when one
engages in certain sexual sins than when, say, one hates one's neighbor;
in this sense many of the sexual sins are far from the worst. It is rather
the chain of destruction that sexual sins tend to leave in their path, a
chain not rightly taken into account by the sinner precisely because she
tends to define her primary motive as love. Thus, whatever the excesses
in which they have engaged, and whatever the futility of rigidly regulat-
ing such matters, moralists who have been preoccupied with sexuality
are onto a significant point: something about who we are as human beings, created not only as biologically sexual beings but for personal relationship with one another, seems to involve staying within bound-
aries narrower than liberated modern people might have guessed, if we
are to avoid serious harm to each other and ourselves. Hence the need
— but also the final inadequacy, as in the case of all "law" — of strictures that define out-of-bounds behavior as sin (always granting the
risk of succumbing to mere prudery that denies the God-given goodness of sexuality in itself).

Money and Sin

It is a commonplace to note that in our day, it is more permissible to
talk about sex than about money in polite society. (Secret, numbered
Swiss bank accounts provide a more sophisticated illustration of persons loving darkness rather than light in this department; but we have
already commented on the prevalence of white-collar crime, with its
obvious economic motivation.) And it is also a commonplace, at least
in certain circles, to note further that the New Testament gives more attention to cautioning against the hazards of money than to elaborating strictures on sex.[31]

31. We grant that the Old Testament frequently counts wealth a blessing accruing to
the righteous (and also, of course, exemplifies somewhat different sexual mores than
the New). For riches as a blessing, see, for instance, 1 Kings 3:13; 1 Chron. 29:12; Ps. 112:1-3;
Prov. 10:15; 13:22; 22:4; Eccles. 5:19. However, the Old Testament also cautions against
trusting in riches (e.g., Ps. 49:6; Prov. 11:4, 28; Jer. 9:23) and indicts usury (e.g., Deut. 23:19;
Ps. 15:5); so the contrast between New and Old is by no means strong.

One thinks not only of the remark that the love of money is a root of all kinds of evil (1 Tim. 6:10), but of Jesus' remark that it is easier for a camel to go through the eye of a needle than for a rich person to enter the kingdom of God (Matt. 19:24; Mark 10:25; Luke 18:25), his warnings against storing up treasure on earth (Matt. 6:21; Luke 12:20-21, 34), and his assertion of the impossibility of serving both God and mammon (Matt. 6:24; Luke 16:13). (See also Matt. 13:22; 19:21; Mark 4:19; 10:21; Luke 8:14; 18:22; 1 Tim. 3:3, 8; Titus 1:7; James 5:1-3; and recall Jesus' blessing of the poor.)

The argument that the problem is not with money as such but with persons' attitude toward it can find a measure of support in these texts; but money has a way of getting an unrelenting grip on people. Money is a form of power, and as Niebuhr said in another context, "there is no ethical force strong enough to place inner checks upon the use of power if its quantity is inordinate."[32] It is hard to defend *whatever* attitude lies behind the fact that so many of us cling to large sums in the face of the deadly poverty of so many others today.[33] Pious and passionate defenses of "property rights," as if such rights were God's first law and as if they properly permit doing whatever we wish with what we own, take really astonishing precedence in many popular discussions over larger concerns of justice, stewardship, and care for one another (and recall that in the Old Testament, land, in particular, was seen as belonging to God, not finally to any individual). Surely we need not shrink from the language of sin in these arenas, even if we can describe our graspingness sympathetically by talking about the emptiness we seek to fill or the anxiety we strive to alleviate or the responsibility for the unpredictable future we seek to take. The point is that beyond a certain minimum that provides for the actual essentials of life, money tends to stand in for God with respect to managing emptiness and anxiety. And thence, of course, it leads us to subordinate everything else to the means of keeping it: the needs of the neighbor, the health of the environment, the lives of two-thirds world peoples.[34] That

32. Reinhold Niebuhr, *Moral Man and Immoral Society* (New York: Scribners, 1960), p. 164.

33. That most of us who read and write books like this stand condemned in this department can be illustrated in that I am entering these words on a not-inexpensive computer.

34. It can blind us even to the desirability of changes that would not in the end cost anything (not to mention those things, like environmental degradation, that will in the

people count their "worth" in dollars rather than by moral criteria says just about all that can be said in this regard — apart from the possible reminder that these are, practically speaking, mutually exclusive alternatives. The generosity of the poor is legendary, as is the tightfistedness of the rich, and makes its own point about the insidious grip of money, as does the visceral reaction many of us have at the thought of a pay cut or other financial loss. Like sex, then, money is not itself sinful but is a prime occasion of sin.

Race and Sin

We have treated the problem of racial prejudice, and particularly the way it affects and has affected African Americans, at some length elsewhere.[35] However, after a century that has surrounded the Holocaust with the Armenian massacre (1915) and "ethnic cleansing" in central Africa and in the Balkans (1990s), and when separatist retribalization is advocated by some as the only way for particular groups to secure their personal and cultural dignity, it would seem that another unequivocal assertion that racial prejudice of whatever stripe and by whoever practices it, is sin, can hardly be superfluous. And the conflicts in Africa and in Europe remind us that fears and stereotypes associated with physical differences are not necessary for murderous intergroup hatreds and rivalries to develop, though an obvious way to identify those one disparages is no doubt convenient.

The problem is nonetheless amplified for African Americans insofar as dark skin color is interpreted, consciously or unconsciously, as a sort of "stain" of sin, and insofar as dark-skinned people are seen as predisposed to sin.[36] Unfortunately, symbolism of language identifying

---

end cost more than we can even imagine): consider the long-standing opposition of California agricultural interests to laws against the short-handled hoe, an instrument whose long-term use cripples farm workers but which was insisted upon because of its supposed economic advantages. When it was finally banned, it turned out that productivity increased rather than decreased (Robert A. Jones, "Short-Handle Hoe: A History of Agony for Dubious Advantages," *Los Angeles Times,* April 14, 1975, pt. II, p. 1+).

35. See *Who We Are,* pp. 100-130.

36. See James H. Evans, Jr., *We Have Been Believers* (Minneapolis: Fortress, 1992), pp. 107-116.

black
vs
white

"white" with cleanliness, purity, and good, and black with dirt, pollution, and evil, is deeply embedded and even found in Scripture itself:
"wash me, and I shall be whiter than snow" (Ps. 51:7; cf. Lam. 4:7; Is. 1:18;
though note well that in the Isaiah passage, the contrast is not with
black but with red). Furthermore, pervasive symbolism of darkness and
light merges with images of black and white, with darkness always as
the negative pole. Thus we find William Blake's lines,

> My mother bore me in the southern wild
> And I am black, but O! my soul is white;
> White as an angel is the English child,
> But I am black, as if bereaved of light.[37]

Note similarly the wrenching tombstone inscription:

> In memory of
> CAESAR
> Here lies the best of slaves
> Now turning into dust.
> Caesar the Ethiopian craves
> A place among the just.
> His faithful soul has fled
> To Realms of heavenly light
> And by the blood that Jesus shed
> Is changed from Black to White.[38]

Even where we find literature using white as a symbol of evil, as in the
woman with skin "white as leprosy" in the "Rime of the Ancient Mari-
ner," part of the power of the image is its dissonance. These embedded
associations are very hard to shake and reside too deep in the consciousness to be dislodged by assertions, however true, that "black is
beautiful." Precisely because of the deep ways that our language and
symbols shape our perceptions, and thence our behavior, Christians
would do well to seek and to substitute other symbols than white and
black for good and evil. We cannot defend on philosophical or aes-

---

37. Untermeyer, *Treasury of Great Poems,* p. 600.

38. Quoted in Joseph R. Washington, Jr., *Anti-Blackness in English Religion, 1500-1800*
(New York: Edwin Mellen, 1984), p. 352. The tombstone is dated 1780.

thetic or traditional grounds what clearly hurts our brothers and sisters and contributes to their oppression.

Racial prejudice refuses to recognize, or at least to honor, the divine image in another human being. It is true, of course, that we fail to honor the divine image in others in a seemingly endless variety of ways, as when we discount the poor or any other group as a group, or treat anyone unjustly; but the peculiar evil of racial prejudice as such is that it responds to nothing over which its victims have the slightest control or which could be changed by any conceivable circumstances.[39] Further, apart from outbreaks of violent conflict, it is a peculiarly insidious sin: ethnic minorities despair most especially at the failure of the *well-intentioned* among the dominant group to admit or even recognize their own destructive attitudes and behaviors. This failure stems at least in part from a refusal simply to listen receptively to what people say: a significant characteristic of sin as self-centeredness is that it is hard to grant the seriousness, or even the reality, of that which is not happening to *us*.[40] And another characteristic is that while we sense immediately the unfairness of anything that *dis*advantages us, we are often not even aware of what unfairly *advantages* us — a manifestation of pride if there ever was one.[41]

As a negative spin-off, precisely because fears of losing something —

39. A black friend of mine recently recounted the story of his son, who has a white girlfriend. The young man remarked to his sweetheart that she had not yet introduced him to her family, and then added the reminder that his being black was non-negotiable.

40. Christian theologians and ethicists do not have a history of distinguishing themselves in this regard. In the middle of the last century, Reinhold Niebuhr, under the guise of his "Christian realism," had a good deal to say about the "cultural backwardness" of black people that justified much sympathy with white prejudices; Paul Ramsey used such ideas as the desirability of maintaining "natural communities" and the need for respect for law and order to warn against the use of sit-ins and economic boycotts; James M. Gustafson and Rachel Henderlite cautioned against trying to go beyond the "possible" in making changes (without quite seeming to perceive that what we really do not *want* to achieve will not be likely to appear "possible"). Once such deep resistance gets linked theologically to, say, the idea of the worthiness of (other people's!) suffering, one can remain impervious to the need for radical change (for the major part of this summary, see Herbert O. Edwards, "Racism and Christian Ethics in America," *Katallagete* [Winter 1971]: 14-24).

41. We are convinced that this factor figures strongly in the affirmative action debates, whatever the merits or faults of particular programs of affirmative action. Obviously, no precise calculus is possible, but no one wants to be on the short end of the stick.

like a position of power and special privilege, or economic advantage, or a head start in obtaining something in short supply (e.g., desirable jobs, marriage partners) — run so deep, everything that looks like it might be an actual difference between certain groups of people becomes a weapon in someone's arsenal. The problem is not just the influence of differing histories and environments, which seems in any case hopelessly to confound efforts to discern differences (as is also true with respect to differences between men and women). It is at least as much the unfortunate fact that were we to discover that a particular group does have strengths and weaknesses somewhat different from our own, we would be prone to define as "really important" what we do well and to devalue the gifts of others, using the data as one more tool of prejudice (not a new problem: see Rom. 12:3-8; 1 Cor. 12:12-26 — we have not been notably successful in "outdo[ing] one another in showing honor," Rom. 12:10; but surely not a problem to be solved by the tactics of some ethnocentrists who see the accuracy of particular assertions as entirely secondary in importance to their psychological effect). The less willing we are to cherish the gifts of each, the more the logic of separatism becomes cogent.[42] Thus sin turns the good gifts of the Creator into means of furthering mutual suspicion and resentment.[43]

---

42. Separatism has the strength of creating a powerful sense of belonging, even if to a smaller group than one might wish. Daniel Day Williams speaks of racism in the context of the passionate will to belong transformed into the will to preserve our way against all others, and of the way this need for belonging can be perverted into absolute hatred of anyone or anything that threatens our security (*The Spirit and the Forms of Love* [New York: Harper & Row, 1968], p. 148).

43. Toward the end of the twentieth and beginning of the twenty-first century, an additional occasion for racial prejudice has been provided by the large number of immigrants in many of our large cities. Since "we" have been here for a long time, no number of reminders sufficiently impresses on us northern European types that we came as immigrants, too — like the Israelites whom the Lord kept reminding that they had once been strangers in the land of Egypt. An influx of people naturally presents challenges, but the racist nature of some concerns is suggested by the refusal of many even to believe the data that suggest that our new neighbors contribute more in taxes than they consume in social services. But even if they did not, Scripture has a good deal to say about how we are to relate to the stranger in our midst, including having only one law for all, and including making active provision by, for instance, leaving gleanings (the point is obviously not that some people deserve only leftovers, but that one must find ways to cover the basic needs of all). For treatment of the stranger, see, among many other texts, Exod. 12:49; 22:21; Lev. 19:34; Num. 35:15; Deut. 10:19; 14:29; 24:19-22; Jer. 7:6; Ezek. 47:23; Zech. 7:10; Matt. 25:31-46.

Gender and Sin[44]

Gender, like race, provides occasion for sin not only in that differences between men and women provoke the fear and anxiety that seem to come with almost all differences, but also because the more powerful group (generally men, in this case) characteristically devalue gifts and functions that are not their own. The history of misogyny makes for unedifying reading.[45] Unsurprisingly, this dismal habit of mind has been turned back on men by some women, who would make "patriarchy" the clue to almost everything that is wrong with the world. It is true, of course, that whoever is in power has more scope for giving expression both to weaknesses and to strengths than do those who are not in power.[46] Thus, certain public institutions and practices may be argued to show the stamp of "male" vices and virtues. By contrast, however much some women might castigate men and wish to control them, they would have difficulty in imposing, say, foot-binding on them, or in executing them as warlocks.

But *are there* specifically male and female sins or tendencies to sin? Some have probed women's actual functioning (particularly in white middle-class society) to conclude that their temptations and sins are indeed unlike men's. Others have sought to ground putatively diverse styles of sin in men and women in the judgment of God following the Fall (Gen. 3:16): since the judgment pronounced bore differently on men and women, it is reasonable to conclude that differing circumstances would generate different temptations.[47] Either way, in a broad

44. See also above, pp. 57-58.

45. For brief treatment see *Who We Are*, pp. 173-76.

46. Note well that this is not to say that those in power are intrinsically more sinful or virtuous, but only that their sins and virtues have an arena for becoming visible and, often, affecting more people.

47. For particularly helpful exploration of this idea, see Mary Stewart Van Leeuwen, *Gender & Grace* (Downers Grove, IL: InterVarsity Press, 1990), pp. 44-48 and passim. She further argues that we should seek to overcome sinful behavioral tendencies resultant from the Fall, and that the constant shifting and reinvention of gender roles may be not a signal of narrowly defined capacities on the part of either men or women, but rather a way of symbolizing the truth that men and women need each other (pp. 69-71). (Some writers with a different viewpoint would, of course, see God's judgment in Gen. 3:16 as something to which women should simply submit and which it is sinful to try to overcome. Others would see the whole longer passage as etiological — a mythical explana-

sense surely the verdict has some truth: varying social and physical environments obviously do provide varying opportunities, both good and bad. Insofar, for instance, as women fail to shoulder the dignity and responsibility befitting those made in the divine image, they sin as surely as do those who mistake responsibility for domination. *Sin* is pervasive and is an equal-opportunity employer, but the shape it takes *(sins)* varies greatly; and it would be a foolish pedagogy that refused to care about particulars, or failed to acknowledge that certain particulars affect whole groups and not just individuals.

However, when we do attend to individuals, this whole approach of seeking out gender-related failings confronts the well-established difficulty of concluding much that is definitive about differences between men and women: "everybody knows" that they are different, but beyond a few established findings (like the *generally* greater verbal proficiency of girls and the *generally* higher activity level of boys), just how is puzzlingly hard to specify. Certain allegedly intrinsic differences between men and women may not hold up very well apart from the strictures and demands of certain disparate environments (like habitual orientation toward "public" versus "private" spheres, to use one common distinction). For instance, a recent survey suggested that female clergy (women who have "public" roles, though in a field in which "servanthood" is theoretically lauded for men as well as for women) apparently do not in fact wonderfully exemplify the ideals of cooperation and mutuality feminists laud as particular gifts of women, but manifest considerable competitiveness.[48]

In any case, precisely because sin by definition has to do with a bro-

---

tion of why things took the shape that the human author of Genesis sees that they in fact have: why snakes crawl on their bellies, why people wear clothes, why there are weeds, why males and females relate as they do. We take the first of these viewpoints as compounding the original problem and the second as denying its moral and religious depth.)

48. "When It Comes to Competition, Women Clergy Are No Angels," *Los Angeles Times*, Jan. 25, 1997. One also recalls George MacDonald's story, "The Wise Woman, or The Lost Princess: A Double Story," in which both the wealthy princess and the humble shepherd girl show themselves prone to rage and conceit: both think they are "somebody." Though this story was written by a man over a century ago, we would be surprised if women as well as men of today could see nothing of themselves in his tale (in *Gifts of the Child Christ*, 2 vols., ed. Glenn Edward Sadler [Grand Rapids: Eerdmans, 1973], 1:199-279).

ken relationship to God, it is not enough — however useful — to look only at social patterns impinging on one's behavior. Swinging from paying no attention whatever to possible gender influences on behavior, to relying too exclusively on them, may allow one to fail to attend to the sins she actually commits, either because her nemesis is stereotypically that of the other gender, or because she absolves herself of responsibility for sins presumably "wired in" by her gender identity on the grounds that she cannot help them. Or, deeply engrained habits of perception may lead both men and women to fail to identify certain sinful attitudes and behaviors as sin at all (as when we act out of unconscious stereotypes), or wrongly to call sinful something that is simply not culturally valued (as when we demean giving attention to faithful homemaking).[49]

We cannot, then, affirm statements like, "women's sin, so far from being the sin of pride, lies in leaving the sin of pride to men,"[50] even though the specific context of this remark has to do with a quite reasonable concern for women gaining a sense of self and taking proper responsibility. The trouble is that in theological context, "pride" has to do with a sense of self that asserts itself over against God and hence can never be a virtue. Women's problems cannot be solved by trading sins; and surely a right apprehension of Christ centers the unfocused life as well as challenges the prideful one. (Furthermore, the woman whose pride manifests itself in, say, self-serving manipulativeness is still guilty of pride, even if she is in a disadvantaged position and sees no other means of asserting herself.) We do not see it as merely fortuitous, and certainly not as indifferent, that many feminist discussions of "sin" have moved away from anything that traditionally merits that name and in the direction of emphasis on our fragility and finitude; away from awareness of the need for redemption coming from outside our-

49. Ted Peters makes the striking observation that early feminist identification of "triviality" as a peculiarly female temptation may actually manifest a buying into the dominant (male) view of what is important rather than a biblical view of what is sinful: "What an idealist characterizes as trivia may actually be the very act of love that makes human life possible" (*Sin: Radical Evil in Soul and Society* [Grand Rapids: Eerdmans, 1994], p. 111). Even in making important and fresh observations, that is, we do not manage wholly to surmount our own culture and its values.

50. Judith Plaskow, *Sex, Sin and Grace* (Washington, D.C.: University Press of America, 1980), p. 92.

selves, to holding ourselves mutually accountable; away, in fact, from relationship to God or attention to Scripture at all, while emphasizing human relationships. For example, Christine Smith characterizes Rita Nakashima Brock's position as involving "a much more self-accepting and potentially empowering definition [of sin]" than one which aligns sin "with blame, punishment, and guilt"; and she quotes her as saying, "sin is a sign of our brokenheartedness, of how damaged we are, not of how evil, willfully disobedient, and culpable we are. Sin is not something to be punished, but something to be healed."[51] One can hardly avoid the conclusion that either these authors wish to define what is traditionally meant by sin out of existence, or else they are confusing sin and certain of its effects. Either way, insofar as they also banish God, they banish not only the fear of punishment but also the hope of redemption. (Some feminists quite explicitly banish anything resembling "God" as traditionally understood, considering this "God" as a prime source of the problems they address. Frequently such women turn to various forms of paganism or goddess-worship as more congenial to their concerns and experience. While we are very far from their position, we do think it important to acknowledge how much of its source is to be found in a sinful sexism.)

51. Christine Smith, "Sin and Evil in Feminist Thought," *Theology Today* 50:2 (July 1993): 21.

8

Original Sin

In analyzing the nature of sin, we spoke of sin both as act and as condition. It is obviously the latter — sin as condition — with which we have to do when dealing with original sin. (It is true that the term "original sin" has sometimes been used to refer to the first act of disobedience on the part of Adam and Eve; but ordinarily, in our day, it refers to the fundamental bent of character in each of us, from which our particular individual sins of commission and omission come.)[1] It is that condition of our hearts, that evil treasure within us, out of which come lying, murder, adultery, and so on, as Jesus said (Matt. 12:35; 15:19). And it is a condition so universal and so evident that Reinhold Niebuhr often called original sin the one doctrine of the church that could be empirically verified.

The Greek fathers of the church regarded original sin as a kind of quasi-metaphysical deterioration of our humanity. Human beings were originally created out of nothing by God; and they are passing back into nothing, deteriorating, decaying spiritually, as a result of sin. They need to have the seed of immortality restored by the sacraments of the church. In the Roman Catholic church, original sin has been seen more as a domination of the higher self by the lower self, due to the loss of original righteousness and the consequent ascendancy of concupiscence.[2] Protestants, by contrast, have avoided thinking of original sin

---

1. That these two meanings of the term are related, we will see below, when we consider solidarity in sin.

2. See above, pp. 59-60.

in metaphysical or ontological categories, such that sin would become a defect in our humanity.[3] They have rather seen it as a corruption of our humanity at the level of the moral and the personal (a view also taken by many modern Roman Catholics). Our humanity is not *essentially* changed (using the term in its traditional Aristotelian sense): we continue to be human; the divine image remains. Rather, its properties, "higher" as well as "lower," are perverted.

Original Sin as Radical Depravity

Especially in Reformed circles, original sin has been understood in terms of radical or total depravity. When Reformed theologians say that we are born sinners, they do not mean, again, that we have lost part of our humanity or that it has deteriorated in an ontological sense; but rather that we are estranged from God in all our faculties and powers, indisposed to do that which is right in God's sight, and deeply inclined to do that which is wrong. "Radical" or "total" depravity should not, however, be taken to mean that we are as depraved as we could be, that we could not possibly be more wicked than we are.

Many have mocked the doctrine on the supposition that it does have this plainly insupportable sense; and it must be admitted that there are certain passages in Calvin that bear this interpretation: for example, chapter 3 of book 2 is entitled, "Only Damnable Things Come Forth from Man's Corrupt Nature," and contains the assertion, "the soul . . . is not only burdened with vices, but is utterly devoid of all good" (*Institutes* 2.3.2). Other passages, however, suggest an extensive rather than intensive definition of radical depravity in human life as we actually experience it; most particularly, Calvin notes as a gift of the restraining grace of God the fact that people are *not* as wicked as they could be (e.g., in the immediately following section, *Institutes* 2.3.3). Thus, his overall thrust would seem to be not to prove that we could do no worse than we do, but rather to ensure that God

---

3. With certain exceptions: e.g., Flacius, who, in the course of the Lutheran controversy with the synergists and the followers of Melanchthon, spoke of an essential corruption of our nature.

and not some virtue of our own is credited for whatever good is manifested.[4]

Were it the case that we could be no more wicked than we are, we
would be incapable even of recognizing or desiring, however imper-
fectly, the good, or of labeling sin as sin. In Pascal's memorable words,
"wretched as we are, and more so than if there were no greatness in
our condition, we have an idea of happiness, and cannot reach it. We
perceive an image of truth, and possess only a lie."[5] (Indeed, it has often been observed that the "good," comparatively speaking, are much
more acutely aware of the heinousness of their own sin than are the
comparatively evil: wickedness has a deadening quality. It has also
been discerned, though, that only the victims really know what sin is:
at least some measure of self-deception spares the perpetrator.) Nor
does belief in total depravity imply that we are ever in the position to
say with confidence that anyone while in this life is so confirmed in
sin as to be beyond the possibility of redemption; though it is proper
to give warning that, so to speak, hell can break through into this
world in the form of the "unforgivable sin."[6] Judgment that anyone
has committed this sin, however, belongs to God and not to the
church. In any case, it is not to this sin that the doctrine of total depravity refers. Rather, the doctrine means that depravity extends to
the whole of the person, sparing no human faculty or power. The intellect is darkened, the will is enslaved, the affections are corrupt. We
are no purer in our thinking than in our desiring; we may sin as
readily when we are happy as when we are angry, sad, or frustrated.[7]

---

4. The Lutheran Formula of Concord, while carefully avoiding speaking of original
sin as an *essential* corruption of human nature, also takes an extreme position: it "rejects
and condemns" the view that would hold "that man's nature and essence are not utterly
corrupt, but that there is something of good still remaining in man, even in spiritual
things, to wit, goodness, capacity, aptitude, ability, industry, or the powers by which in
spiritual things he has strength to undertake, effect, or co-effect somewhat of good"
(Formula of Concord, Art. I, neg. 6, in Philip Schaff, *The Creeds of Christendom*, 6th ed., 3
vols., rev. David S. Schaff [1931; Grand Rapids: Baker, 1983], 3:102).

5. Pascal, *Pensées*, #434.

6. See above, pp. 142-43.

7. Recall the behavior of fans at public concerts and sports events. For instance, after the Pirates' World Series victory in 1971, celebrators engaged in arson and theft, destroyed property, drank heavily, danced nude, and committed a dozen rapes (*Los Angeles
Times*, Oct. 18, 1971, pt. I, p. I).

And if the accent in the Reformed tradition has been on the will, the twisting and impotence of volition, this emphasis should not be taken to obscure the larger affirmation that implicates every aspect of us in alienation from God's purpose.

Regarding the corruption of the powers of thought, Charles Williams, for instance, spoke of "that lack of intellectual clarity produced by the Fall";[8] he clearly meant here something that is culpable, not a defect for which we are blameless); and Alexander Miller wrote, "the power of rationality which was for the wholesome mastery of the world to the glory of God, becomes an instrument for the subjugation of the world to the service of this man."[9] In a helpful chapter, Rollo May remarks on how we must *conceive* before we can *perceive:*[10] it follows that insofar as our conceptions are marked by sin, they cannot be simply corrected by supposedly neutral empirical observations. This problem relates not only to that of experimenter bias, but also to that of the functioning of paradigms in science, as elaborated by thinkers such as Michael Polanyi and Thomas Kuhn: paradigms define what counts as fact, what is worthy of investigation, and so on. It is thus a serious mistake to suppose that science offers a safe objectivity that is utterly lacking in, say, religious faith. We emphasize that corruption of thought is not a matter of falling prey to something like non sequiturs in logic: these are more a matter of finitude. Rather, to add unsubtle illustrations to the subtler problems besetting not just science but all thought, one thinks of smart criminals and of devoting intelligence to committing perfect crimes; of James's devilish in contrast to heavenly wisdom (James 3:13-18); of the twisted rationality that calls the wisdom of God foolishness and laughs at the gospel (1 Cor. 1:18-25; Acts 17:32); or of the perverse bent of mind that leads the thief, asked why he robs banks, to respond, "That's where the money is."

Emphasis on the scope of sinfulness is not inconsistent with our earlier discussion of degrees of sin precisely because we understand radical depravity in an extensive rather than in an intensive sense. The theologian who affirms the truth of radical depravity is not observing

---

8. In *Charles Williams: Essential Writings in Spirituality and Theology*, ed. Charles Hefling (Cambridge and Boston, Mass.: Cowley, 1993), p. 36.

9. Alexander Miller, *Faith and Learning* (New York: Association Press, 1960), p. 64.

10. Rollo May, *Love and Will* (New York: W. W. Norton, 1969), chap. 9, esp. pp. 236-37.

a world different from that of the commonsense person who sees it as a fact too obvious for comment that some people are more wicked than others. Nor does she wish to foster a kind of "miserable sinner Christianity" that focuses more attention on the magnitude of human failings than on the love and grace of the Christ who redeems us. (Actually, minimizing the depth of sin minimizes the work of Christ in redemption.) The theologian, however, might be less likely than others to be surprised by the failings of the "good," and also less surprised at the failure of the dream of "progress," especially in the moral realm. She most certainly does intend to object to those who would make a kind of bagatelle of the problem of sin — from those who rejected with deep offense Kant's discussion of radical evil (a remarkable philosophical analysis which attributed universal radical evil — corrupting the ground of our actions, based on the ascendancy of self-love, and inextirpable by human powers — to humankind[11]), to those who think the sin problem can yet be solved by technology or environmental engineering. Furthermore, that whole faculties are corrupted, and not just encroached upon, by sin may be seen in the great sins committed by the great: note, for instance, what happens when a Martin Luther turns anti-Semitic; or consider the vicious brilliance of Cesare Borgia, a sort of epitome of the Renaissance prince.

The theologian might also ponder that it is not easy but hard to become a *complete* sinner: Herod was fool enough to swear an oath to a dancing girl and evil enough to kill John the Baptist, but still he did the latter for his oath's sake (Matt. 14:5-10, Mark 6:22-28); the chief priests paid Judas for betraying Jesus but had scruples against putting blood money in the treasury (Matt. 27:3-6). Terrorists must have an astonishing amount of single-minded persistence, skill, and daring, as well as suicidal selflessness; it is surely both inaccurate and unjust to call them "cowards." (The disinclination to attribute any virtue to such people is understandable but ignores exactly the point we are making: a person of no actual strengths cannot be an effective terrorist. We do well not to corrupt our own language and powers of perception as we view such people.) Selfish and wicked people may continue to be drawn to a Mother Teresa or a St. Francis: even they retain a capacity to recognize and often to long after the good. Even Nazism's gas chambers were a

---

11. Kant, *Religion Within the Limits of Reason Alone*, pp. 15-39.

sort of testimony to the fact that people trained to merciless cruelty could not reliably bear actually to see what they were doing — but found a way to do it anyway.[12]

Nonetheless, although we affirm that we are seldom as evil as we could be, there have been sobering reminders in the just-past century of how quickly the "ordinary" person can descend to depths of evil — reminders that should chasten us in our consideration of this whole question. It is still perhaps barely possible to hope, for instance, that Nazism, in all its scope and horror, was some kind of moral aberration; yet it may rather be the case that it demonstrates how easily, under certain circumstances, the moral values of ordinary people can be co-opted for evil.[13] (The famous Milgram experiments, designed after the Second World War to test the hypothesis that ordinary people will in fact "obey orders" to do what they believe to be life-threatening harm to an innocent and protesting victim, demonstrated that about two-thirds of almost all groups of people will indeed be compliant under a dismaying array of circumstances (a few Christian Reformed folk resisted better than most). Similarly, Philip Zimbardo's 1971 "prison experiment" at Stanford University transformed randomly assigned volunteer college student "guards" and "prisoners" into abusive sadists and sniffling neurotics, respectively, in a mere six days (the two-week experiment was halted early because the effects were so devastating). Zimbardo's research leads him to believe that "most people can be made to do almost anything if you put them in psychologically compelling situations, regardless of their morals, ethics, values, attitudes, beliefs, or personal convictions."[14] At the very least, such studies should warn us that the reservoir of evil in all of us is deeper than we know, and that barriers against its eruption are shockingly fragile. Optimism about human tendencies does not hold up well under examination. (François Mauriac wrote in his Foreword to Elie Wiesel's *Night*, speaking of trainloads of Jewish children standing at Austerlitz station: "this dream [of progress] . . . vanished finally for me before those

---

12. Michael Polanyi, *Personal Knowledge* (New York: Harper & Row, 1962), pp. 205-6; see the whole chapter "Conviviality" for the persistence of good and its relentless vitiation by evil in the human enterprise.

13. See Victoria J. Barnett, "Germans and the Past: Stories, Secrets, Silences," *Christian Century* 111:23 (Aug. 10-17, 1994): 755-57.

14. Quoted in Joan O'C. Hamilton, "Zimbardo," *Stanford* (Sept. 1990): 30.

trainloads of little children" — before he even knew that or how they were to be exterminated.)[15]

Not only are all of our faculties corrupted, so that there is no "Archimedean point" of moral integrity on which we can stand to deliver ourselves, but also all of our individual actions — our best ones as well as our worst ones — are marked by sin (including our theological reflections on the topic!). Brunner saw a kind of illustration of this point in the fact that all of our achievements — as may be seen especially readily in discoveries in science and technology — turn out to be sources of death as well as of life to us.[16] Religion itself becomes the occasion for heinous crimes: it has been said that we never do evil so completely and cheerfully as when we do it from religious conviction[17] — a truth illustrated in crusades and jihads, inquisitions and witch trials. Moved by pride and self-centeredness, we assert ourselves over against the authority of God our Maker, and over against the rights and claims of our neighbor. In what we do, we do not incline to love God supremely; and we love ourselves in our neighbor rather than loving our neighbor as ourselves. Paul, for instance, counted the whole of his former, scrupulously religious, life as dross (Phil. 3:4-7). The insufferability of the "righteous" is a commonplace of literature, including the depiction of the scribes and Pharisees in the Gospels: the point here is not to doubt anyone's sincerity but simply to observe that it misfires insofar as love for the good transmogrifies into the longing to see oneself as good. C. S. Lewis commented on a woman who "lives for others" and concluded, "You can always tell the others by their hunted expression."[18]

---

15. François Mauriac, "Foreword," in Elie Wiesel, *Night*, trans. Stella Rodway (New York: Avon, 1960), p. 7.

16. Brunner, *Christian Doctrine of the Church, Faith, and the Consummation* (Philadelphia: Westminster, 1962), p. 272.

17. Pascal, *Pensées*, #894. For a particularly violent example, one may take the St. Bartholomew's Day massacre of the French Huguenots — a massacre carried out by Christian fanatics and involving all strata of the society. Medals were struck in Paris and in Rome in celebration of the massacre (see *History of Christianity*, ed. Clyde Manschreck [Englewood Cliffs, NJ, 1964], pp. 141-45). Shakespeare, too, wrote of the corrupted good that is worse than the simply bad: "sweetest things turn sourest by their deeds;/Lilies that fester smell far worse than weeds" (Sonnet #94, in *A Treasury of Great Poems*, ed. Louis Untermeyer [New York: Simon & Schuster, 1955], p. 278).

18. C. S. Lewis, *The Screwtape Letters* (New York: Macmillan, 1961), p. 123.

Rollo May remarked that the person who tries to be good all the time will turn not into an ethical giant but into a prig[19] — an example of the "paradox of moralism" that parallels the paradox of hedonism. Each of these paradoxes seems to relate profoundly to what we might call the moral quality of the universe. If happiness could be obtained by seeking it out directly, the merely reasonable person would devote herself to doing so, letting the world go hang in the meantime. If real goodness could be attained by concentrating upon becoming good, the saint would be one who implicitly made God and others means to the end of the cultivation of her own character instead of seeking them as those to be loved for themselves: her attention would, that is, be exactly wrongly focused. Or, looked at from a different angle, these paradoxes reveal something corrupt at the root of our acts and impulses: our "natural" desires for pleasure and for a goodness of our own are deeply self-centered and so twisted that they cannot reach their own proper ends but tend instead to destroy self and others. Even the effort to rid oneself of excessive self-concern may intensify it. Thus, at the superficial level, the paradox is simply the observation that we cannot reach certain goals by aiming at them; at a deeper level, the paradox points to our profound moral inability to do that which we ought to do, to love what we ought to love, or to will as we ought to will (which we shall take up further below). The same truth is symbolized by the village of Morality in *Pilgrim's Progress* and, in a different way, by the character Ignorance, who insisted that his heart was a good one, and that he never would believe that it was bad; but who at last discovered "that there was a way to Hell, even from the Gates of Heaven, as well as from the City of Destruction."[20] Ignorance of the depth of one's sin must be seen as sinfully motivated by the desire to think well of oneself, and hence it is culpable.

Nor can we simply "be ourselves" unself-consciously, as if the desires of our hearts, except insofar as they have somehow been inhibited by society, were pure and were the route to both virtue and self-realization (as Romanticism, with its belief in basic human goodness, suggested). Attempts to rear children without curbing their "natural"

---

19. Rollo May, *Power and Innocence* (New York: Delta, 1972), p. 238.

20. John Bunyan, *Pilgrim's Progress*, ed. Roger Sharrock (Baltimore: Penguin, 1965), pp. 50-51, 185, 186, 205.

self-expression have been disastrous illustrations of the epigram that a wicked person is but a child grown strong. The problem cannot plausibly be construed merely in terms of the power of example to influence choices: were that the case, whence the preponderance of bad examples and the weakness of good ones? What comes out when we cast inhibitions aside unmistakably shows the marks of sin even in the choice of examples to heed; and sin thus indulged, far from being a means of self-realization, profoundly disfigures us. Like all sin, it traps rather than liberates us, as Jesus' and Paul's language of slavery to sin makes clear. (However, just because there is no such thing as a pure act or pure motive because there is no pure person to engender such an act or motive, we are in the position of having to "sin boldly" [Luther] if we are to do anything at all. The point here is to avoid the scrupulosity that leads to paralysis: relying upon grace, in the knowledge that all we do, or refuse to do, will manifest our character as sinners, is a very different matter from denying the fact or importance of sin — but further exploration of this question belongs to the discussion of sanctification.)

Original Sin as Universal

Everything we have said may rightly be taken to imply that sin reaches not only to every aspect of certain individuals, but to every aspect of all individuals. Not only pagans but also Christians, not only adults but also children, not only criminals but also saints, are sinners.

This idea is not much to our taste. A letter from the Duchess of Buckingham to Lady Huntingdon, patron of the Calvinistic wing of the Evangelical Revival, expresses profound disgust at the very idea that sin in all its depth should be universal: "It is monstrous to be told that you have a heart as sinful as the common wretches that crawl on the earth. This is highly offensive and insulting, and I cannot but wonder that your ladyship should relish any sentiment so much at variance with high rank and good breeding."[21] Charles Spurgeon, in contrast, re-

21. Quoted in Albert Edward Bailey, *The Gospel in Hymns* (New York: Charles Scribner's Sons, 1950), p. 115. For an example in literature, consider Swift's king of Brobdingnag, who was astonished at Gulliver's historical account, "protesting it was

flected with great sadness and seriousness on Moses' life and his being
forbidden to enter the promised land because he had once spoken unad-
visedly, concluding, "Who can be faultless when even Moses erred?"[22]

The affirmation that all are sinners, applied to little children, especially offends: we often speak sentimentally of the innocence of children. And it is true, of course, that we do not hold children fully accountable for their actions until they are old enough to understand
what they are doing and why it is wrong (just as we do not hold people
with limited intellectual capacity fully accountable for their actions).
However, the utter self-centeredness of small children that can in one
sense be attributed to "nature" is in another sense almost a parable of
sin and will shortly, as we said above, show itself as the full-blown article if not appropriately disciplined.[23] For instance, as Piaget observed,

---

only a heap of conspiracies, rebellions, murders, massacres, revolutions, banishments;
the very worst effects that avarice, faction, hypocrisy, perfidiousness, cruelty, rage, madness, hatred, envy, lust, malice, and ambition could produce" (*Gulliver's Travels*, p. 76),
implying that things might be quite different in other parts. Yet even Swift's more ideal
society, that of the Houyhnhnms — ruled by reason — is flawed by Christian standards,
for the Houyhnhnms show no natural affection (they are not, note, ruled by *love*) and
force Gulliver from their island.

22. Spurgeon, *Lectures to My Students* (New York: American Tract Society, n.d.), p. 45.
A practical consequence of recognition that all are sinners is knowledge that in matters
of law and ethics, it is invariably sinners who will sit in judgment on other sinners.
Thus, we seek a balance of power among branches of the government, give police power
to enforce justice in the civilian realm but have a civilian police commission to hold the
police accountable, and know that ethics committees can themselves become corrupt. A
twist on the whole matter — but one that also shows our sinfulness, taking shape this
time not in corruption so much as in self-righteousness and self-interest — is that sometimes we will entertain the possibility that others may be falsely accused only if we are
wrongly fingered ourselves. We are much readier to assume our own innocence than
that of others. Thus, for instance, former California State Senate President James R.
Mills favored continuing the state senate's Un-American Activities Committee until he
found out that their file included his name. Then he announced he would move post
haste to abolish it (*Los Angeles Times*, Mar. 12, 1971, pt. 1, p. 1).

23. See Augustine, *Confessions* 1.6.8; 1.7. He suggested that the infant's lack of physical
strength, not its will, constitutes its innocence, as he observed the extreme willfulness
and enviousness of small children. And reflecting on his own boyhood pride, thefts, and
quarrelsomeness, he concluded, "as riper years succeed, these very sins are transferred
from tutors and masters, from nuts and balls and sparrows, to magistrates and kings, to
gold and manors and slaves" (1.18.30). There is a parallel here with the divine image: we
hold it to be present in infants but more fully manifested as they mature.

children fail to understand each other because they think they do understand, and they also speak simply from their own point of view
without processing the other person's — a state of affairs not unknown
in conversations between adults.[24]

By the time people reach the age of accountability, they seem universally to manifest what we might call an uneasy sense of self — an
awareness that they do not themselves measure up to what they expect
of others, to what they ought to be, to what they affirm to be right and
good. It will not do to be satisfied with tracing this discomfort back to
the strictures under which one was reared: those strictures (however
faultily they may have been conceived or applied) themselves came out
of a sense of oughtness, of what should and should not be done. Nor
will it do to dismiss this phenomenon by observing that its actual content may differ significantly from culture to culture. We do not deny
that culture leads to at least some variation in what might be called the
material definition of sin: the knowledge of God that we have through
creation (Rom. 1) is subject to all the imperfect apprehension and dis-
tortions to which any human knowledge is prone. But whatever the
specific standards may be, and whether those standards might from a
given perspective appear lax or rigid, people go against the good that
they know. That the issue is the human heart and not the unreason-
ableness of particular standards is neatly demonstrated both by cultural variations and by the fact that making the "rules" more permissive does not solve the problem. The malaise is not banished, for
instance, by reconceiving most of the "seven deadly sins" as virtues,
though in our day this malaise may no longer be labeled a "sense of
sin" but rather be renamed a "guilt complex" or an "inferiority complex" or "poor self-esteem." But even when we discard the traditional
label and have been well taught not to accuse ourselves, we know that
something is wrong — something that the rationalization that of
course no one is perfect will not quite fix.[25]

Furthermore, while the universality of sin as traditionally understood may be denied, no one can evade death; and death, Paul said,

24. See Polanyi, *Personal Knowledge*, pp. 206-7.

25. See D. M. Baillie, *God Was in Christ* (New York: Charles Scribner's Sons, 1948), pp.
162-63; also C. S. Lewis, *Mere Christianity* (London: Fontana Books, 1952), pp. 18-19;
Hendrikus Berkhof, *Christian Faith* (Grand Rapids: Eerdmans, 1979), p. 193.

came by way of sin (Rom. 5:12; 6:23; cf. Luke 13:1-4; James 1:15).[26] Pagans and Christians, adults and infants, criminals and saints, are subject to death — if not sooner, then later.[27] Death grants no one immunity or special status.

> By a late ritual in Austria the corpse of the emperor was ordered to be carried to the door of an abbey. The chamberlain who leads the cortège knocks at the door. A friar opens the window and asks: "Who knocks?" — "The Emperor." — "I know no man of that name." The chamberlain knocks again. "Who is there?" — "The Emperor Francis Joseph." — "We do not know him." Third knock, and the same question. After reflection, the chamberlain now answers: "Brother Francis." Then the door opens to receive a comrade in the army of death, on equal terms with all souls.[28]

This universal reign of death, especially in the suffering and terror it so often brings, can be seen as confirming that all are indeed sinners.[29]

26. See above, pp.72-79, on the consequences of the Fall; and below, Appendix I, Physical Death as Existential Reality.

27. "It is not so much that there are deaths as that death can be seen as an all-embracing structure. It can be seen as the manifestation of a power which negates every human possibility and renders life ultimately meaningless. And thus St. Paul can speak of the entire creation as subjected to futility and decay (Rom. 8:20-21)" (L. R. Bailey, *Biblical Perspectives on Death* [Philadelphia: Fortress, 1979], p. 104).

28. Eugen Rosenstock-Huessy, *The Driving Power of Western Civilization* (Boston: Beacon Press, 1950), pp. 55-56. The theme of death as universal and death as an equalizer is a common one in poetry; see, for instance, Thomas Nashe, "In a Time of Pestilence"; Francis Beaumont, "On the Tombs in Westminster Abbey"; Thomas Gray, "Elegy Written in a Country Churchyard" (all in Untermeyer, *Treasury of Great Poems*, pp. 331, 382, 555-59). (The translations of Elijah and Enoch [2 Kings 2:11; Gen. 5:24; Heb. 11:5] are curious exceptions that prove the rule. A rather impressive amount of silence has been bestowed on these cases with respect to the specific issue of the breaking of the association of sin and death — for surely these men were, like all humans, sinners. About all we can suggest is that as recipients of a special act of God, they exemplify the important truth that God's sovereignty is not limited by any "natural" constraint. The association of sin and death is indeed penal; death is not just an unfortunate biological reality.)

29. We have already granted that the person who is a convinced naturalist will, of course, see it as confirming no such thing, but only that the human animal, like all animals, is mortal. For an array of interesting biblical examples associating original sin and the universality of death, see Jonathan Edwards, *Original Sin*, ed. Clyde A. Holbrook, *The Works of Jonathan Edwards*, vol. 3 (New Haven: Yale University Press, 1970), pp. 206-19. He

The Biblical Basis of the Doctrine of Original Sin

Like the doctrine of the Fall with which it is closely associated, the doctrine of original sin has been scored as being longer on theological consequences than it is on direct biblical support. Where, some query, does it say that human motives and behaviors are inevitably corrupted at their spring, and identify that spring with Adam and Eve? And those who answer this question substantively tend to point not to the Hebrew Old Testament (which does not, in fact, refer to the Genesis account as the source of sin and evil in the world) but to the intertestamental literature, particularly 2 Esdras:[30]

> For the first Adam, burdened with an evil heart, transgressed and was overcome, as were also all who were descended from him. (2 Esd. 3:21)

Or again:

> It would have been better if the earth had not produced Adam, or else, when it had produced him, had restrained him from sinning. For what good is it to all that they live in sorrow now and expect punishment after death? O Adam, what have you done? For though it was you who sinned, the fall was not yours alone, but ours also who are your descendants. (2 Esd. 7:116-18)

The idea of original sin is, then, a "late" concept, interpreting the data

---

argues that the fact that death has historically fallen heavily on infants [and still does, in many parts of the world] — who cannot be supposed to be able to profit from the reality of death by, say, reflecting upon it as a means of curbing sin — makes implausible the arguments of those who say it is really given for the benefit of the individual who dies rather than coming as judgment.

30. See also 2 Esd. 4:30. 2 Bar. 23:4 and 48:42-43 might be noted, but with the caveat that this work is later than Paul. It does suggest, though, that the idea of tracing human sin back to Adam was "in the air" (see K. Congdon, "The Biblical Doctrine of Original Sin," *Irish Theological Quarterly* 34 [1967]: 20-36). Congdon further notes that these sources do not mention *inheritance* of sin, but make individuals responsible for their own transgressions (e.g., 2 Bar. 54:15, 19). Barr observes that Is. 43:27, "Your first ancestor sinned," refers not to Adam but to Jacob or other early Israelites ("The Authority of Scripture," in *Christian Authority: Essays in Honour of Henry Chadwick*, ed. G. R. Evans [Oxford: Clarendon Press, 1988], p. 67).

of the Old Testament and of human experience in what may be argued
to be only one of several possible ways.[31] And it is surely true that the
Old Testament provides a great deal of material ready to be interpreted.
In approaching this material, we frankly acknowledge that we do use
the concept of progressive revelation, which means that the way the
New Testament utilizes the data carries great weight for us.[32] Thus, we
consider Paul's particular appropriation of Genesis 3 in Romans 5:12 to
be highly significant — "sin came into the world through one man, and
death came through sin" — about as close as one could come to affirming original sin without actually using the term.

Paul's purpose of making a comparison of Adam and Christ leads
him to emphasize the account in Genesis 3. The rest of the Old Testament, however, does not lack support for the idea of original sin, in the
sense that it depicts all as sinful (hardly a likely outcome were there no
predisposition to sin). Ecclesiastes 7:20 says, "Surely there is no one on
the earth so righteous as to do good without ever sinning" (see also
1 Kings 8:46; 2 Chr. 6:36; Ps. 130:3; 143:2; Job 14:4; Prov. 20:9; and while
Job 15:14-16 and 25:4 are the deliverances of Job's friends, they may still
be taken as an expression of the common understanding of universal
human impurity). Isaiah 53:6 declares that all, like sheep, have gone
astray and turned to their own way. And Psalm 14 asserts that there is
no one who does good, but all alike are perverse. Genesis 6:5 affirms
the extent of sin in terms as strong as found anywhere in Scripture:
"The LORD saw that the wickedness of humankind was great in the
earth, and that every inclination of the thoughts of their hearts was
only evil continually." After the Flood, God promised never again to
curse the ground, not because humankind had now reformed, but
rather because "the inclination of the human heart is evil from youth"
(Gen. 8:21; see also Jer. 17:9, cf. Jer. 6:7). And beyond specific texts, the
pervasiveness and inescapability of sin underlie the whole system of
sacrifice and atonement that was key to the religious life of God's people under the Old Covenant.

In the Gospels, we find this same basic apprehension of sin implied.
The petition in the Lord's Prayer that our debts (Matt. 6:12) or our sins

---

31. See James Barr, *The Garden of Eden and the Hope of Immortality* (Minneapolis: Fortress, 1992), p. 18; also Paul Ricoeur, *Symbolism of Evil* (Boston: Beacon, 1967), p. 4.
32. See *God, Creation, and Revelation,* pp. 144-45.

(Luke 11:4) be forgiven presumes universal sinfulness, as does the role of Jesus as the one who will save the people from their sins (Matt. 1:21; also John 1:29). Jesus does not hesitate to address a group with the assumption that they are evil (Matt. 7:11; Luke 11:13; see also John 8:44). In the General Epistles, we find the unequivocal assertion of 1 John 1:8-10: "If we say that we have no sin, we deceive ourselves, and the truth is not in us. If we confess our sins, he who is faithful and just will forgive us our sins and cleanse us from all unrighteousness. If we say that we have not sinned, we make him a liar, and his word is not in us" (see also Heb. 2:17; James 5:16; 1 Pet. 2:24; Rev. 1:5). In short, one is hardly confined to the deliverances of Paul for attestation of the reign of sin.

When one does turn to Paul, though, one can find a particularly vehement and sustained indictment of the sinful predilections of humankind. After the lengthy detailing of vices and failings in Romans 1 and 2, Paul in Romans 3 quotes Psalm 14, as well as excerpts from other psalms and from Isaiah 59, in the strongest terms:

> "There is no one who is righteous, not even one; there is no one who has understanding, there is no one who seeks God. All have turned aside, together they have become worthless; there is no one who shows kindness, there is not even one." "Their throats are opened graves; they use their tongues to deceive." "The venom of vipers is under their lips." "Their mouths are full of cursing and bitterness." "Their feet are swift to shed blood; ruin and misery are in their paths, and the way of peace they have not known." (Rom. 3:10-17)

The climax comes with the final line: "'There is no fear of God before their eyes'" (Rom. 3:18). This is the heart of the matter — the lack of reverence, of awe, of an awareness on the part of the sinner of what a right relationship with God means. And all, Jew and Gentile alike, are under the power of sin: "all have sinned and fall short of the glory of God" (Rom. 3:23).[33] Galatians 3:22 speaks of all things being imprisoned un-

---

33. It has been argued that certain aspects of Paul's preceding argument, especially Rom. 2:13-14, but also what some judge to be the "overstatements" of chapters 1 and 2, mean that Paul's line of reasoning scarcely justifies his conclusion (see, for instance, Sanders, "Sin, Sinners," *Anchor Bible Dictionary*, 6:45). However, we have already said that a doctrine of radical depravity does not mean that no one ever heeds her conscience or

der the power of sin. In Ephesians 2:1-3 the figures — "dead through trespasses and sins"; "we were by nature children of wrath, like everyone else" — are different but are certainly just as devastating, making plain not that we have become passive (the rest of the passage allows no such thought), but rather that we are past the point of no return so far as our own strength is concerned. And we have already commented on the way Paul links the universality of death to the universality of sin (Rom. 5:12-14; 6:23; cf. 1 Cor. 15:56). It is difficult indeed, then, to avoid the conclusion that Scripture as a whole provides strong testimony to the depth and universality of sin, a depth and universality articulated by the doctrine of original sin.

---

does anything lawful; and if our own society provides any parallels, we doubt that Paul could be convicted of overstating the corruption of his.

Shadows

A Sermon Preached by Marguerite Shuster
at Fuller Theological Seminary Chapel
February 20, 2002

This is the message we have heard from him and proclaim to you, that
God is light and in him there is no darkness at all. If we say that we have
fellowship with him while we are walking in darkness, we lie and do not
do what is true; but if we walk in the light as he himself is in the light, we
have fellowship with one another, and the blood of Jesus his Son cleanses
us from all sin. If we say that we have no sin, we deceive ourselves, and
the truth is not in us. If we confess our sins, he who is faithful and just
will forgive us our sins and cleanse us from all unrighteousness. If we say
that we have not sinned, we make him a liar, and his word is not in us.
My little children, I am writing these things to you so that you may not
sin. But if anyone does sin, we have an advocate with the Father, Jesus
Christ the righteous; and he is the atoning sacrifice for our sins, and not
for ours only but also for the sins of the whole world.

I JOHN 1:5–2:2 (NRSV)

A cartoon depicts an old priest looking down in dismay at his congregation, packed into the last few rows of pews and leaving the entire front of the church empty. His obviously unnecessary announcement that there are plenty of seats down front has no impact whatever. So, next frame, he's out in front of the church, putting as an announcement on the sign board, "ALL SINNERS MUST SIT IN THE REAR." Final frame, he is peering down at the whole congregation gathered so close under the pulpit that they're practically climbing it; and he pleads futilely that there are plenty of seats in the rear.

Sin. It's not most people's favorite word. Many people would rather do just about anything (including something so radical as sitting in the front row in church) than frankly admit that they are sinners. Avoiding

the idea is easier than it used to be, these days. People may say they are
not too sure what counts as sin anymore: they tell themselves in all seriousness that so many things are gray and ambiguous. They're not at all
sure that thinking of oneself as a sinner is healthy; in fact, they've been
strongly instructed that it's not. Besides, there are plenty of other ways
of understanding what they and other people do, without dragging in
God and a bunch of medieval categories. And since most things, looked
at carefully and with compassion and with a sense of a person's history,
have a character that is anything but transparently clear, people don't
necessarily appreciate texts like this one, that has room for light and
darkness only — two categories, mutually exclusive, without even a recognition of the gray shadows in which most of our activity takes place.

Shadows, where shapes shift and outlines are blurred. Shadows,
where we neither see nor can be seen clearly. Shadows, where we don't
know for sure how to label what we can barely discern. Shadows, where
people do as they like, or at least do as they feel compelled to do, and
no one calls sin, sin.

An old *New Yorker* cartoon showed Adam and Eve being driven out
of the Garden of Eden by an angel with a flaming sword. Adam remarked, "My dear, we live in an age of transition."[1] Devastating exile for
disobedience to God becomes "an age of transition," a mere matter of
change, for which no one is personally responsible and about which one
needn't feel too bad. Redefinition is, in fact, a very handy tool for dealing with what used to be called sin. Take the Seven Deadlies — you
know, pride, envy, lust, sloth, gluttony, covetousness, and wrath — those
sins that in one way or another cover most of our serious failings. From
a slightly different perspective, they're no problem at all — in fact, just
the sort of thing a healthy, well-adjusted Christian should aspire to.
Pride? Call it excellent self-esteem, and you'll see that it's quite necessary
to functioning well, really a virtue. Envy? Nothing but a keen sense of
justice, that accurately perceives how unequally and unfairly things are
distributed. Lust? Surely everyone knows by now that those urges are
the perfectly normal result of biological drives that cause neurosis or
worse if suppressed. Just find expression for them in some meaningful
auxiliary relationship between consenting adults, and you will be spared

---

1. Quoted in Robert McAfee Brown, *Frontiers for the Church Today* (New York: Oxford
University Press, 1973), p. 65.

damaging frustrations. Sloth means that you take good care of yourself. Gluttony is a way of appreciating the finer things in life. Covetousness, called high aspirations, is the sort of thing that motivates you to do your best. And wrath, well, everyone knows what suppressed rage does to your health, so by all means let her rip. Actually, properly interpreted, the Seven Deadly Sins become practically a duty, surely nothing that could get in the way of one's relationship with God or neighbor.

And if the Seven Deadlies, in their new garb, can be celebrated, surely nothing of a lesser nature should be cause for guilt. George MacDonald once told the story of a little girl who was obsessed by guilt and feared that she had committed the unforgivable sin because, when she was getting dressed one day, she used a pin in a way she had been forbidden to use it.[2] Such a small thing, a thing of no consequence. Surely only a diseased fancy could turn a tiny, childish disobedience into an ultimate issue. Must there not be something terribly wrong with any religion that could, by any means, produce such fear in the mind of a child? Well then, change the name and do not call such a disobedience a sin. She, and we, still have fellowship with God, we say.

However, for those of us who aren't good at renaming and who have trouble persuading ourselves that what we are doing is really perfectly all right, or at least of no importance, there is another way of living in the shadows: we can simply deceive ourselves and convince ourselves that what we are doing is really quite different from those behaviors that we name quite accurately and rightly deplore in others. It's like the personnel manager of a large corporation who was continually plagued by employee problems. One night, while perusing the newspaper, he read an article about how stress and tension drive some people to drugs. "I can understand that," he said to his wife. "I'd probably be on drugs myself if I weren't taking tranquilizers."[3] Or how about military tribunals, free to try and execute people in the dark, in secret? Obviously reprehensible tools of oppressive regimes? Or merely a rational response to terrorism on our own soil? Surely *we* are nothing at all like *them*? (I am very glad if the secrecy provision, for instance, ends up being eliminated; but the point is that the large majority of the American public appear to have been ready to accept such tribunals in their worst form.)

2. C. S. Lewis, *George MacDonald: 365 Readings* (New York: Macmillan, 1947), #11.

3. Pastor's Professional Research Service, October-December 1989.

Sometimes, of course, the manifestations of self-deception about sin are quite a lot subtler, and more painful and touching. The case of Puritan preacher Cotton Mather particularly moves me. He was a man of astounding achievements, producing 388 separate volumes and an equally large collection of unpublished works in an age long before secretaries and duplicating machines, much less word processors, and this in the midst of a busy pastoral ministry with much community involvement. His home life was tragic: two wives and thirteen of his fifteen children died prematurely. Despite all this achievement and tragedy, he has been described as "the Puritan hypocrite historians loved to hate."[4] How so? Well, one historian says,

> Mather was constantly beset by the classic Puritan double-bind of doing the right works for the wrong reasons. Unlike his illustrious contemporary, Benjamin Franklin, who wore his ambition and pride on his sleeve, Mather tried to convince himself and others that all his good works proceeded from grateful thanksgiving, not prideful self-justification. This, of course, led to feelings of guilt in Mather and charges of hypocrisy from others, because the pride was impossible to erase. Still, Mather tried. And the harder he tried the guiltier he felt, creating a spiral of ambition, remorse, and renewed ambition that rose to ever greater heights.[5]

We try, try hard, to say and believe that we have not sinned. And as long as we stay in the shadows, hiding from ourselves at least as much as from anyone else, we at least half-way suppose that we can keep the illusion going, even if it isn't quite working. We will try, desperately hard, to keep it going and not to face any other possibility.

That's why, no doubt, Luther said that, "Only he can pray profoundly who has been shocked profoundly."[6] Only those who have been brought up short and shocked by themselves are really ready to be addressed by the gospel. It's like the event writer Tobias Wolff describes from his childhood, when he had been part of an inadequately staffed

4. Harry S. Stout, "What Made Cotton Run?" *The Reformed Journal* 35:8 (August 1985): 24.

5. Stout, "What Made Cotton Run?" p. 25.

6. Quoted by Karl Heim, *Jesus the World's Perfecter* (Philadelphia: Muhlenberg, 1961), p. 53.

after-school archery club. The boys soon gave up fixed targets for the big domestic cats used to having the run of the yard; and when the cats wisely decided to make themselves scarce, the boys started hunting each other. Wolff says,

> The game got interesting. All of us had close calls, close calls that were recounted until they became legend. The Time Donny Got Hit in the Wallet. The Time Patrick Had His Shoe Shot Off. A few of the boys came to their senses and dropped out but the rest of us carried on. We did so in a resolutely innocent way, never admitting to ourselves what the real object was: that is, to bring somebody down. Among the trees I achieved absolute vacancy of mind. I had no thought of being hurt or of hurting anyone else, not even as I notched my arrow and drew it back intent on some movement in the shadows ahead. I was doing just that one afternoon, drawing my bow, ready to fire as soon as my target showed himself again, when I heard a rustling behind me. I spun around.
>
> Sister James had been about to say something. Her mouth was open. She looked at the arrow I was aiming at her, then looked at me. In her presence my thoughtlessness forsook me. I knew exactly what I had been doing.[7]

Ah, yes. Those moments come when the light shines and we are shocked by knowing exactly what we are doing. "God is light and in him there is no darkness at all. If we say we have fellowship with him while we walk in darkness, we lie and do not do what is true. . . . If we say that we have no sin, we deceive ourselves, and the truth is not in us. . . . If we say we have not sinned, we make him a liar, and his word is not in us." Strong stuff. Sin and God are utterly incompatible. The light shines, and the shadows vanish, and the sinfulness of sin becomes undeniably clear.

And you know what? Much as we dread it, that is tremendously good news. It is good news because for sin, faced, repented of, and confessed, there is an answer. But for the vague sense of unease we have when we are telling ourselves that our behavior is really perfectly all right, or at least unavoidable, and that any foibles are hardly worth mentioning, there is no answer but the tactic of the positive thinker

7. Tobias Wolff, *This Boy's Life* (New York: Atlantic Monthly Press, 1989), pp. 8-9.

who resolutely intoned, flying in the face of all the evidence, "Every day, in every way, I'm getting better and better."[8] And for the person who, like Cotton Mather, needs desperately to see his behavior as something other than it really is, the spiral of self-deception drives him deeper and deeper into misery. By trying to define sin out of existence, we deprive ourselves of our only remedy.

The little girl who was disobedient in her use of a pin didn't need to be told that it didn't matter. She knew it did matter because she knew it was wrong to disobey. Cotton Mather didn't need to be reassured that he was not prideful because it wasn't true and there was no way to make such a reassurance stick. These approaches, intended to be kind, actually prefer darkness to light. What the little girl and the Puritan divine both needed was to be forgiven. They needed to get out of the shadows of self-justification, see their sin for what it was, and recognize that Jesus Christ died and rose again to cleanse them, once and for all and also day by day, from these very sins. In a deep sense, they needed not more tolerance for sin but less, along with a stronger reliance upon God's grace, sufficient for the sins of the whole world.

So William Cowper, the noted poet and hymn-writer, discovered during a time of despair prior to his conversion. He found himself unable to believe, unable to repent, unable to feel sorrow for his sin. Then a friend came to visit him and spoke to him about the depth of sin that affects every human being without exception. Instead of driving Cowper deeper into despair, as one might suppose, this message was to him a source of hope, putting him in the same position as everyone else. And when his friend proclaimed to him the all-atoning efficacy of the blood of Jesus Christ, he said, "I saw clearly that my case required such a remedy, and had not the least doubt within me but that this was the Gospel of salvation."[9] Later he wrote those famous words,

> There is a fountain fill'd with blood
> Drawn from Emmanuel's veins;
> And sinners, plung'd beneath that flood,
> Lose all their guilty stains.

---

8. Émile Coué.

9. Quoted in D. L. Jeffrey, *A Burning and a Shining Light* (Grand Rapids: Eerdmans, 1987), p. 461.

"If we walk in the light, as he himself is in the light, we have fellowship with one another, and the blood of Jesus his Son cleanses us from
all sin. . . . If we confess our sins, he who is faithful and just will forgive
us our sins and cleanse us from all unrighteousness. . . . I am writing
this to you so that you may not sin. But if anyone does sin, we have an
advocate with the Father, Jesus Christ the righteous; and he is the atoning sacrifice for our sins, and not for ours only but also for the sins of
the whole world."

Do not deceive yourself. Hope is to be found, not in the shadows,
but in the light. Do not be robbed of forgiveness by the rationalizations
and excuses that suggest that you need none. Rather, let your sin shock
you. Let it drive you to Christ. There you will find mercy, and cleansing,
and help, in him who died and rose again for our salvation.

9
========

Problems of Freedom

Moral Inability

The charge most frequently brought against the traditional doctrine of original sin is that it contains a fundamental antinomy: it implies that humankind is unable to keep the counsel of perfection, and hence it undercuts all moral responsibility. If sin is unavoidable and inevitable in all of our actions and in the use of all of our faculties, then how shall we be motivated even to aspire to do better than we do?[1] Liberal theology in particular has rejected this doctrine as a counsel of despair, offensive to a proper view of the nobility, worth, and dignity of those invested with the divine image and working against our duty to emulate the example of Jesus, who has shown us the full potential of our humanity. But if the history of the past century has taught us anything, surely it is that Liberalism has consistently underestimated the human potential for evil.

The Augustinian tradition, as we have said, has repudiated the thought that sin is a defect of nature, an ontological defect, by saying that Adam and Eve were created "able not to sin" *(posse non peccare)*. However, it has also insisted that we are indeed now dead in trespasses

---

1. Turning this argument more or less on its head, William Hordern argues that it is not surprising that sin should take advantage of the view that humankind cannot save themselves in order to justify itself: that is precisely the nature of sin (*The Case for a New Reformation Theology* [Philadelphia: Westminster, 1959], p. 141).

and sins and that there is no possible solution to the sin problem short of a supernatural experience of grace which may appropriately be described as a "new birth" or "new creation." Thus, it is true that the Augustinian tradition — and, we believe, the biblical witness — contains two affirmations that are hard to hold together using strict canons of human logic: we are now incapable of doing the good by our own power; and we are responsible for our sinful state.[2] For all its emphasis on sin as endemic and something from which we cannot possibly save ourselves, Scripture never implies that this condition somehow exonerates us. To the contrary, in Scripture this radical character of moral evil exacerbates our guilt before God. When the psalmist says, "Indeed, I was born guilty, a sinner when my mother conceived me" (Ps. 51:5), he is not excusing himself and pleading not to be blamed, but rather confessing how deep and fundamental his sin problem is. And so it is throughout the literature of Christian piety: those who confess their sins of the deepest dye do so not to defend themselves but to underscore their exceeding sinfulness. It is precisely because we know that our sinful acts stem from our sinful hearts that we recognize our sin as so desperate. Particular acts, however they might be evaluated, are indications of how truly sinful we are. Our hearts recognize this fact more truly than our heads can explain it.

One recalls the famous incident of the sixteen-year-old Augustine stealing pears, not because he was hungry but simply because stealing was wrong: "O God, behold my heart, which Thou hadst pity upon in the bottom of the bottomless pit. Now, behold, let my heart tell Thee what it sought there that I should be gratuitously evil, having no temptation to ill but the ill itself. It was foul, and I loved it; I loved to perish, I loved mine own fault, not that for which I was faulty, but my fault itself."[3] He goes on for several sections trying to sort out and understand his own behavior but he cannot, eventually quoting Ps. 19:12: "Who can understand his errors?" [the NRSV reads "detect" instead of "under-

2. These apparently dueling affirmations are not peculiar to the Christian tradition but appear to lie deep in the human psyche. Ricoeur remarks on the plea of a Babylonian suppliant, "Why should the suppliant beg to be *released* from what he has *committed* if he did not know obscurely, if he did not know without knowing, if he did not know enigmatically and symbolically, that he has put upon himself the bonds from which he begs to be released?" (*Symbolism of Evil* [Boston: Beacon Press, 1967], p. 153, emphasis his).

3. Augustine, *Confessions* 2.4.

stand": obviously the latter reading is essential to Augustine's meaning]. This analysis (not to mention Rom. 7:13-25), not so incidentally, confutes the old Scholastic argument that we do not really choose evil *as evil*, but only insofar as we regard what is actually bad as good or pursue some intended good in that which is objectively evil.[4] It may be that much or even most of our sinning is of this latter type; but sin at its heart is quite capable of saying, "Evil, be thou my good"[5]: that is the mystery of iniquity.

In short, the example of Scripture and of the saints in Christian history teaches us to use the doctrine of original sin existentially, not as a way of explaining and therefore exonerating our behavior, but rather as a way of acknowledging the terrible depth and insoluble nature of our moral problem.

Even so — even if we try to be clear about the right *use* of the doctrine for the Christian person, so as to avoid engendering fatalism or quietism — the theoretical question still presses itself upon us. How do we escape the reasoning of Immanuel Kant, who held that the measure of our responsibility is our ability: if we say, "I ought," we necessarily imply, "I can"?[6] First of all, to say that the natural person this side of the Fall is not able not to sin *(non posse non peccare)* does not mean that she is subject to some sort of physical or metaphysical determinism. Her understanding is not darkened in the sense of the understanding of a person who is limited by, say, a brain injury leaving her with an IQ

---

4. For a sophisticated form of this argument, see Pannenberg, *Anthropology in Theological Perspective* (Philadelphia: Westminster, 1985), p. 118.

5. Milton, *Paradise Lost*, 4.110.

6. Theologian Robert McAfee Brown spoofed the famous dictum, "I ought, therefore I can," on the frontispiece of one of his books, thus: "I ought, therefore . . . — I. Kant" (*The Hereticus Papers* [Philadelphia: Westminster, 1979]). One suspects that a Pauline take on the effects of the law as well as a keen wit bore on this rejection of the seemingly unimpeachable Kantian logic. Kant himself considered freedom to be a necessary postulate of practical reason, *given the moral law,* but he did not think reason could independently fathom the nature and possibility of this freedom (see his "Theory of Ethics," 2.4, in *Kant: Selections,* ed. Theodore M. Greene [New York: Scribners, 1957]). Pascal also affirmed the incompetence of reason in this arena, but on the grounds of its corruption by sin; and he argued to a very different conclusion, namely, that humankind is incomprehensible apart from the doctrine of original sin: "And how should it be perceived by his reason, since it is a thing against reason, and since reason, far from finding it out by her own ways, is averse to it when it is presented to her?" (*Pensées,* #445, cf. #434).

of 30, which will not allow her to manage outside of an institution. Her will is not enslaved like the will of the person who has been tortured and subjected to psychotropic drugs, so that she is no longer capable of free and responsible decision. Nor is her moral inability like the inability of an animal to write poetry or to compose music. Were human inability of this kind, then we would be speaking of persons who had no understanding left to be enlightened, no will left to be renewed, no affections left to be cleansed and purified. On the contrary, we continue to insist that humankind by definition are those with a transcendent freedom that forms the basis of their responsibility.[7]

However, just as human freedom is not the freedom of the Creator but that of the creature, given within the limits of finitude; so human freedom is also curtailed, after the Fall, by our moral bankruptcy. Our freedom to be who we are is bounded not just by creaturehood but by morally alienated creaturehood. Kierkegaard employed the analogy of the knight who, before battle, was free to join either army. Afterwards, when he had been defeated and taken captive, he offered his services to the winning side under the same conditions as before — an offer that is obviously foolish under the changed circumstances. It is not the case that what we have freely chosen, we can freely undo; nor is it the case that we do not bear responsibility for our predicament.[8] "Sin which does not imply the enslavement of the will is not sin at all in the true sense."[9]

Scripture uses almost unbelievably strong figures to emphasize our moral impotence. For instance, Jeremiah 13:23 says that the Israelites can no more do good, being accustomed to doing evil, than an Ethiopian can change the color of her skin or a leopard, her spots. Jesus like-

---

7. See *Who We Are*, pp. 53-89.

8. Noted by Karl Heim, *Jesus the World's Perfecter* (Philadelphia: Muhlenberg, 1961), p. 57.

9. Ott, *Theology and Preaching* (London: Lutterworth Press, 1965), p. 96. Force of habit provides a minor but nonetheless telling example of a partial enslavement of the will. Even in neutral areas, habit is very difficult to break: how many of us make certain turns automatically when driving, even when we actually intended to go a different way. Where habit attaches to appetite, the problem is yet worse: those addicted to drugs or alcohol may be physically free from dependence after a stay in a detoxification facility, yet the impulse to turn to the problem substance is by no means gone. Knowledge that we should do differently makes little difference. Difficult though it may be, however, habits *can* be broken: this is where force of habit diverges from real moral inability.

wise appeals to nature, saying that a sound tree cannot bear bad fruit, neither can a bad tree bear good fruit (Matt. 7:17-18); and he follows the similar affirmation in Matthew 12:33 with the words, "You brood of vipers! How can you speak good things, when you are evil? For out of the abundance of the heart the mouth speaks. The good person brings good things out of a good treasure, and the evil person brings evil things out of an evil treasure" (Matt. 12:34-35; see also Luke 6:43-45). These figures from nature are, of course, only analogies that cannot be pressed absolutely, lest we lose all sense of responsibility for sin. We are not sinners in quite the same sense that a leopard is a leopard or a fig tree is a fig tree. Nonetheless, the very fact that such figures can be used at all heavily underscores the inability of the sinner to do what is good. That, after all, is their point. And Scripture also makes explicit transformation of this theme into the moral key: not only does Paul speak of slavery to sin (Rom. 6:16-19); he also says that those who are unspiritual are *unable* to understand the gifts of God's Spirit (1 Cor. 2:14) and that those who are in the flesh *cannot* please God (Rom. 8:8). Such texts compel the theologian who would be faithful to them to confess that she cannot, in herself, do the good in any ultimate sense of the word. We have from within nature freedom only to be people who are sinful, estranged from God and from their neighbor. It takes a sovereign, gracious, free act of God to restore us. Scripture is clear and emphatic on this point, while being equally clear that God continues to require humankind to do what they ought to do. And this is our human misery, that we are aware of what we ought to be; and we know, at the deepest level of our awareness, that we cannot be it. The proper end of this awareness, then, must be faith in Jesus Christ: the law that weighs us and finds us wanting stops the mouth of pride and self-sufficiency, in order that it might, by the grace of the Holy Spirit, open the mouth of faith that calls upon the Lord for salvation. The only alternative is the despair of Judas. Hence Dante appropriately writes over hell's entrance, "Lay down all hope, you that go in by me":[10] hope depends utterly upon grace.

One way of thinking about moral inability is by analogy to what we call *character*: we sometimes say of a person whom we perceive as having

---

10. Dante, *Hell*, trans. Dorothy L. Sayers, *The Divine Comedy*, vol. 1 (Baltimore: Penguin, 1949), 3.9.

integrity that she would be "incapable" of doing this or that; while we find it equally impossible to conceive that another person, of lesser moral stature, could act truly selflessly. In neither case is the person's behavior determined by something we could identify as being other than what she herself is; and it is determined at a level we would see as being somehow "higher" or more fundamental than that of mere appetite or impulse: she who has a weak character is driven by appetite and impulse; she who has a strong one is not. Either way, she is not seen as lacking responsibility for her choices on the grounds that she chooses in accord with her character, even though we acknowledge that character is shaped at least in part by many outside forces, as well as by prior choices. Furthermore, we tend to have more confidence in the goodness of the character of those who on the one hand are not too sure of their own virtue and righteousness, and who on the other hand are not too eager to find external excuses for their actions. Our experience — and our knowledge of ourselves? — leads us to distrust protestations of purity and innocence, and it also leads us to distrust self-justifying approaches to their absence. Those who have seen a little of life and of themselves, that is, enter a sort of assumption of universal sinfulness into their calculations. (We might also remark in passing that the importance but also the final impotence of character bears importantly on both the strengths and the weaknesses of "virtue ethics.")

It follows that the charge that the doctrine of moral inability is inimical to all moral achievement, is really a false charge; for that doctrine leads us to the one source of help. As C. S. Lewis put it, reflecting on the human impossibility of truly surrendering and repenting, "it needs a good man to repent. And here comes the catch. Only a bad person needs to repent."[11] Therefore, a commitment to humankind's essential goodness and self-sufficiency that promotes self-assurance proves deadly in the end. The reason is that we are, as a matter of fact, morally bankrupt; and just as proper diagnosis is essential to adequate therapy in the physical realm, so it is in the spiritual realm. A falsely optimistic view leaves us in our bondage to death. But when our need is

---

11. C. S. Lewis, *Mere Christianity* (London: Fontana Books, 1952), p. 56. Similarly Donald Baillie, who observes that a wrong will cannot put itself right: that is precisely what is wrong with it, that it does not *wish* to put itself right ("Philosophers and Theologians on the Freedom of the Will," *Scottish Journal of Theology* 4:1 [March 1951]: 113-22).

brought home to us by the Spirit, and God's word of judgment drives us from our false refuge in self-confidence, then we become open to the Gospel. And only the Gospel of the redeeming grace of God provides the true antidote to our deep and endemic alienation, our sin, that is the source of our moral inability.

Pelagianism

Pelagianism, repeatedly condemned as heresy in the fifth century, takes its name from the British monk Pelagius, who, upon coming to Rome in A.D. 400, was dismayed by the state of conduct of the inhabitants and was convinced that greater moral effort was required. Augustine's prayer, "Give what thou commandest and command what thou wilt," shocked him.[12] Pelagius claimed that humankind is created "as well without virtue as without vice,"[13] though basically good, and that character is the fruit of action. (Augustine, of course, argued exactly the reverse: it is not that we are what we do, but that we do what we are; and what we are is sinners.) According to Pelagius, people fall as individuals when they follow the bad example of Adam, or grow into fuller realization of the divine image when they exercise righteousness. He argued that it would be unrighteous and cruel of a holy God to demand of humankind what they cannot perform or to condemn them for what they cannot help. He claimed, indeed, that because of the possibility granted by God, humankind could be without sin, if only they freely used their wills so as to conform to God's commandments.[14]

By no means was Pelagius' position self-indulgent, as may tend to be the case with Romantic or psychologically oriented philosophies that suggest that all will be well if we give natural impulses free rein (on the grounds that we are naturally good). Rather, his practice was ascetical in its thrust and deeply serious in its moral aim. In the sense that he admitted the power of bad example, the pressure of an environment created by bad examples, and the force of bad habits, he took sin very

---

12. Henry Bettenson, ed., *Documents of the Christian Church,* 2nd ed. (London: Oxford University Press, 1963), p. 52.

13. Pelagius quoted in Bettenson, *Documents,* p. 53.

14. Bettenson, *Documents,* pp. 52, 53.

seriously.[15] His whole purpose was to nerve people to strive to do better.

Pelagius' views, and these views as reflected in and developed by Dutch Arminianism and classic Liberalism (which latter tends to emphasize more the good example of Jesus, which we should emulate, rather than the bad example of Adam), founder not on their quite proper affirmation of human dignity, but on their failure to balance this affirmation with an equally serious consideration of human misery and the extent to which our freedom to do the good has been lost. This failure produces the sort of superficial and optimistic anthropology that shatters on the hard facts of radical evil in our society. (We might note in passing that Wesleyan Arminianism, because rooted in an Augustinian doctrine of original sin, differs from the Liberal forms of Arminianism. Wesley saw clearly the need for radical renewal, for rebirth, though he also believed that humankind retained from within nature the ability to cooperate with grace [a sort of semi-Pelagian stance].)

Today, a whole array of "can-do" mental hygiene theorists, pop psychologists, self-help gurus, and even church growth promoters seem to have embraced avidly the most unchastened forms of Pelagianism, focusing on its positive perspective and neglecting altogether its ascetical roots. They have an easy time spreading the doctrine, for Pelagianism seems on the face of it like a perfectly commonsense interpretation of our ordinary experience of ourselves (until, that is, we come up against recognition of a sin that defeats us). Without denying for a moment that Pelagius himself was a Christian of holy intentions, we would still insist on recalling the church's longstanding judgment that Pelagianism is a heresy that in the end undercuts our understanding of grace and of the necessity of the work of Christ and the Holy Spirit.[16]

15. See George Vandervelde, *Original Sin* (Amsterdam: Rodopi N.V., 1975), pp. 10-14.
16. Note the comment in *God, Creation, and Revelation*, p. 290, on the full deity of the Holy Spirit and the saving efficacy of the work of the Spirit: this affirmation is profoundly anti-Pelagian.

Free Agency

Does honesty then require us at last to do what we have thus far so ada-
mantly refused to do, and declare that the language of human freedom
has no meaningful content? That is, we have refused to understand the
divine sovereignty in terms of a causality that would make God the
only real actor in history.[17] We have insisted, when speaking of humankind created in the divine image, that human beings are self-
transcending, responsible subjects whose spiritual lives must not be
made otiose and meaningless by mechanistic, deterministic anthro-
pologies.[18] Do the Fall and sin make these protestations empty when
we consider our actual relationship to God and to the external world?

On the one hand, of course, the whole nature of sin is to destroy
freedom: that is what the biblical language of *slavery* to sin entails. But
on the other hand, common sense protests that we act and choose
freely all the time: which door shall I go through? which brand of deter-
gent shall I buy? shall I have apple or berry pie for dessert? If the door is
blocked by the secret police, or a workers' strike means that the store is
out of a favorite brand, or the restaurant just sold the last piece of
berry pie, we may be distressed by political or economic or merely incidental external constraints on our freedom to do as we choose; but we
do not attribute our frustration to our sin or to any fundamental inability to choose as we wish.

Part of the difficulty here is that "freedom" bears so many and such
widely varying meanings, from freedom from external coercion or from
the relentless unfolding of a fully mechanistic universe on one end, to
the silent internal protest of a prisoner in solitary confinement on the
other, with meanings that rest on possession of certain kinds of knowledge or power — like freedom to read a rare book in a foreign language —
somewhere in between.[19] Another part of the difficulty is that it is hard
to construe what freedom might mean apart from a goal or a *direction* of
action made desirable by knowledge or by appetite: someone lost in the
woods may be free to proceed in any direction, but that "freedom" is not

17. *God, Creation, and Revelation*, p. 357.

18. *Who We Are*, passim, but esp. pp. 72-77.

19. For one listing of thirteen different senses of the word, see Finley Carpenter, *The
Skinner Primer: Behind Freedom and Dignity* (New York: Free Press, 1974), chap. 3. The Augustinian meaning we shall espouse is not among them.

much use if she has no idea in which direction help lies. *More* choices don't help much if one does not perceive a *good* or desirable choice. Freedom, that is, is meaningless without a context of values of some sort.[20] For our purposes here, we will leave aside questions of external constraint, important as these are in the life of human communities; questions of knowledge or power that one may gain or fail to gain (without denying that one is sometimes culpable for failure, say, to learn one's math or to maintain one's physical strength); and even questions of native endowment and of environment, insofar as these do not fatally compromise capacity to function as an agent. We will consider only the freedom implied when we say "I" as the subject of an action, thought, intention, or desire, meaning that that action, thought, intention, or desire is in some important sense our own. Note that this mysterious "I" is to be identified with neither reason nor appetite, but transcends them and judges them — or judges itself when it sees itself as, say, wrongly overcome by passion or as wrongly using reason in the service of cowardice. "Sees itself"; "judges itself": there is that self-transcendence of the human agent that we can neither explain nor deny.

First, then, we reaffirm and insist that humankind even as fallen, even as sinners incapable of doing the truly good, do act — act in such a way that we must speak of the source of their action as themselves, and not simply of their biology or their environment. Certain things take place because someone decided to do something; had she not decided to do it, it would not have happened. Nor are people mere pawns of fate, God, or the Devil. Obviously, forces of all kinds that are beyond their control bear in upon them: they are not insulated from a whole vast complex of influences and determinants. But even so, human agency is not a mere psychological illusion, or a joke played by evolution to ensure that humans keep striving; rather, it is human agents who process the various influences and determinants. Luther, drawing on Augustine, put matters in a way that is too easy to misinterpret as an essential denial of human willing when he wrote, "man's will is like a beast standing between two riders. If God rides, it wills and goes where God wills. . . . If Satan rides, it wills and

20. And when I think of *my* freedom, I think in the context of *my* values, not of the values someone else might wish to impose. It is worth remarking that even defenses of freedom tend to manifest the very self-concern from which Christians might rightly pray to be freed, and ignore that context of responding in love to God's love that we actually experience *not* as choice, but still as true freedom.

goes where Satan wills. Nor may it choose to which rider it will run, or which it will seek; but the riders themselves fight to decide who shall have and hold it."[21] That God often works through means, including human willing, does not mean that human willing is not real. No; human beings are personal subjects, not physical objects or dumb beasts.[22] "Will" is a meaningful term only in the context of personal agency.

Second, human beings are, by their very nature as created by God, responsible to him: they must give account to God for their actions, render up an answer for them in a context in which these actions cannot be assumed to be neutral or of no importance. They cannot evade this responsibility, however much they may seek to hide or justify themselves. God will not allow Cain to escape the question about his brother. Even those, on the other end of the spectrum from the evaders and deniers, who are plagued by neurotic guilt feelings or convictions of being responsible for that which was not in fact in their power may be seen as experiencing distorted manifestations of the deeper truth that to be human is to be responsible.[23] (It may indeed be that the false guilt experienced by many victims is not negative in every respect, but testifies to an insistence on that basic component of personhood: victims cannot allow victimization to deprive them of their sense of themselves as responsible agents.)

Third, human agency and responsibility imply the presence of choices: the mysterious human power of self-transcendence means that humans do not operate like animals, out of instinct however refined and marvelous, but by making conscious decisions. Not that there are

---

21. Martin Luther, *On the Bondage of the Will*, trans. J. I. Packer and O. R. Johnston (London: James Clarke & Co., 1957), pp. 103-4.

22. That this view depends in some sense on a dichotomistic anthropology has been widely assumed (and we have argued for such an anthropology in *Who We Are*). For instance, in his 1957 Gifford Lectures, published as *The Freedom of the Will* (London: Adam & Charles Black, 1958), Austin Farrar begins his whole discussion of various determinisms with the mind-body problem; and he concludes that after all the various sorts of causality have had their play, the human being still has to *decide* what he or she will do. There is something irreducible about conscious decision.

23. We do not intend to deny Ricoeur's important observation that human consciousness of responsibility, stemming from interdictions and fear of punishment, precedes consciousness of being an author or agent of one's actions (*Symbolism of Evil*, p. 102); and we certainly do not intend to blame victims in a roundabout way by positively acknowledging their feelings of responsibility. The point is simply that it may be intolerably dehumanizing and debilitating to see oneself as utterly stripped of agency.

no unconscious springs of action (of which more shortly), but humans take a position with regard even to these unconscious drives and predilections and their effects. It is simply not the same thing to die in one's sleep from carbon monoxide poisoning coming from a poorly vented heater, as it is to die from carbon monoxide poisoning as a result of hooking up the car exhaust to the car interior: the former is a chemical event; the latter is suicide. Even giving up one's choices by submitting absolutely to the will of another is an expression of the will, of decision, not a refutation of it.[24] Similarly, when one says that she does something "against her will" or "against her better judgment" (in circumstances in which she is not being coerced), she means that she does not like the probable consequences of her action but considers choosing differently to be still worse. People speak of seeing themselves as having certain options even under conditions of extreme constraint. We laugh at the child who says rebelliously, "I may be sitting down on the outside, but I'm standing up on the inside"; but we do not laugh when a prisoner of conscience says something altogether similar.[25] A deep inner volition transcends particular circumstances.

That last affirmation of a deep inner volition brings us to the crux of the matter for this particular discussion. The three affirmations we have just made are affirmations of a very real human freedom which must not be denied at the cost of our humanity itself. Yes, we affirm: we can (at least often) do what we will; and when we do what we will, we act freely. But that is not the fundamental question. The fundamental question is whether we can will aright. To that fundamental question, a great host of thinkers, non-Christian as well as Christian, have given a negative answer.[26]

Those who have thought deeply about these matters observe that our willing springs from a primal disposition of spirit (will in the sense of

24. See Ricoeur, *Symbolism of Evil*, pp. 123-24.

25. Recall the famous lines of Richard Lovelace: "Stone walls do not a prison make,/ Nor iron bars a cage" (*A Treasury of Great Poems*, ed. Louis Untermeyer [New York: Simon & Schuster, 1955], p. 472).

26. For examples, see Arthur Schopenhauer, *Essay on the Freedom of the Will*, trans. Konstantin Kolenda (Indianapolis and New York: Bobbs-Merrill, 1960), chap. 4. Schopenhauer is concerned not specifically with willing *aright* but with any freedom of the will at all at this deeper level. His basic conclusion is that what we will springs necessarily from what we are, from our character.

voluntas, in classical terms) that is not itself consciously chosen. While Scripture does not have a single word for this primal volition, "heart" perhaps comes as close as any. We are told, for instance, to keep our heart with all diligence, since from it flow the springs of life (Prov. 4:23). The blessing of the New Covenant is precisely a new heart, in place of the stony heart of unbelief (Jer. 31:31-33; Ezek. 36:26). Such a gift is a prime necessity, for, "Who can say, 'I have made my heart clean; I am pure from my sin'?" (Prov. 20:9). The question assumes the answer, No one; and hence it corresponds to the conclusion we have reached about the depth and extent of human sinfulness. Since the Fall, that is, the primal disposition of the human will — of all human wills — is bent in the direction of evil. It is not just that both intellect and passions are themselves corrupted, as we have said earlier, but that even when we do know what is good and right, we cannot do it (Rom. 7, of course; but altogether similarly Ovid, who gives his Medea to say, "I see and approve the better course; I follow the worse":[27] the experience is universal, not a Christian aberration). The key point is that we find ourselves utterly unable to do as we ought even when we see alternatives and do not experience ourselves as fatally constrained from without: the bondage is deep within us, not imposed from the outside. And we are baffled at ourselves. After we are done with all of our explanations and excuses, we are beset with the conviction that we both could and should have done differently. But worse, if we are yet more honest, we know with a terrible certainty that faced with just the same circumstances again, despite our firm resolve, we would do the same wrong thing. It is not choice that we lack, but power to choose aright.[28] Likewise with unworthy impulses that arise unbidden: we do

---

27. Quoted by Norman Fiering, *Moral Philosophy at Seventeenth-Century Harvard: A Discipline in Transition* (Chapel Hill, N.C.: University of North Carolina Press, 1981), p. 115; see the whole of chap. 3 for an illuminating discussion of will and intellect.

28. In Calvin's words, "Man will then be spoken of as having this sort of free decision, not because he has free choice equally of good and evil, but because he acts wickedly by will, not by compulsion. Well put, indeed, but what purpose is served by labeling with a proud name such a slight thing?" (*Institutes* 2.2.7; see also 2.3.5). A striking example here is Dmitri Karamazov's conversation with Alyosha about a particularly base and dishonoring deed that he knew he would carry out. He spoke of it as that "'which will come to pass, though I'm perfectly free to stop it. I can stop it or carry it through, note that. Well, let me tell you, I shall carry it through. I shan't stop it. I told you everything just now, but I didn't tell you that, because even I had not brass enough for it. I can still pull up; if I do, I can give back the full half of my lost honour to-morrow. But I shan't

not consciously will them; we cannot consciously prevent them; yet we recognize them as without doubt our own. The spring itself is polluted. No amount of "will power" can correct the will, any more than a dirty spring can cleanse itself with its own water.[29] The bubbling up of the spring is impenetrable to thought and imagination alike.

Such self-knowledge conflicts sharply with the dictates of popular culture. It would appear that the modern romance with self-help literature and motivational speakers plays hard on the conviction that *of course* we can and should do better, that "thinking we can" and "feeling better about ourselves" are the keys to progress. Some 50,000 people are allegedly seeking to enter the motivational speaking business, and droves of large companies solicit their services both as speakers and as writers of inspirational messages.[30] Presumably all of this energy implies that people think at least some sort of result is being achieved. But the real question is not whether certain stimuli may move us to do differently, and even in some practical sense to do better, than we might otherwise do: the answer to that question is obvious and is certainly allowed by our affirmative points about human freedom. The real question has to do with the deeper dispositions on which our more superficial volitions rest; and the more we focus on the superficial, the more we may deceive ourselves about, or lose touch entirely with, these deeper dispositions.

Modern psychoanalyst Leslie Farber gets at the distinction especially profoundly, and in contemporary language, when he speaks of two interdependent realms of the will. The first is unconscious, manifested when we act as whole persons, subjectively freely, in a particular direction (but not toward a specified goal, which shifts will to the second realm). The second is conscious and goal-directed — what we aim to achieve by will power, working step by step. As he puts it,

---

pull up'" (Dostoyevsky, *Brothers Karamazov,* pp. 186-87). There is more desperation than defiance in Dmitri's knowledge of himself.

29. Thus Berdyaev remarks, "Man's moral dignity and freedom are determined not by the purpose to which he subordinates his life but by the source from which his moral life and activity spring" (*Destiny of Man* [New York: Harper & Row, 1960], p. 80). Surely this distinction is a false one when we are speaking of the Christian life as a whole; but the point that moral striving and noble ends alone cannot save us stands.

30. See Bonnie Harris, "'I *Am* the Next Big Thing'," *Los Angeles Times,* April 18, 2001, p. A1+.

The problem of will lies in our recurring temptation to apply the will of the second realm to those portions of life that not only will not comply, but that will become distorted under such coercion. . . . I can will knowledge but not wisdom; going to bed, but not sleeping; eating, but not hunger; meekness, but not humility; scrupulosity, but not virtue; self-assertion or bravado, but not courage; lust, but not love; commiseration, but not sympathy; congratulations, but not admiration; religiosity, but not faith; reading, but not understanding.[31]

One recalls Augustine complaining about the recalcitrance of the male sexual organ, or Rollo May describing the impotent patient who "is trying to make his body to love when *he* does not love."[32] (Utilitarian attempts to capture the deeper qualities will simply imitate their public face. By contrast, on the positive side, "when the job is a labor of love, the sacrifices will present themselves to the worker — strange as it may seem — in the guise of enjoyment":[33] the inner disposition transforms the outer experience). The very fact, which Sayers remarks, that moralists deem dutiful sacrifice more admirable than the act that springs from love shows the depth of sinful pride, for one can will dutiful sacrifice but cannot will love. Again Farber,

> My answer, then, to the question, what is the nature of the experience of the man who seeks to purchase with his will some semblance of those qualities of being that cannot or should not be willed, is that eventually it is will itself that increasingly becomes his experience, until the private voices of subjectivity and the public occasions from life that might raise this voice are almost stifled, if not silenced. To put the matter somewhat differently, *what is* in his experience gives way to *what should be,* as decreed by his will.[34]

Subjectivity and the world fade, and powers that cannot be willed atrophy — an outcome that looks remarkably like a direct goal of the

31. Leslie Farber, *The Ways of the Will* (New York and London: Basic Books, 1966), p. 15.
32. Rollo May, *Love and Will* (New York: W. W. Norton, 1969), p. 280.
33. Dorothy Sayers, *The Mind of the Maker* (New York: Living Age Books, 1956), p. 130.
34. Farber, *Ways of the Will,* p. 25.

motivational speaking industry, which exists to pooh pooh the seriousness of inner and outer obstacles. Worse yet, from a theological point
of view, we may simply become blind to the broken quality of "what is,"
to our sinfulness — and to the complete impotence of our will (in the
first sense) to be other than it is. (We ought not, of course, to go to the
other extreme and suppose that will in the second sense is unimportant, and that we might as well do as we please since, after all, we can't
help it: that stance is itself a choice of the will in the second sense, and
one which other people will rightly judge negatively. The point is rather
a sober assessment of what is and what is not in our power.)

From this analysis, it will follow clearly enough that we reject the
idea that fallen humankind has what has been called the power of contrary choice (*liberum arbitrium indifferentiae,* in classical terms): the power
to choose between two alternatives — most particularly, the power freely
to choose the good and refuse the evil. Although this freedom has long
been fundamental to the Eastern Church's understanding,[35] it is possible to ask if it is even a coherent idea, at any level beyond choosing between apple and berry pie on a dessert menu, and perhaps even there. To
be truly indifferent before a choice is to be unable to choose at all except
by the merest caprice or impulse or arbitrary act (consider the long and
unhelpful discussions when two people really do not care which restaurant to select for dinner).[36] And to be putatively neutral about a *moral*

35. For example, very early, Justin: "unless the human race have the power of avoiding evil and choosing good by free choice, they are not accountable for their actions"
(*Apology* 43, ANF vol. 1, p. 177); also Clement of Alexandria: "neither praises nor censures,
neither rewards nor punishments, are right, when the soul has not the power of inclination and disinclination, but evil is involuntary" (*Stromata* 1.17, ANF vol. 2, p. 319). Fiering
remarks on denial of radical evil in Classical Greek culture by virtue of its intellectual-
ism (the will must follow the dictates of the reason), and notes that Pelagianism and
Arminianism are actually closely tied to the intellectualist theory. He further notes an
anomaly in intellectualist thinking: if the will *must* follow the dictates of the intellect,
the question of freedom arises in a different way (*Moral Philosophy at Harvard,* esp. pp.
113-24, 137). See also Reinhold Seeburg, *Text-book of the History of Doctrines,* vol. 1, trans.
Charles E. Hay (reprint, Eugene, Oregon: Wipf and Stock, n.d.), pp. 294, 328. Seeburg
notes the probable Greek influence on Pelagius, p. 332.

36. Dante captures the image of those who refuse to choose in his depiction of the
Vestibule of Hell. Sayers comments, "The spirits rush aimlessly after the aimlessly whirl-
ing banner, stung and goaded, as of old, by the thought that, in doing anything definite
whatsoever, they are missing doing something else" (notes on Canto 3, *Hell,* p. 89).

choice is to set ourselves alongside God as ultimate judges of good and evil — which sounds all too much like the temptation eventuating in the Fall in the first place. How can we choose at all without some kind of motive? How can we consider a will to be a good or admirable will if it is no more inclined to the good than to the bad?[37]

The more significant a choice is, the clearer it becomes that approaching it neutrally is as undesirable as it is impossible. Imagine sending out a half-dozen proposals of marriage so as to have maximum freedom of selection. Or imagine saying yes to a proposal of marriage about which one felt the same as about half a dozen others simply on the grounds that it happened to be on the top of the letter pile.[38] Imagine Luther at the Diet of Worms saying, "Well, there are good arguments on both sides, but I guess I'll go with what I've written." Imagine Paul saying not that necessity was laid upon him to preach the gospel, not woe to him if he did not preach (1 Cor. 9:16); but that it seemed like as good a career choice as any. Such suggestions fatally trivialize our identity and motives at their deepest levels. The deeper and more central a motive is to our personhood, the less we are open to alternatives.

And our deepest trouble is that, since the Fall, our will at this fundamental level is bent: it is biased toward evil. That bias does not mean that no acts are better than any others, that all choices are equal; but it does mean that we do no acts out of wholly pure love of God and neighbor. Self-love always intrudes and distorts, sometimes more, sometimes less; but the more we know of ourselves, the more dismayed we are at the hidden corruption of even our best acts. Precisely when we want to choose purely, we discover how very unfree we are.[39]

---

37. Thus the Reformed have held that even the freedom of Adam and Eve in the Garden was not marked by this sort of indifference, but was specifically a freedom to obey: they began with a positive (though mutable) inclination toward the good. Similarly Heim: "It is an indication of our being far from God that the question what we have to do arises at all, that a decision in favour of God's will is necessary at all" (*Jesus the Lord* [Philadelphia: Muhlenberg, 1961], p. 71).

38. Truer to the experience of love is this Elizabethan poem of unknown authorship: "Her hair the net of golden wire,/Wherein my heart, led by my wandering eyes,/So fast entangled is that in no wise/It can, nor will, again retire;/But rather will in that sweet bondage die/Than break one hair to gain her liberty" (Untermeyer, *Treasury of Great Poems*, p. 266).

39. One suspects that so-called free-will theists and those who advocate an "open" view of God have not sufficiently taken the depth of human sinfulness into account (or perhaps consider it less devastating than we do).

That deep discovery of our bondage to our sin may lead at last to the discovery of the truth that Augustine spoke long ago: the essence of freedom is bondage to God's will. It is not unlimited choices among which we struggle and debate, but the limits befitting our status as God's beloved creatures, that free us to be who we are meant to be and to find true fulfillment in responsible relationship to our Maker.[40] It is not the agonizing effort to do our duty at whatever cost, but finding — as a gift of a new heart with the law written upon it rather than imposed from the outside (to be had fully only in the state of glory) — that our deepest inclinations lead us where we *ought* to go at the same time as they take us where we *want* to go.[41] Then we shall be as unable to sin *(non posse peccare)* as we are now unable to refrain from sinning *(non posse non peccare)*. When Christ makes us free, we shall be free indeed (John 8:36; cf. 2 Cor 3:17; Rom. 6:16-22).

> Make me a captive, Lord,
> And then I shall be free;
> Force me to render up my sword,
> And I shall conqueror be. (Matheson)

Solidarity in Sin[42]

That all are sinners — that "there is no one who is righteous, not even one" (Rom. 3:10) — must be the sober conclusion reached by any honest observer of humankind. The doctrine of the Fall purports to tell us why this is the case: something went desperately wrong at the very beginning of the human story, something that marked all of history. But

40. By contrast, Ricoeur speaks profoundly of "the evil infinite of human desire — always something else, always something more" (*Symbolism of Evil,* p. 254). Recall that it was Milton's Satan who thought it preferable to reign in hell rather than serve in heaven (PL 1.263) — better to be unhappy without limits than to be happy with them. Yet surely misery is itself a sort of limiting condition, which is a point worth considering when we think about what we intend to affirm when we affirm freedom.

41. To take a common and trivial example, imagine two children at mealtime. The first is given a choice of eating her despised vegetables or getting no dessert. The second happens to like the vegetables and is confronted with no choices at all. It is not hard to discern which will be the happier dinner table.

42. See above, "Parties to the Covenant," pp. 12-13.

how? To say that Adam and Eve fell, so all their offspring are sinners, sounds on the face of it neither plausible nor just. Having made this point, Pascal argues that reason must simply submit in the face of this mystery that is so central to our identity.[43] Others have by no means been so modest.

One early view (dependent, in its more literalistic forms, upon strict monogenism)[44] is that we were all in some sense present in Adam, or that the "seed" derived from him was corrupt. That Augustine held such a view is clear: "we all were in that one man, since we all were that one man. . . . [A]lready the seminal nature was there from which we were to be propagated. . . ." Again, "In the first man . . . there existed the whole human nature, . . . and what man was made, not when created, but when he sinned and was punished, this he propagated, so far as the origin of sin and death are concerned.[45] The *in some sense* part of the "present in Adam" is important, though: the church's

43. "It is, however, an astonishing thing that the mystery furthest removed from our knowledge, namely, that of the transmission of sin, should be a fact without which we can have no knowledge of ourselves. For it is beyond doubt that there is nothing which more shocks our reason than to say that the sin of the first man has rendered guilty those who, being so removed from this source, seem incapable of participation in it. . . . Certainly nothing offends us more rudely than this doctrine; and yet, without this mystery, the most incomprehensible of all, we are incomprehensible to ourselves. . . . Whence it seems that God, willing to render the difficulty of our existence unintelligible to ourselves, has concealed the knowledge so high, or, better speaking, so low, that we are quite incapable of reaching it; so that it is not by the proud exertions of our reason, but by the simple submissions of reason, that we can truly know ourselves" (Pascal, *Pensées*, #434).

44. For a brief note on monogenism, see *Who We Are*, pp. 391-92.

45. Augustine, *City of God* 13.14; 13.3. However, it is not clear that his view should be understood *simply* in a physical way. Alongside his convictions of seminal identity, he also held the opinion that while infants were born guilty because of the act by which they were generated, it was not the act itself but the lust that (Augustine believed) inevitably accompanied the ardor of the act of procreation that was the problem (*On Marriage and Concupiscence*, 1.27; 2.14). Augustine tended (e.g., in *On Forgiveness of Sins, and Baptism*, 1.11; 3.14) to put heavy weight on ἐφ' ᾧ in Rom. 5:12 as meaning "in whom" (that is, Adam) or "in which sin" all sinned, an interpretation now rejected by the vast majority of commentators. Calvin, too, could speak of "inherited corruption"; of being "descended from impure seed"; of infants whose "whole nature is a seed of sin" (*Institutes* 2.1.6, 8), though he immediately attributed the "contagion" not to physical generation but to the fact that "it had been so ordained by God" (2.1.7, also note 11). "Inheritance" begins to sound much more like a metaphor than like a mechanism.

theology, both early and more recent, intends to say that the whole of human nature is vitiated by sin.[46] That is not an idea that can be readily accommodated by modern views of heredity, based on scientific understandings of genetics. Thus, ideas of "hereditary sin" become increasingly problematic as our understanding of the mechanisms of heredity grows. Let it be clear that human nature is not something that can be corrupted by a genetic mutation. And even if it could be, if we were speaking of that sort of physical change, we would leave the realm of sin and enter that of illness. Even if one produced such an effect, one would not produce responsibility for it. There could be no *guilt*.[47] Recall, of course, that the pervasive biblical language involving our being heirs is not based on physical heredity. We may be called children of the Devil (e.g., John 8:44; Acts 13:10) or of God (esp. Rom. 8, *passim*); to be "Abraham's children" involves not mere descent but orientation of life (John 8:39-41); and to be "heirs with Christ" (Rom. 8:17) does not entail being physically related to him.[48] Slippage between this rich metaphorical usage and the sort of usage that would provide a physical mechanism for the transmission of sin will simply result in confusion. Thus, it seems best at this stage of history to put aside the thought of hereditary sin, insofar as we

46. For helpful remarks, see Otto Weber, *Foundations of Dogmatics,* 2 vols., trans. D. Guder (Grand Rapids: Eerdmans, 1981), 1:610-11.

47. An additional problem with hereditary views has sometimes been suggested: if transmission of sin takes place at a biological level, why are we presumably marked only by Adam and Eve's first sin, and not by those that came later? Questions of this sort underscore the pervasive weakness of the position. Appeals to genetic determinism echo earlier appeals to the stars as the inexorable cause of our behavior, which appeals were eloquently rejected by Dante (". . . If the world now goes with crooked gait/The cause is in yourselves for you to trace" [*Purgatory* 16.67-83]) and by Shakespeare (". . . an admirable evasion of whormaster man, to lay his goatish disposition to the charge of a star! . . . I should have been that I am, had the maidenliest star in the firmament twinkled on my bastardizing" [*King Lear* 1.2.116-30]).

48. Even Jesus' words to Nicodemus, that "What is born of the flesh is flesh" (John 3:6), do not establish *how* this result comes about but simply state our condition apart from the work of the Spirit. We must admit, however, that the traditional understanding of the virgin birth as important to the idea of Jesus' sinlessness does seem to suggest the thought of physical transmission of sin — and makes salient the logic of the Roman Catholic doctrine of the immaculate conception of Mary (which we reject for lack of scriptural ground), when we understand the equal physical contribution of the woman to the heritage of the child.

mean thereby a sinful condition produced as the inevitable result of biological processes.[49]

The seemingly obvious alternative to hereditary explanations of the transmission of original sin would be an environmental explanation: once evil was introduced into the environment, it kept exerting its influence, not only as bad example but also because of negative pressures now experienced by individuals. There is some truth here: we have acknowledged at various points the power of environment.[50] It is quite correct to observe soberly that "Every sin strengthens the dominion of evil in the world and increases the weight of transgressions burdening other men and posterity."[51] We as perpetrators of sin and not just as victims of it do well to take that point into account. The point is further strengthened when we consider sin embedded in the structures of society, such that no one is directly responsible for ongoing evils, and such that any action one takes will produce further evil. Even so, the problem is not just the theological one of why we should not then side with Pelagius — why, by a mighty act of will, we could not then achieve restoration by imitating Christ (making his death on our behalf superfluous except as a model of extraordinary love); but the logical one of why evil spread with such abandon in the

---

49. Actually, the hereditary view of the transmission of sin has always been beset with difficulties, as manifested in part in the ancient conflict between creationists and traducianists with respect to the origin of the soul in the individual. Does God create each soul afresh? Then how does he escape the charge of being the direct cause of sin, since each person is marked by sin from the beginning? It will not do to locate sin solely in the body, as if it were matter that was somehow corrupting. Is the soul somehow passed on from parents to child? How, then, do we avoid seeing the soul as material? (For brief summaries of the traditional positions, see Charles Hodge, *Systematic Theology*, 3 vols. [Grand Rapids: Eerdmans, reprint 1981]: 2:68-76; James Franklin Bethune-Baker, *An Introduction to the Early History of Christian Doctrine*, 5th ed. [London: Methuen & Co., 1933], pp. 302-5.) Scripture is silent on the subject, though both sides find texts that they can interpret in their favor. Today, the whole conflict will strike many as being entangled in an excessive dualism. Note, however, Weber's interesting remark, "the 'I' which says, 'I believe,' is not simply the same thing as the human soul which is subject to the work of psychology. . . . In this regard, are not the proponents of Creationism right in a way which they will scarcely be aware of themselves?" (*Foundations of Dogmatics*, 1:478).

50. Even Augustine, for all of his anti-Pelagianism, did not deny that we imitate Adam's sin (e.g., in *On Forgiveness of Sins, and Baptism*, 1.10).

51. Piet Smulders, *The Design of Teilhard de Chardin*, trans. Arthur Gibson (Westminster, MD: Newman Press, 1967), p. 174.

first place, if the human were not somehow bent in the way we have argued above.[52] We have also observed above that those reared in virtually identical environments may respond differently.[53] The environmental view has widely been seen as seductive but as inadequate to the actual depth of evil (not to mention that the Bible does not speak as if the environment is the fundamental problem). One recalls by contrast Chesterton's famously brief response to an invitation to readers of England's *Daily Mail* to tell what was wrong with the world — he wrote, "Dear Sir, I am. Yours sincerely."[54]

The way the Reformed tradition in particular has dealt with the question of how we are all involved in our first parents' sin is by way of imputation, a theologically rich concept that is crucial to the doctrine of salvation. The idea is a judicial one, whereby the debt of one may be reckoned to the account of another, as when Paul says to Philemon regarding Onesimus, "If he has wronged you in any way, or owes you anything, charge that to my account" (Philem. 18). Today, sponsors are held responsible for the acts of refugees; cosigners of loans, for the default of the other party; and so on. We speak in the context of salvation of our sin not being "reckoned" to us (Rom. 4:6-8; 2 Cor. 5:19), but rather being imputed to Christ and his righteousness being imputed to us: Christ is not made a sinner in the sense that he is personally defiled by sin and is guilty in his own person before God (2 Cor. 5:21); rather, when our sins are imputed to him, he is *reckoned* by God the Father to be a sinner, treated as if he were a sinner.[55] We, in turn, are reckoned righteous in him as we receive him by

---

52. Jonathan Edwards pressed this latter argument (see Smith, *Changing Conceptions of Original Sin* (New York: Scribners, 1955), pp. 29-30.

53. See pp. 121-22.

54. Altogether similarly, "Sophocles has in Oedipus dramatized the greatest and wisest of men seeking the cause of human ruin. And he finds that cause, not in another as he expects, but to his horror and despairing dismay he finds it in himself" (Roland Frye, *Perspective on Man* [Philadelphia: Westminster, 1961], p. 102).

55. The biblical vocabulary of imputation includes most prominently חשׁב in Hebrew and λογίζομαι in Greek (used to translate חשׁב in the LXX, as well as being used in the NT). The Hebrew term is used in commercial settings associated with debts, and appears as a fixed idiom meaning "reckon something to someone's account" in a variety of passages (see K. Seybold, חשׁב, *Theological Dictionary of the Old Testament* [Grand Rapids: Eerdmans, 1974-], vol. 5). See especially Gen. 15:6, where Abram believed God and it was *reckoned* to him as righteousness; and Ps. 32:2, where those are said to be happy to whom the LORD imputes no iniquity. Λογίζομαι is used of imputing faith

faith. Something profound takes place here that does not correspond to the individual worthiness of the persons involved.[56]

Paul in Romans 5:12-19 — the key passage for discussion of imputation of Adamic sin (but also see 1 Cor. 15:21-22) — suggests a direct analogy between the work of Adam at the beginning of the age and the work of Christ at its end: "Therefore just as one man's trespass led to condemnation for all, so one man's act of righteousness leads to justification and life for all. For just as by the one man's disobedience the many were made sinners, so by the one man's obedience the many will be made righteous" (Rom. 5:18-19). There can be no doubt that Paul intends to include under the bane of Adam's sin those who did not themselves commit that sin, just as he includes under the blessing of Christ's righteousness those who are not themselves righteous. To maintain the parallel quality of the argument, it is logical to interpret the key verb καθίστημι as meaning something like "were constituted" (carrying, therefore, a meaning like that of imputation) rather than as "were made" or "became" in the sense of "were caused to be inwardly." As we were constituted sinners in Adam, and only then confirmed the sinfulness in our own persons (Rom. 5:12, 17: death holds sway over all through one person's sin; but all humans do proceed to sin for themselves); so we are constituted righteous in Christ while we are yet sinners, and the full realization of that righteousness awaits what appears to be eschatological confirmation (Rom. 5:16-19: note the future in v. 19). It must be admitted, though, that the passage as a whole is slippery, and one may wonder if Paul actually intended to answer the "how" question at all. It may instead be that he simply wished to assert the "that," with the larger goal of exalting the work of Christ.[57] The

---

(Rom. 4:3-12; Gal. 3:6; James 2:23) and of not imputing sin (Rom. 4:7-8; 2 Cor. 5:19) (see H. W. Heidland, λογίζομαι, *Theological Dictionary of the New Testament* [Grand Rapids: Eerdmans, 1964-75], vol. 4). Clearly, then, the idea is biblical, even though it is sometimes scored today as being coldly legalistic.

56. On the alleged injustice of imputing sin to us, see Augustine's remarks in *On Man's Perfection in Righteousness*, 15 (NPNF, first series, vol. 5).

57. Augustine puts the greatness of grace thus, commenting on Rom. 5:16: "[W]e have derived from Adam, in whom we all have sinned, not all our actual sins, but only original sin; whereas from Christ, in whom we are all justified, we obtain the remission not merely of that original sin, but of the rest of our sins also, which we have added" (*On Forgiveness of Sins, and Baptism*, 1.16).

Fall and redemption are both theological realities the inner working of which remains hidden from our view.[58]

We might repeat that, as a matter of fact, none of the proposed mechanisms for transmission of sin "works." We are merely told that sin enters the world "through" (διά) one man (Rom. 5:12). (According to Heim, this usage should be understood to imply the satanic agency behind sin. John's usage [e.g., John 8:44; 1 John 3:8] supports this view.)[59] Even if we affirm imputation, as we do, we are not told how being *counted* a sinner relates to *being* a sinner: that there is no necessary connection is shown by the case of Jesus. Rather, as we have said, we find both suggested in the same passage (Rom. 5:12-21), which has to do more with judgment and grace, death and life, than with specifics of the transmission of sin (similarly 1 Cor. 15:21-22). As Dubarle remarks, Paul seems simply to take for granted that sin has spread from Adam to all.[60] Barth's remark that the connection between our first parents' sin and our own is best seen simply as established by God, seems to us to be well taken.[61]

The obscurity with regard to specifics bears on the much-controverted matter of how we can carry an "alien" guilt — guilt for a sin that not we but our first parents committed, since guilt, of all things, would appear to have to be our own to qualify as guilt at all. (The answer to Q. 18 of the Westminster Shorter Catechism, to take a single example, explicitly includes guilt for Adam's sin, along with want of original righteousness and corruption of our whole nature, in the original sin that we bear.) Scripture does not appear to be troubled by this question, any more than the Old Testament is troubled by the guilt associated with even unintentional incurring of uncleanness. As Quell remarks, "the Hebrews never attained to any sharp terminological dis-

---

58. There is of course a vast literature both on the nuances of the doctrine of imputation (immediate or mediate, etc.: pushed, we would affirm immediate imputation) and on the specifics of the exegesis of Rom. 5:12-19. For a brief and helpful discussion, see Herman Ridderbos, *Paul: An Outline of His Theology*, trans. J. R. DeWitt (Grand Rapids: Eerdmans, 1975), pp. 95-100.

59. Karl Heim, *The World: Its Creation and Consummation* (Edinburgh and London: Oliver and Boyd, 1962), pp. 123-24.

60. A. M. Dubarle, *Biblical Doctrine of Original Sin* (London: Geoffrey Chapman, 1964), p. 171.

61. Barth, *Church Dogmatics*, IV/1: 510-11.

tinction between sin and guilt, since there was not the slightest doubt as to the causal connection between abnormal action and abnormal state."[62] There is an objectivity in the Old Testament view of sin and guilt that seems to be similarly assumed in the New Testament. Our protestations against this state of affairs seem to come more at the theoretical level, as we contemplate what we construe as abstract "fairness," than at the existential level, as our consciences testify to our responsibility. In our hearts, we may recognize, when we are being strictly honest — and most especially as we are taken up by grace — that however it may have come about, our first parents' sin *is* our own; we have owned it and acted on it. All of our evasions of responsibility echo Adam's laying the blame for his fault on "the woman whom you gave to be with me" (Gen. 3:12): one way or another, we want to believe, it must really be God's fault in the end.

Obscure though the "how" may be, the very least we may conclude is that Adam and Eve's act, and the act of Christ, both have unique significance for the whole of humanity — Adam and Eve's act somehow putting all under the sway of sin, as evidenced by the universality of death; and Christ's, offering a gift of righteousness not in any fallen human being's power.[63] These must not be dissolved into a general and amorphous assertion that we are not isolated monads but are involved inextricably with one another. Fundamental theological affirmations must not be reduced to sociological truisms. Provided we keep the uniqueness of the theological affirmations in mind, however, the reality of solidarity in sin may still rightly remind us that we are indeed not isolated monads but are involved inextricably with one another. Even the ambiguities of the biblical witness may help us to affirm that this interweaving with others is not on the basis of biology or social influences or matters of representation and imputation alone, but all of these and doubtless more besides. Consider: even if we live in a democracy, in which we choose our representatives and can hardly conceive how Louis XIV could have declared, *"L'état, c'est moi"* ("I am the state"), we are still at war if our President declares war. Furthermore, the "givenness" of our situation in Adam, despite its unique universality, is

---

62. Quell, "ἁμαρτάνω," *TDNT,* 1:279.

63. See, for instance, John Murray, "The Imputation of Adam's Sin — II," *Westminster Theological Journal* 19:1 (November 1956): 25-44.

not otherwise altogether unlike the givenness of our birth in a particular location, with a particular culture, at a particular point in history, to particular parents, with a particular genetic endowment: none of these do we choose; and with respect to each of them, the choices already made by many others affect us in the most profound manner possible. Everyone is born not only into history, but with a history. To reject this plain fact by complaining, "It's not fair," is to refuse to receive life as a gift — a gift given in and for fellowship — and suppose we can be our own makers.[64]

Considering the actual contingencies of human existence, then, it can hardly be surprising that Scripture deals throughout in terms of corporate and not just individual calling and responsibility. It may be that ideas about a "corporate personality," especially when this personality is reified, may be a bit overdrawn; yet truth remains in them.[65] Recall that the whole idea of a covenant community, the whole idea of the election of a particular people, is by definition corporate; when the nation is constituted under Moses, Moses says, "I am making this covenant, sworn by an oath, not only with you who stand here with us today before the LORD our God, but also with those who are not here with us today" (Deut. 29:14-15). The Israelites are taught to tell their children of future generations, "the LORD brought *us* out of Egypt"

64. L. Gregory Jones recently wrote on the question of reparations to the African-American community in the context of repentance and coming to terms with our past, rather than acting as if we supposed we had no past ("Truth or consequences," *Christian Century* 118:16 [May 16, 2001]: 23). For a fascinating argument that we are more the product of our parents' intentions and omissions than they themselves are, and that our own acts and ideas are more likely to bear fruit in others than in ourselves, see Eugen Rosenstock-Huessy, *The Christian Future or The Modern Mind Outrun* (New York: Scribner's, 1946), pp. 221-23. He asserts that our freedom is given us not for ourselves but for others, for the race.

65. The formulations of H. Wheeler Robinson (an early work is *Corporate Personality in Ancient Israel* [Philadelphia: Fortress, 1964]; articles originally published in German, 1936, 1937) have particularly come in for criticism; but note Walter Wink's much later observation of the shifting back and forth from singular to plural forms of "you" in Rev. 2 and 3, with a preponderance of the singular: "It is the *angel* who is held accountable for the behavior of each of the congregations, and yet the congregation is virtually indistinguishable from the angel" (*Unmasking the Powers* [Philadelphia: Fortress, 1986], p. 71; see also p. 192 n. 7). Robinson believed and explicitly says that the contrast of Adam and Christ in 1 Cor. 15:22 "draws all its cogency from the conception of corporate personality" (*Corporate Personality*, p. 12).

(Exod. 13:16). New Testament imagery of the church is likewise corporate: consider the Body of Christ, or the spiritual house constructed of living stones, to take just two examples. Images of this kind work strongly against visions of strictly individual self-fulfillment or even simply individual responsibility and freedom, hard as that may be to stomach for those raised with the mantra that they must be motivated just by what is right for them.

Images of solidarity in grace bother us less, though, than those of solidarity in sin. What do we say about God "punishing children for the iniquity of parents, to the third and the fourth generation of those who reject [him]" (Exod. 20:5; see also Jer. 32:18, etc.: examples can be greatly multiplied); or destroying the whole family of Achan, including infants and sucklings, because Achan had transgressed the Law, and hence "Israel has sinned" (Josh. 7)? The psalmist prayed to the LORD, "Do not remember against us the iniquities of our ancestors" (Ps. 79:8). Or what about Jesus' words to the Scribes and Pharisees, laying upon them "all the righteous blood shed on earth, from the blood of righteous Abel to the blood of Zechariah son of Barachiah, whom you murdered between the sanctuary and the altar" (Matt. 23:35)? How do we then also affirm Ezekiel 18:1-4, which explicitly sets aside the saying about the children's teeth being set on edge because the parents have sinned, and instead insists, "it is only the person who sins that shall die"?

It would seem that we need, first, not only to judge Scripture by Scripture and acknowledge that general acceptance of a principle does not necessarily entail accepting every aspect of every instance of the principle; but also, second, to acknowledge soberly that our own involvement in sin is far deeper than we generally admit. With respect to the first point, we might note both that those weighted with the sins of others have in fact very usually sinned in their own persons; and that when they have not, as in the special case of infants, both texts like Ezekiel 18 and the words of Jesus in the New Testament about the kingdom being given to little children (Matt. 19:14; Mark 10:14; Luke 18:16) should be taken as decisive (decisive, that is, against charging the infant children of sinners with their parents' guilt). For instance, Israel is told way back in Deuteronomy 25:17-19 that when she is given rest from her enemies, she shall requite Amalek for deeds Amalek committed when Israel was journeying out of Egypt. Only in another generation is this commandment carried out, against Amalek in the person of Agag, whose *own* sword "has made women childless" (1 Sam. 15; such was also the case of the Scribes and Pharisees Jesus condemned; see also Jer. 16:11-12: "It is because your ancestors have forsaken me, says the LORD, and have gone after other gods and have served and worshiped them, and have forsaken me and have not kept my law; *and because you have behaved worse than your ancestors*" [emphasis added]; similarly, Lev. 26:40; Lam. 5:7, 16). And whereas Revelation 18:6 alludes to Psalm 137:8, it does not continue the allusion to include verse 9, which calls those happy who dash the enemy's little ones against the rock. The doctrine of solidarity in sin ought not to be understood fatalistically, that is, so as to make anyone assume that she bears no personal responsibility but is simply the pawn of her ancestors' choices.

With regard to the second point, remember that an excessive individualism is a fault no less serious than fatalism; and the nature of both fatalism and individualism as sins can be demonstrated by the ease with which we swing from one to the other, depending on which shows the greatest promise for getting us off the hook. Young people who cheat on exams argue not only that "everyone does it," but that pressures put upon them to get into a good college really demand that they do it. They are perfectly moral people; it's the system that is bad.[66] If, however, African-Americans or Japanese-Americans ask for reparations for years of slavery or internment, those who would have to pay (and who, not so incidentally, have benefited in many indirect ways from the labors of these people) argue that they were not present — probably not even born yet — when any of these things took place, so why should anyone lay responsibility on them? We have a very keen sense of what is "fair" when we are personally involved; and we generally manage to perceive anything that would be costly to us as unfair by definition. To put it another way, we tend to be highly individualistic with respect to our supposed "rights," and quite group-oriented with respect to (not!) taking personal responsibility. The exact opposite would be more godly.

Sometimes these sinful predilections are in fact overcome in moving ways (which shows the importance of our responsible agency). In

66. A recent high school graduate argued in exactly these terms on a National Public Radio broadcast in May of 2001.

the time of Nehemiah, the Israelites gathered and confessed both their own sins and the iniquities of their ancestors (Neh. 9:2). In more recent times, surviving leaders of Germany's Confessing Church spoke in their famous "Stuttgart Declaration of Guilt" of 1945 of "solidarity in guilt" and accused themselves of inadequacy in their resistance to Nazism, despite all of their efforts.[67] Or take the more mundane example of the editors of a student newspaper in Canada who decided against publishing athletic news because they saw glorification of athletes in the media as contributing to scandals in athletics and to making university sports into big business: they saw themselves as sharing the guilt, that is.[68]

More common, though, is the way sinful predilections lead to the good intentions of a person being subverted or manipulated by others. Consider the striking paragraph in *War and Peace* where the young count Pierre's plan to ease the lot of his serfs is seen by his cleverer stewards as simply giving insight into how they could maneuver him for their own ends.[69] Both acceptance of community responsibility for evil and frustration in the pursuit of good, however, show that we cannot live in a fallen world without being entangled in evil. To deny that entanglement involves either extreme naïveté or a reprehensible hardening of the conscience.

Right use of the doctrine of solidarity in sin, then, entails seriousness about our interrelatedness and firmness about our hope. We have insisted all along that our humanity is constituted through relationship with God and neighbor. If our awareness of our own sin leads us to further knowledge of our kinship with all who have sinned, and if that knowledge increases rather than decreases our sense of the scope of our personal responsibility, we will have taken steps in the right direction. In the end, though, our power to see our entanglement in and

---

67. Clyde L. Manschreck, ed., *A History of Christianity* (Englewood Cliffs, NJ: Prentice-Hall, 1964), pp. 516, 532-33. Not until 1990 did the government of East Germany (its first democratic government) express "sorrow and shame" and ask forgiveness for the Holocaust; but it did finally do so (Tamara Jones and Tyler Marshall, "E. Germany Takes Holocaust Blame," *Los Angeles Times,* April 13, 1990, Part I, p. 1+).

68. Noted by D. D. Williams, *Spirit and the Forms of Love* (New York: Harper & Row, 1968), p. 152.

69. Tolstoy, *War and Peace, Great Books,* vol. 51 (Chicago: Encyclopaedia Britannica, 1952), p. 211.

responsibility for the world's sin will be no greater than the robustness of our confidence in God's promise of new life in Christ.[70] And it is to a very robust hope that Paul points us in Rom. 5:12-19, given by One who, despite his own sinlessness, stands with us and for us in our sin.

70. Thus, the student who garbled a response to an exam question which asked her to write out the Apostles' Creed, by stating that she believed in "the communion of sins and the forgiveness of the saints," said something true and important in spite of herself!

10

Civil Righteousness

The modern reader, living in a pluralistic world and exposed both to the failings of Christians and to the moral praiseworthiness of actions of many non-Christians, is likely to object sharply that the whole foregoing argument flies in the face of both experience and charity. Fair-minded observers would be hard-pressed to conclude either that Christians excel others in general righteousness, or that Buddhists or Muslims or Hindus or atheistic humanists do not sometimes act in ways that a Christian might be proud to emulate. Is there not a sort of churlishness, a sort of lack of gratitude — a big sin for a Reformed theologian! — in the ideas of radical depravity and moral inability? And is not this churlishness made the more reprehensible in that it impugns the extraordinary nobility of others while claiming to cover the lack of nobility of every ordinary Christian with the "alien righteousness" of Christ?

To this complaint, we should respond first of all by acknowledging with thanksgiving every manifestation of genuine nobility or moral excellence, whether by exceptional individuals (Gandhi, Socrates, Plato, Marcus Aurelius . . .), humanitarian organizations (Amnesty International; the International Red Cross . . .), or the anonymous, unbelieving neighbor next door who selflessly, patiently, and cheerfully cares for disabled and demented parents. To dismiss such achievements as "splendid vices," insofar as they are the works of unbelievers, strikes us as deeply unjust.[1]

---

1. The sentiment that the virtues of the heathen are but splendid vices is often, and

As a matter of fact, the instincts of some of the early church Fathers went much in the other direction. Justin Martyr, for instance, simply assumed that Moses was the earliest writer of all, and that a virtuous pagan like Plato must have gone down to Egypt and learned morality from Moses — neatly assimilating pagan achievements into the fold of God's covenant people.[2] He, like Eusebius later, in a move that fore-shadows Rahner's "anonymous Christians," claimed that the noble people of earlier ages were Christians, even if they did not know it.[3] That such moves will not work today is too obvious for comment, not least because many people of other faiths or of no faith strenuously ob-ject to being called Christians, even if the one so labeling them intends only a compliment. (Such moves also presume that Christians are in general more characterized by moral excellence than others are, which is unfortunately difficult to demonstrate, at least in our day.) The point, however, is that these Fathers did not find it easy to dismiss the virtues of pagans. Even Augustine entertained the thought that God might have an elect people among the heathen before Christian times, people who "lived according to God and pleased Him"; he cited in par-ticular the example of Job.[4] Clement more modestly affirmed simply that truths the ancient philosophers may have espoused came by di-vine inspiration.[5]

It would seem to be best to say, as the Reformed tradition generally has, that every sign of good in the world, human or natural, should be attributed to God's common grace.[6] As the familiar hymn puts it,

---

with considerable reason, attributed to Augustine, who made statements closely ap-proximating that one. Schaff, however, notes this idea "in this form and generality" is not to his knowledge to be found in Augustine's writings, and that it is a view Augustine himself could not consistently maintain (*History of the Christian Church*, 5th ed., 8 vols. [1910; Grand Rapids: Eerdmans, 1953]: 3:810; 842).

2. Justin Martyr, *Hortatory Address to the Greeks*, 20 (ANF, vol. 1).

3. Justin, *Apology* 1.46 (ANF, vol. 1); *Antiquity of Christianity*, 4.6 (NPNF, series 2, vol. 1).

4. Augustine, *City of God*, 18.47.

5. Clement, *Exhortation to the Heathen*, 6 (ANF, vol. 2).

6. John Murray defines common grace as "every favor of whatever kind or degree, falling short of salvation, which this undeserving and sin-cursed world enjoys at the hand of God" (*Collected Writings*, 4 vols. [Edinburgh: Banner of Truth Trust, 1977], 2:96). More warmly, Herman Bavinck: "There is thus a rich revelation of God even among the heathen — not only in nature but also in their heart and conscience, in their life and his-tory, among their statesmen and artists, their philosophers and reformers. There exists

This is my Father's world:
He shines in all that's fair.

(Babcock)[7]

The God who makes his rain to fall and his sun to shine on just and unjust alike and does not limit his love to those who love him (Matt. 5:43-48; Luke 6:32-35), the God who says that "the children of this age are more shrewd in dealing with their own generation than are the children of light" (Luke 16:8), has not distributed his gifts in a way that allows one to discern Christians from non-Christians by analyzing these gifts. The "good things" the rich man who wrongfully ignored Lazarus enjoyed were not *in themselves* bad things just because they were not eternal things (Luke 16:19-31). Much though it may surprise us, it may well be the case that even those gifts, and those favorable circumstances of birth and environment, that promote outward righteousness are not allocated in a way that favors Christians. Perhaps that is why, as Abraham Kuyper said, "the world goes better than expected and the church worse than expected."[8] That does not make the gifts any less from God or mean that they are not real blessings, but it does put their final worth in rather different perspective. We need, then, to find ways of affirming what is good without thereby making that good an ultimate one.

Outward works of righteousness make the world run better for ev-

---

no reason at all to denigrate or diminish this divine revelation" ("Common Grace," trans. R. C. Van Leeuwen, *Calvin Theological Journal* 24:1 [April 1989]: 41; translation of original address given in 1894). Calvin is clear enough on the substance here, though he seldom uses the actual term (see, for instance, *Institutes,* 2.2.12-17; 2.3.4). The Lutheran tradition has been closer to the Roman Catholic tradition in being willing to attribute civil righteousness (not understood to be saving righteousness, or to be continuous with saving righteousness) to free will, to that remaining excellence that human beings have as human (Augsburg Confession XVIII); the Arminian tradition has seen civil righteousness as continuous with saving righteousness.

7. Richard Mouw takes the second line as the title of his book dealing with common grace (Grand Rapids: Eerdmans, 2001). Keble's final line in the poem for the third Sunday in Lent is altogether similar: "There is no light but Thine: with Thee all beauty glows" (*Christian Year* [New York: Frederick A. Stokes, 1827], p. 115). The whole poem affirms common grace.

8. Quoted by John Riches, "Berkouwer on Common Grace," *Theology* 78:660 (June 1975): 304.

eryone: that is why we have laws to restrain outward unrighteousness. To suggest that they do not matter would undercut the whole basis of civil society. Scripture itself speaks often enough, and with a measure of approval, of the good works practiced by Christians and non-Christians alike (e.g., Luke 6:33; Rom. 2:14, 15; James 1:17; 1 Pet. 2:14). But even to label the works "outward" is to say that one is not probing motives or heart attitudes.[9] As a matter of fact, certain motives that are clearly sinful from a Christian perspective, like pride and love of human praise and the deep impulse toward self-justification, may prompt chaste and self-sacrificial behaviors that overcome the temptation to more outward sins, much to the benefit of the well-ordered society.[10]

True virtues require right motives as well as right actions if they are to count as virtues.[11] This affirmation may seem to set an unrealistically high standard. Note, however, that the more modest principle that what is bad in itself may yield some temporal good — even if it has some limited truth — is one that goes very sour very fast. Reason itself betrays us because it justifies whatever it sees as necessary to its ends. "In our time, for example, terrorism and torture are no longer primarily instruments of passion; they have become instruments of political rationality. . . . Furthermore, the empirical rationality of terrorism and torture has become so apparent that to question their use is to risk the accusation of irrationality."[12] Again, Oliver Thomson: "Most of the man-made suffering in the world has not been attributable to delinquents, criminals, deviants, or other people who rejected the moral norms of their societies, but to those who followed the norm very diligently, who were heroes of their own time, who had the intellectual power or authority to rationalise the cruelties they were committing."[13] Polanyi likewise notes that

9. Recall the discussion above of sins and crimes (pp. 110-12): something may be a sin without it being subject to the condemnation of the civil law, or be illegal without being a sin.

10. See, for instance, Augustine's remarks in *On Marriage and Concupiscence*, 4; as well as his harsh analysis of the Roman love for glory as the motivator for Roman virtue, of which he concludes that those who have sought and received honor from human beings have received their reward, according to the Gospel principle (*City of God*, 5.13-15; cf. Matt. 6:2, 5).

11. See the discussion by T. H. Irwin, "Splendid Vices? Augustine for and Against Pagan Virtues," *Medieval Philosophy and Theology* 8:2 (Fall 1999): 105-27.

12. George M. Kren and Leon Rappaport, *The Holocaust and the Crisis of Human Behavior* (New York: Holmes and Meier, 1980), p. 140.

13. *A History of Sin* (New York: Barnes & Noble, 1993), p. 258.

civic culture rests upon coercion — a fact that is sometimes masked by shared convictions and by moral rhetoric, but that will be revealed soon enough under pressure.[14] Thus, if civil order becomes the all-important value, disaster follows close behind as far as other human values are concerned. This whole convoluted situation shows the complexity of the relationship of Christ and culture generally: affirm too little, and one impugns God's creation and gifts; affirm too much, and one is consumed, literally or figuratively, by temporal goals.

In any case, the civil magistrate and the courts do not concern themselves with the inner life of an individual unless that person has committed, or is suspected of having committed, an overt act against the laws of the society. Thus, if a man has a motive for wishing his wife dead, that fact may lend credence to the charge that he killed her; but he could also be condemned for the murder wholly apart from establishment of a motive if the evidence against him was sufficient. The law, however, would take no notice of the fact that this man hated his wife if the hatred found no outward expression. Similarly, when immediately following the World Trade Center attacks, a young man on the New York streets shouted that the United States was getting what it deserved, he was momentarily apprehended and isolated, and his backpack was searched. Then, as he had broken no laws, he was immediately — and in our view rightly — released. Jesus, by contrast, in the Sermon on the Mount, spoke of inner attitudes of anger or lust themselves being subject to judgment: only the one who loves God with heart, soul, mind, and strength, and her neighbor as herself, truly meets the requirement of the law (Matt. 22:37-39; Mark 12:30-31).[15] And who could possibly say that she has achieved *that* standard?

This distinction between the depth dimension and the visible act is key to the judgment that all the acts of the unredeemed are sinful (and so are all the acts of the redeemed, this side of the eschaton). Thus, in

---

14. See the whole illumining discussion in chapter 7, "Conviviality," in his *Personal Knowledge*.

15. Similarly enough, though of course from a different perspective, Kant: "the mode of thought which sets down the absence of such vice as being conformity of the *disposition* to the law of duty (as being virtue) — since in this case no attention whatever is paid to the motivating forces in the maxim but only to the observance of the letter of the law — itself deserves to be called a radical perversity in the human heart" (*Religion within the Limits of Reason Alone*, p. 33; see also pp. 42-43).

response to a courteous letter from Pelagius early in their conflict, Augustine wrote, "Pray for me that God may really make me that which you already take me to be."[16] Altogether similarly, Luther remarked, "In the eyes of the world I may be pious and do all that I should — but in God's sight it is nothing but sin."[17] Knowing their own hearts, Augustine and Luther knew their hidden faults. Surely we know at least something of our own as well, if we are honest. Not, perhaps, that there is no instance in which we do freely and spontaneously what the law requires: it may be that a person may act with utterly unpremeditated courage and selflessness in a moment of crisis. But then there is the aftermath, with the lurking desire for gratitude, for appreciation, for recognition. . . . Pride — that great epitome of sin — sneaks in, if not in the initial impulse, then all too soon in the outcome.[18] It would be safe to assume that the problem is universal.[19]

We do not have to peer into the private lives of others to draw the conclusion that clay feet cripple us all. Indeed, it can seem petty and ungrateful to snoop out the private failings of the great. We would do better to emulate their accomplishments than to seek to cheapen them. Yet, we should not be surprised when failings present themselves. Gibbon, for instance, in his great volumes, gives example after example of noble Romans acting in the most admirable ways, who nonetheless also manifested striking lapses; Augustine likewise details ways in which the allegedly "noble heathen" fell short.[20] Some have even suggested that

16. Quoted by Schaff, *History of the Christian Church*, 3:792.

17. Quoted by Heim, *Jesus the World's Perfecter* (Philadelphia: Muhlenberg, 1961), p. 42.

18. In Milton's "Samson Agonistes," Samson's father Manoa cautions him against the temptation to refuse mercy and be "over-just, and self-displeas'd/For self-offence, more then for God offended" (ll. 514-15). Or, as Bavinck put it, "There is nothing more difficult for man than to be saved by grace and to live on gifts. It is this which far transcends the reason, the power, and the nature of man" ("Common Grace," p. 59). "Haughty eyes and a proud heart — the lamp of the wicked — are sin," says Prov. 21:4: what the sinner takes for light, God counts darkness.

19. As Pascal said, "Vanity is so anchored in the heart of man that a soldier, soldier's servant, a cook, a porter brags, and wishes to have his admirers. Even philosophers wish for them. Those who write against it want to have the glory of having written well; and those who read it desire the glory of having read it. I who write this have perhaps this desire, and perhaps those who will read it" (*Pensées* #150; see also nos. 100, 147-153).

20. For just a couple of examples among many, note Gibbon on Belisarius (*Decline and Fall*, chap. 41) and Augustine on Cicero (*City of God*, 2.27).

the greater the individual, humanly speaking, the more likely he or she is to manifest great faults, which judgment, as we have noted above, corresponds strikingly to what one would anticipate if all of our faculties are indeed corrupted. The largeness of the power will manifest itself in large capacity for both good and evil. Something approximating this outcome on a national level could be seen in twentieth-century Germany, the home of unparalleled cultural and scientific achievement, and also of the unparalleled horror of the Holocaust. As secular writers on the Holocaust concluded, in a sobering paragraph,

> What remains is a central, deadening sense of despair over the human species. . . . Along with this despair there may also come a desperate new feeling of vulnerability attached to the fact that one *is* human. If one keeps at the Holocaust long enough, then sooner or later the ultimate personal truth begins to reveal itself: one knows, finally, that one might either do it, or be done to. If it could happen on such a massive scale elsewhere, then it can happen anywhere; it is all within the range of human possibility, and like it or not, Auschwitz expands the universe of consciousness no less than landings on the moon.[21]

Dig deep enough, and what one finds can produce nothing but darkest dismay. The Holocaust, and other disasters of the twentieth century, demonstrate beyond all possible doubt that human nature can break all restraints, and that the vast majority of "good people" will not only not prevail; they very often will not act at all, or even allow themselves to notice. Even the blindness of science to moral values may teach us that our "virtues" are fragile indeed against the real threats that face us.

None of this is to deny the less and more of the range of sins of both the Christian and the non-Christian. As we have said before, the differences are real enough, as long as we are thinking about actual effects in this life.[22] But as Brunner observed, when we distinguish varying degrees of virtue and vice, we are looking at the virtues and vices of sinners, redeemed or unredeemed as the case may be; we are not distinguishing between those who are sinners and those who are not.[23] It is

---

21. Kren and Rappaport, *The Holocaust and the Crisis of Human Behavior*, p. 126.
22. See above, "Degrees of Sin and of Culpability," pp. 137-43.
23. Brunner, *Creation and Redemption*, pp. 110-12.

not that the unbeliever necessarily lacks virtue: she may display a great deal more virtue than the believer. Rather, it is faith that she lacks; and "without faith it is impossible to please God" (Heb. 11:6); "whatever does not proceed from faith is sin" (Rom. 14:23).[24] In a striking passage in one of his sermons, John Wesley wrote,

> A man may be of a compassionate and a benevolent temper; he may be affable, courteous, generous, friendly; he may have some degree of meekness, patience, temperance, and of many other moral virtues. He may feel many desires of shaking off all vice, and of attaining higher degrees of virtue. He may abstain from much evil; perhaps from all that is grossly contrary to justice, mercy, or truth. He may do much good, may feed the hungry, clothe the naked, relieve the widow and fatherless. He may attend public worship, use prayer in private, read many books of devotion; and yet, for all this, he may be a mere natural man, knowing neither himself nor God; equally a stranger to the spirit of fear and to that of love; having neither repented, nor believed the gospel. . . . Beware, then, thou who art called by the name of Christ, that thou come not short of the mark of thy high calling. Beware thou rest not, either in a natural state with too many that are accounted *good Christians;* or in a legal state, wherein those who are highly esteemed of men are generally content to live and die.[25]

The reason for that warning is not a narrow-minded exclusivism, but rather a sober analysis of what human beings are really like when one looks beneath the surface. The depth of sin means that "no one living is righteous" before God (Ps. 143:2); that "those who are in the flesh cannot please God" (Rom. 8:8); that "all our righteous deeds are like a filthy cloth" (Isa. 64:6). It is the flip side of the coin on the obverse of which is written the much-quoted and crucial truth that faith without works is dead; this flip side means that works not done out of whole-souled love for God and trust in him continue to be sinful works at

---

24. This point echoes Kierkegaard's famous definition, that "the opposite of sin is not virtue but faith," which he offers in specific connection to Rom. 14:23 (*Fear and Trembling* and *Sickness Unto Death,* trans. Walter Lowrie [Garden City, NY: Doubleday, 1954], p. 213).

25. John Wesley, "The Spirit of Bondage and of Adoption," *Works,* vol. 5 (Master Christian Library, version 6 CD from Ages Digital Library, 1998).

bottom, even though they may contribute positively to our common life.

To say anything else is to deny all that has gone before and finally to imply that a Savior is, after all, a sort of luxury, or an aid for those who are unfortunately less competent or more compromised than others, rather than an absolute necessity for all humankind. If the heroes and moral athletes could make it on their own, Nietzsche's claim that Christianity is a sort of "slave religion," an expedient for the weak who are taking revenge upon the strong, would indeed have merit. But it was not from a position of felt moral failure that Paul proclaimed that he counted all of his past achievements rubbish for the sake of being found in Christ; it was rather from the pinnacle of Israelite heritage and personal achievement (Phil. 3:2-11). From that place of seeming triumph, he rejected all claims he might bring on the grounds of his own righteousness — not, note, because he counted it hypocritical, but because encountering Christ revealed to him that it was not enough.[26] Even virtue is dangerous if it masks the need for redemption. This testimony of one who *succeeded* by all ordinary criteria is critical, not least because the better we discern our own moral failures, the more our feelings of shame and our sense of the need to be just to those we see as more righteous than we are may lead us astray theologically. Why should we be saved and not they, we may cry? But the answer involves all the difference between a sinner's rush of gratitude toward Another and her making of a personal moral claim — which, for sinful and fallen creatures, is all the difference between heaven and hell.

---

26. Even the distinction between the inner and the outer may deceive: moral sincerity is an "inner" quality, but it is not the same thing as faith in Jesus Christ. Jonathan Edwards in particular decries the tendency to assume that if a person is morally sincere, then surely all must be well ("An Humble Inquiry into the Rules of the Word of God, Concerning the Qualifications Requisite to a Full Communion in the Visible Christian Church," in *Works of President Edwards,* 4 vols. [New York: Jonathan Leavitt and John F. Trow; Boston: Crocker and Brewster; Philadelphia: Geo. S. Appleton, 1843], vol. 1, pp. 83-192, passim) — a point we do well to heed in a contemporary society where we seem to care about "authenticity" and "sincerity" in others more than we care about truth and righteousness. We seem to find ourselves in something of an anomalous situation: we may continue to admire heroes, and yet we do not wish to face any outward constraints, even by those values that might promote heroism. This problem, needless to say, is an entirely different one than that posed by observing that those who do not share our faith may sometimes appear to embody our values better than we do ourselves; but it may be at least as characteristic of our day.

I'd Rather Do It Myself

A Sermon Preached by Marguerite Shuster
at La Verne Heights Presbyterian Church, La Verne, California
Lord's Day, August 26, 2001

Beware of the dogs, beware of the evil workers, beware of those who mu-
tilate the flesh! For it is we who are the circumcision, who worship in the
Spirit of God and boast in Christ Jesus and have no confidence in the
flesh — even though I, too, have reason for confidence in the flesh. If any-
one else has reason to be confident in the flesh, I have more: circumcised
on the eighth day, a member of the people of Israel, of the tribe of
Benjamin, a Hebrew born of Hebrews; as to the law, a Pharisee; as to
zeal, a persecutor of the church; as to righteousness under the law, blame-
less. Yet whatever gains I had, these I have come to regard as loss because
of Christ. More than that, I regard everything as loss because of the sur-
passing value of knowing Christ Jesus my Lord. For his sake I have suf-
fered the loss of all things, and I regard them as rubbish, in order that I
may gain Christ and be found in him, not having a righteousness of my
own that comes from the law, but one that comes through faith in Christ,
the righteousness from God based on faith. I want to know Christ and the
power of his resurrection and the sharing of his sufferings by becoming
like him in his death, if somehow I may attain the resurrection from the
dead.

PHILIPPIANS 3:2-11 (NRSV)

"I'd rather do it myself!": parents may hear those words with a certain
measure of trepidation, recalling, say, the devastating impact on the
crystal goblets the last time the little darling wanted to "help" set the
table for guests. Kids are always assuming that they can do things that
are as a matter of fact beyond their ability, and their capacity for making messes is virtually inexhaustible. In the end, though, good parents
are glad that they at least want to try. That's how they learn, parents in-

tone. Imagine if they just sat on their hands? Besides, it's not news that this is an individualistic and achievement-oriented society. We admire those who struggle until they succeed, especially if they do it "on their own" in the face of obstacles. Those people inspire us, help us to believe that we just might be able to do the same. And if we don't have immediate access to the right set of examples, a bumper crop of inspirational literature and motivational speakers is waiting to help us out: a recent *Los Angeles Times* article says that approximately 50,000 people are seeking to enter the motivational speaking field, encouraged by the insatiable appetite for their wares.[1] "You can do it!" "You can do it!" "You can do it!" The thought that maybe we *can't* do it is a sort of heresy.

This enthusiasm for achievement can even spill over into the moral arena, despite the well-grounded observation that contemporary society is not exactly a hotbed of virtue. Still, when William Bennett wrote a book on virtues a few years ago, it made the *New York Times* bestseller list. That means, as one reviewer put it, that "a lot of supposedly amoral Americans have been willing to put down over $25.00 for 800 pages of improving literature."[2] Something in us responds to the thought of cultivating a better character, and we are ready to pay for insight into how to do it. If a Christian were to ask how all of this fits in with her faith, though, as contrasted with other faiths or no faith at all — what any of this interest in moral self-improvement has to do with Christianity — she is likely to be a bit puzzled. Christians are supposed to be nice, moral, people, right? Isn't that what Christianity is about? Lots of people seem to assume so. And yet. . . . Something seems wrong here.

One painfully obvious part of the trouble is, of course, that lots of studies show that those who identify themselves as Christians do not on the average do noticeably better than anyone else on almost any measure of virtue or morality we might wish to consider. Let's not kid ourselves: we don't shine on the moral or ethical achievement charts. Furthermore, when we look candidly at adherents of other faiths, or at certain pagans of other ages — the Hindu Gandhi, the pagan Greek

1. Bonnie Harris, "'I *Am* the Next Big Thing,'" *Los Angeles Times* (April 18, 2001), p. A1+.

2. Jean Porter, "The Moral Life according to William Bennett," *Christian Century* 111:27 (October 5, 1994): 896.

philosopher Socrates, the pagan Roman emperor Marcus Aurelius, to take just a few striking examples — we see qualities of life and character to which any Christian might rightly aspire. Closer to home, I imagine most of us could name adherents of other faiths, or of no faith at all, who put us to shame: they simply seem to be better people than we are — more generous, more kindly, more reliable, more patient. Somehow, it appears, they have "done it themselves" — out of idealism and effort, or however, they have achieved something admirable. It would be blind and ungrateful of us to refuse to admire it. These people may be exceptions — that's why we pick them out as examples — but isn't it exceptions that put our casual assumptions to the test? And especially given our own really shocking failures, aren't all of these "exceptions" a very considerable challenge to the supposed superiority of Christianity?

All of this not only raises the question of what Christianity has to offer the virtuous non-Christian; it also makes many folks anxious about Christian claims in a deeper sense: how dare we even hint that people who are plainly better people than we are, are lost without Christ, whereas we are saved? Isn't it supremely presumptuous for us to deny that they have found a way that works for them? And we can hardly be surprised that non-Christians see Christians as astonishingly arrogant to suggest that they have access to God that others do not. Talking that way is not only not nice; it doesn't even sound very plausible. It's a big problem — a problem that comes up in almost any serious conversation about the status of different religions and their adequacy as ways to God. Or, if you don't want to generalize to the status and adequacy of other religions as such, what about the fate of the individual high-achiever: surely provision is made for such folks?

Like most tough problems, this one is not exactly new. Paul gets at it by talking about his own experience as an observant Jew, as a non-Christian. He lists his own qualifications, that include both those he had by heritage and those he attained by his own moral effort: "if anyone else has reason to be confident in the flesh, I have more: circumcised on the eighth day, a member of the people of Israel, of the tribe of Benjamin, a Hebrew born of Hebrews; as to the law, a Pharisee; as to zeal, a persecutor of the church; as to righteousness under the law, blameless" (Phil. 3:3b-6). When he speaks here of confidence in the "flesh," he doesn't mean circumcision alone, taken as a sign in one's physical body of one's religious identity, but rather he means every-

thing a human being can achieve on his own at his highest and best —
that's the broader sense of "flesh" as it is used here. About all of that,
Paul makes the astonishing claim that he was "blameless": not only did
he do all that was positively required, but also he did not omit anything
the Law enjoined.

In modern American dress, it might sound something like this (you
will note that I am joining church and state together, since Judaism
had and has both religious and political aspects): "Feel good about myself? Of course, and with reason! I was baptized at exactly the right
time and reared by believing parents. They were not just Americans, but
people whose ancestors came over on the Mayflower and who have
been faithful to the most cherished American ideals of liberty and justice from the very beginning. I not only embraced these ideals myself,
but I struggled for them: I joined the Marines — the toughest, most
elite form of service — and zealously fought against those who threatened the American dream. I left nothing undone in service to God and
country; indeed, I went above and beyond the call of duty in every area
of life. What more could anyone possibly ask?"

Now imagine the American version of Paul continuing, "I've come
to see it all as loss." *Loss.* Not neutral, not just inadequate, but *loss.* The
American heritage, the religious background and training, the patri-
otic war effort, the struggle to be a sort of saint — all of it, lumped together as loss. *Worse than nothing* — that's what *loss* is. If you are not feeling objections rise up, I don't think you've gotten the point. What Paul
says is shocking. How could everything many of us hold most dear be
worse — worse! — than nothing at all?

Paul answers that it is worse than nothing at all because it is an alternative to gaining Christ, to belonging to him, to being found in him.
Christ's righteousness is not something we can add to our own, to im-
prove it a little or to help it along, to make what is already good better.
No; it is a flat alternative. If I cling to my own righteousness, insist
upon doing it myself, I shut myself off from Christ's righteousness.
Unreasonable? Perhaps, but Jesus, of course, spoke in much the same
way. One must sell all to gain the pearl of great price or to buy the field
with the wonderful treasure. One must scrap all of one's old ideas
about righteousness, for tax collectors and sinners, Jesus said, would
enter the kingdom of God before the "good people" of his day. It made
people plenty mad then, too. Make no mistake about it: Paul, following

Jesus quite precisely, is turning everything we think we know on its head, calling our most cherished achievements "refuse" (for which he uses a potentially vulgar and unpleasant word, in case we are at risk of missing the point). You'd rather do it yourself? Warning! The path may be attractive and the company well-regarded and the achievements satisfying in their way, but it all leads, well, nowhere or worse in the end. Achievement apart from Christ does not count. *Ultimately*, that is.

It's a terribly touchy point. Wouldn't you prefer, right now, that your neighbor be a pagan philanthropist rather than a Mafia hit man? Face it: wouldn't you rather your neighbor be a pagan philanthropist of high ideals and unimpeachable character, than be like a lot of Christians you know? In our common life together, a virtuous character, however achieved, is a long way from being "refuse." It counts a lot. And as a matter of fact, theologians have always granted that point, claiming that whatever we find in our world that is good and helpful and true is a manifestation of what they have called "common grace," that gift of God's goodness found in all he has made. They have even insisted that God positively requires virtuous behavior in the public arena. It is not a bad thing to thank God for the human decency of your non-Christian neighbor!

But — and it is a huge BUT — that human decency which we rightly affirm and for which we rightly thank God is not the same thing as salvation, and that is Paul's point. It's not a matter of two moral standards, one higher than the other: Paul makes clear that he as a Pharisee reached the top as far as human moral achievement is concerned. But that is not enough. The righteousness that depends on Christ cannot be adequately defined in external moral terms, and that tends to confuse us. It rather has to do with the inside, with the depths of our hearts and how they are oriented. It's bigger, not smaller, than our ordinary ideas of righteousness; and we trust that that moral righteousness where we continue to fail so miserably will indeed at last be fully realized, when sin is finally defeated. But the point is, no moral achievement on human terms, no matter how exceptional, can change the heart and provide either a vital relationship to Christ or the hope of resurrection, and that's why Paul calls such achievement *refuse*. Heroic examples can, in fact, be a fatal temptation to those of us who, in our heart of hearts, really would prefer to be seen as noble than to admit that we desperately need to be saved. I'm reminded of the

"Herman" cartoon where his wife says to Herman, sitting at his type-writer, "Writing your autobiography! Who's it about?" Most of us would sort of like our autobiographies to be about us; but the Christian's autobiography is fundamentally about Christ.

You see, when by a supreme effort we conquer those impulses of our lower nature that do not fit our image of who we should be, pride, that great fountainhead of sin, almost inevitably creeps in, and that is fatal. The Jews themselves knew that. Isaiah, in a familiar line from our Old Testament lesson, spoke of all of our righteous deeds as like filthy rags (64:6). And a story from one strand of the Jewish tradition tells of a preacher who was giving detailed instructions to two brothers on how to conduct themselves throughout the day, and how they should review the day before they went to sleep. He concluded, "And when a man calculates his hours and sees that he has not wasted a moment in idleness, when his heart beats high with pride, then — up in Heaven — they take all his good works, crush them into a ball, and hurl it down into the abyss."[3] It's not that the problem wasn't known; but how could it be avoided? We can't fix it ourselves, because we are the problem.

Molding ourselves after our own ideals always risks changing the outside without really dealing with the inner character, like the time Dennis the Menace proclaimed, while painting spots on poor Ruff, "We're playin' fireman, and Ruff's gonna be our Dalmatian!" Anyone who has a Dalmatian, as I do, knows that you do not achieve their special character by painting spots on some other kind of dog! It's the inside as much as the outside that makes a real Dalmatian. Anyone who knows her own heart knows that her best motives are mixed and her best acts are at least subtly self-interested and corrupt: the inside does not match outside. That is true of the saint and hero as well as of the more obvious sinner.

What is more, when we are busy making ourselves in our own image of what is required, we have also shut ourselves off from whatever God may have for us that others or even we ourselves do not in fact know about. Even our ideal image is too limited. Everyone knows that new circumstances and especially new relationships may reveal to us something we need to do or be that we never even imagined on our own.

3. Martin Buber, *Tales of the Hasidim: The Early Masters,* trans. Olga Marx (London: Thames and Hudson, 1956), p. 106.

You've had experiences like that, right, when meeting someone new shows you something entirely new about yourself? Shut up in ourselves, we'll never see it.

So, in a way that deals with these problems of pride and of hidden sin and of limited vision, Paul speaks *not* of how we can better remake ourselves by trying harder, but rather what he discovered out of his own astonishing experience of meeting Christ, of conversion. His new knowledge came not out of striving, but out of what happened to him and took him wholly by surprise. So now, he presents the goal of being found in Christ, of having a righteousness that is not his own — not made by his own efforts, out of his own understanding of the Law — but that comes through faith in Christ. It's a righteousness that provides for something absolutely new and unforeseen, so new and unforeseen and beyond his control that Paul speaks a bit tentatively even of his hope: "if somehow I may attain the resurrection from the dead," he says, not so much doubting Christ's promise as knowing that he cannot rely upon himself and have confidence in himself. We have trouble taking the whole idea in because we have been trained to be doers, and Paul speaks here of what can only be done for us. That's why, when near the beginning of *The Lion, the Witch and the Wardrobe*, Lucy wants to hurry up and go to rescue her friend Mr. Tumnus the faun, Mr. Beaver tells her, "'The quickest way you can help him is by going to meet Aslan, . . . once he's with us, then we can begin doing things.'"[4] Doing things matters, but they must be done in relationship with Christ. Go meet Christ first. None of what I am saying will make the least bit of sense if you have not had a life-changing encounter with Christ.

But even if we have, the image Paul gives us of what doing things in relationship with Christ entails is a long way from the daydreams of ourselves as heroes that we may have entertained as children. You know; the ones in which, overcoming all obstacles single-handedly, we do what no one else could have done, become the object of the admiration and adoration of all, and are rewarded with everything we always wanted — images that supremely feed our pride. Need I remark that Paul's life wasn't like that? Not only did he *regard* his past accomplishments as rubbish, but he says he actually suffered the loss of all things (recall his life as an itinerant, persecuted evangelist, where even the

4. C. S. Lewis, *The Lion, the Witch and the Wardrobe* (New York: Collier, 1970), p. 77.

churches he founded himself were all too often not only mired in conflicts but also on his case personally). His aspirations changed absolutely, so that he put desire for Christ's righteousness in the place of
his own. He linked even the longing to know the power of Christ's resurrection indissolubly to sharing his sufferings by becoming like him
in his death. The two cannot be separated. They are lumped together
using only one article in the original text. Resurrection power united to
suffering, together for a whole earthly lifetime: it's not the stuff that
looks like great material for motivational speakers. Would you care to
write advertising copy for that agenda? Not much good news here for
heroes.

But you know what? There's the best news in the world here for anyone who is not a hero, or for heroes who even dimly perceive that they
are not exactly as they appear to be on the outside, as sometimes hits
most of us when we are alone.

Oh, there are times, in our youth, in our strength, when we are ex-
ulting in the height of our powers and when the future spreads out vast
with promise, that we indeed want to do it all ourselves, take credit for
it, enjoy the excellence of what we have gained by our own grit and idealism. But as someone said in a *Newsweek* article of some years ago,
"Celebration of the self, after all, is a game young people play; it is no
way to deal with decline and death."[5] When we are old, or tired, or defeated, and have the bitter taste of our own helplessness lingering in
our mouth, and see little that does not smell of death or futility in
front of us, the thought that the way of true life has to do with the
power of resurrection and with the present sharing of Christ's sufferings is the best news in the world. Do you identify with one who turns
her ankle before reaching the first plateau on the climb up the moral
mountain? Paul's word is the best news in the world for you. Or do you
identify with Paul himself, who reached the very peak of accomplishment and, looking down, saw nothing but the other side of the mountain? It's the best news in the world for you, too. Paul gives us testimony from the top, the testimony not of an underdog, not of a
"spoiler" jealous of the attainments of others, but of one who has
"made it"; and we can trust his conclusion: "Whatever gains I had,

5. Kenneth Woodward et al., "A Time to Seek," *Newsweek* 116:25 (December 17, 1990):
56.

these I have come to regard as loss because of Christ. More than that, I regard everything as loss because of the surpassing value of knowing Christ Jesus my Lord. For his sake I have suffered the loss of all things, and I regard them as rubbish, in order that I may gain Christ and be found in him, not having a righteousness of my own that comes from the law, but one that comes through faith in Christ, the righteousness from God based on faith. I want to know Christ and the power of his resurrection and the sharing of his sufferings by becoming like him in his death, if somehow I may attain the resurrection from the dead" (Phil 3:7-11).

That, friends, is the Christian hope and the Christian promise to all who will come to Christ and put Christ first: a righteousness that comes from God through faith in Christ, and resurrection power now and in the future. Don't settle for trying to do *that* yourself.

Physical Death as Existential Reality

Death as Curse and Mystery

Because of the overwhelming impact of death on human experience, we cannot do justice to a discussion of the effects of the Fall without taking up directly the subject of death as existential reality.[1] Indeed, it serves as a sort of case study of the effects of the Fall. The first thing we must say about it is that death confronts us as both mystery[2] and curse,[3] as something we cannot comprehend and as something that arouses in us a deep sense of *wrongness:* even the ex-

---

1. That death has a large place in theology appears in that the topic belongs in certain aspects to the loci of Atonement and of eschatology. At this stage, our focus is on elaborating the impact of death as a physical fact.

2. This mystery parallels the mystery of life (see *Who We Are,* pp. 376-79): while we can describe certain chemical and biological characteristics of each, yet they both escape purely materialistic categories. As Brunner puts it, "The belief that science, biology, physiology, neurology, have given us a knowledge of what death is, so that talk of the mystery of death merely rests upon ignorance, is itself the product of a superstition. Materialism is not science, but metaphysics" (*The Christian Doctrine of the Church, Faith, and the Consummation,* p. 382). Insofar as life is the gift of God, separation from life is not purely "natural." That sin separates humankind from God and, consequently, from life, makes sense in the biblical context.

3. Very early (Delumeau notes works of Theophilus of Antioch and of Irenaeus [*History of Paradise,* pp. 232-33]), death was construed as a mercy, instituted that sin might not be immortal. Be that as it may at the theoretical level, the theory operates at a level of abstraction far removed from our more visceral responses.

pected death that ends a long life or the anticipated death that ends a long suffering — the deaths we are most likely to see as "natural" or "merciful" — yet come, despite the best efforts of reason, as a sort of surprise and assault to many of those most closely affected by them. Even when they provide relief, they are yet mourned rather than celebrated. This reaction, we believe, results not from a stubborn bit of psychopathology or the programming of an evolution that rewards creatures that resist death; it rather represents a primitive knowledge that death is evil, the result of sin. "You are dust, and to dust you shall return" (Gen. 3:19), we have said, is not a mere law of nature like "water flows downhill"; it is a threat. "The wages of sin is death" (Rom. 6:23). That wrenching reality of the threat comes home all the more clearly when the one who has died is a lover, a friend in her prime, or, most especially, a child.

One recalls the torment of Luther when his beloved daughter lay dying, and he thought he should be willing freely to relinquish her to God but could not. He said, "I love her very much; if my flesh is so strong, what can my spirit do? God has given no bishop so great a gift in a thousand years as he has given me in her. I am angry with myself that I cannot rejoice in heart and be thankful as I ought."[4] One feels that his heart spoke more truly than his head to the human realities. Or take Augustine's description of his reaction to the death of a dear friend: "At this grief my heart was utterly darkened; and whatever I beheld was death. My native country was a torment to me, and my father's house a strange unhappiness; and whatever I had shared with him, wanting him, became a distracting torture. Mine eyes sought him everywhere, but he was not granted them; and I hated all places, for that they had not him; nor could they now tell me, 'he is coming,' as when he was alive and absent. I became a great riddle to myself."[5] Surely everyone who has grieved deeply recognizes these sentiments and can only acknowledge that all of life would be cheapened beyond recognition were death suddenly to be experienced as nothing more grievous than the disposal of a few fingernail clippings. That Christians do not grieve "as those who have no hope" (1 Thess. 4:13) does not

4. Quoted in *A History of Christianity,* ed. Clyde L. Manschreck (Englewood Cliffs, NJ: Prentice-Hall, 1964), p. 52.
5. Augustine, *Confessions* 4.9.

mean that they do not grieve. (We insist upon that judgment despite Augustine's view that his grief was inordinate [his friend's death took place before Augustine's conversion].)

Death is an enemy, indeed the last enemy (1 Cor. 15:26; Rev. 20:14). The New Testament does not neutralize it by interpreting it as a natural process.[6] Refusal of that knowledge leads to the vacuous ideal of those who "propose to reconcile death with happiness. Death must simply become the discreet but dignified exit of a peaceful person from a helpful society that is not torn, not even overly upset by the idea of a biological transition without significance, without pain or suffering, and ultimately without fear."[7] Such a vision condemns itself. Far more compelling are the visceral reactions of biologist and physician Lewis Thomas, who reflects on the outrage and grief that well up when one sees even an animal dead on the highway, and further remarks: "At the very center of the problem is the naked cold deadness of one's own self, the only reality in nature of which we can have absolute certainty, and it is unmentionable, unthinkable."[8]

Death Avoided

Death is certain and death is unthinkable. Humans are in the position, says Pascal, of people in chains, all condemned to death, who each day see certain of their number killed and must await their turn without hope of reprieve.[9] Under these circumstances, it is hardly surprising both that there should be numerous attempts to avoid facing this reality and that such attempts should take on a somewhat forced and unconvincing quality. Plain words about death have been resisted at least as assiduously as were plain words about sex in Victorian days: indeed,

---

6. Rudolf Bultmann, "θάνατος, κτλ," *TDNT*, 3:7-25.

7. Philippe Ariès, *The Hour of Our Death*, trans. Helen Weaver (New York: Alfred A. Knopf, 1981), p. 614.

8. Lewis Thomas, *The Lives of a Cell: Notes of a Biology Watcher* (New York: Bantam, 1974), pp. 55, 113. However, it is Thomas's visceral reaction that we here credit, not his later (p. 116) conclusion that we shall need somehow to naturalize death and not suppose we can hide it — a conclusion much like that of the many who try to make scientific scrutiny go bail for theology and faith.

9. Pascal, *Pensées*, #199.

euphemisms like "pre-need memorial estate" (cemetery plot) and "loved one" (corpse) show rather more creativity than the substitution of, say, "limb" for "leg." More surprisingly, even the plain fact of death has been denied: in 1965 when Elisabeth Kübler-Ross was looking for dying persons to interview, the heads of the hospitals and clinics to whom she addressed herself protested, "Dying? But there are no dying here!" There could be no dying in a well-organized and respectable institution. They were mortally offended.[10] Assorted mental health professionals have brought such dishonesty and its negative effects on the terminally ill to our attention, so that we can no longer engage in it quite so naively. And yet the impulse toward denial is powerful and persists.

Death at a Distance

One of the most striking characteristics of the impact of death is how much that impact depends upon immediacy and individuality: we seem to be more personally affected by the death of a pet dog at close hand than by the death of thousands of people in a distant flood, more repulsed by the rat the cat just brought to a bloody end than by the blood-stained streets shown in a newscast of a war or riot. Partly, of course, it may be that mass death and disaster simply overwhelm our emotional ability to respond, and our intellectual sense of obligation falls prey to "compassion fatigue" in a world in which one catastrophe after another confronts us on the evening news. But partly, distance makes death seem unreal. Many pilots who drop bombs could not inflict the same injuries if they had to do so by hand, one by one, seeing clearly what they were doing. Many movie viewers who seem to have a taste for ever-increasingly violent and gory films would doubtless insist that they are not themselves violent and know what they are seeing is not "real" (though one suspects that movies and newscasts get blurred in the consciousness, given the commonal-

---

10. Ariès, *Hour of Our Death*, p. 589. Karl Rahner said that it is hope that allows the Christian not to conceal from herself "the comfortless absurdity of death" ("Ideas for a Theology of Death," in *Theological Investigations*, vol. 13, trans. David Bourke [New York: Seabury, 1975], p. 179).

ity of the medium, and that incessant exposure makes the death they depict seem in general illusory). In any case, distance means that there is nothing one *has* to do, not much that one *can* do. And what we do not immediately engage, we can allow to slip readily from consciousness.

Removal of individual death to the hospital, as has often been noted, likewise achieves this distancing effect; and it also removes the dying person from the context of her individual existence and places her in the midst of many others who are not, like the rest of us, simply going on with their lives. Death does not take place where we live. Death does not demand that we deal with it directly; indeed, we say to ourselves, we are not qualified to deal with it directly. With the best of conscious intentions, we conspire to allow it to take place behind our backs.[11]

Death Redefined or Defied

A more direct approach to death's terrors is to redefine or defy them. A very old method, expressed by Epicurus, for instance, is simply to derogate the terrors as foolish. For a long time one did not exist; for a short time one lives; then one does not exist again. Not to exist was not terrible in the first place; why should it be later?[12] But can one be certain that the second state parallels the first? As Hamlet put it, "To sleep, perchance to dream — ay, there's the rub."[13] Maybe death is nothingness, or as peaceful as sleep. But if there should be distressing dreams?

11. The possibility of distancing death is a modern one, not known on a large scale in days before weapons of mass destruction, mass media, and institutions — whether hospitals or hospices — that become defined as the usual, ordinary place to die. In Scripture, Old Testament and New, deaths that do not take place in battle or by murder or accident typically take place in the home, in the midst of life. However, while there may be certain psychological advantages to allowing death a measure of immediacy, death does not thereby turn into a friend. For a detailed analysis of changes in historical styles of relating to death — a history of changes that itself suggests the hypothesis that nothing quite "works" — see Ariès, *Hour of Our Death*.

12. D. J. Enright, ed., *The Oxford Book of Death* (Oxford: Oxford University Press, 1983), p. 8.

13. William Shakespeare, *Hamlet*, 1.2.

Or, perhaps death is an illusion (Christian Science)[14] or "the final stage of growth" (the title of a collection edited by Elisabeth Kübler-Ross). We go on after death, but just in a different way; and the new way will surely be better. Well, again, perhaps. Grateful as we should be to Kübler-Ross for seeking to understand and humanize the process of dying, there is something subtly coercive and, many will feel, emotionally false about the effort to make death simply natural; and the leap to defining it as "growth" rests not on science but on a highly speculative philosophical commitment (note that these — death as natural and death as growth — are positions with no necessary relationship to one another, nor did Kübler-Ross's eventual embracing of the latter position appear substantively to alter her understanding of the former).[15]

While acceptance might be the most rational response to an objective and neutral fact, it fits less well the characterization of death as judgment. Note how we respond to other effects of the Fall. We cannot eliminate pain in childbirth and weeds and distorted relationships between the sexes, but we do not generally advocate passivity before them, either. Although "natural" in the sense of being common to our condition, these elements of the curse remain enemies to be combatted. Thus, we resonate with the poet:

Do not go gentle into that good night;
Rage, rage against the dying of the light.[16]

Or again:

---

14. A position we take to be artificial and hollow, being more persuaded, *mutatis mutandis,* by the following limerick of unknown authorship:

There was a faith healer of Deal
Who said, "although pain isn't real,
When I sit on a pin,
And it punctures my skin,
I dislike what I fancy I feel."

15. See the discussion in Lucy Bregman, *Death in the Midst of Life: Perspectives on Death from Christianity and Depth Psychology* (Grand Rapids: Baker, 1992), chap. 2.

16. Dylan Thomas, "Do not go gentle into that good night," in Enright, *Oxford Book of Death,* p. 39.

Down, down, down into the darkness of the grave
Gently they go, the beautiful, the tender, the kind;
Quietly they go, the intelligent, the witty, the brave.
I know. But I do not approve. And I am not resigned.[17]

The poets capture the sense of offense and resistance appropriate to a
Christian estimate of death as *not* merely natural (and we further recall
that nature itself is God's creation, not an independent source or measure of values).

Likewise contrasting with a "healthy-minded" view of death as not
really so bad after all is the stark view of someone like Ernest Becker,
who, like Kübler-Ross, believes death must be faced up to rather than
avoided; but who takes something of a heroic and defiant stance before
it. For him, "nature" is not benign but malignant: "The soberest conclusion that we could make about what has actually been taking place
on the planet for about three billion years is that it is being turned into
a vast pit of fertilizer."[18] In the face of "the real despair of the human
condition," one must not blink or deceive oneself about one's prospects; all one can do is "fashion something . . . and drop it into the confusion."[19] Perhaps it seems strange that we have located such defiance
among ways of avoiding death, since it tries so hard to face it head on;
yet a shrill titanism that shouts into the wind of death as much fails to
deal with it as a passive acquiescence that allows one simply to be carried along by it.

Death Delayed

Far from treating death as inevitable, parts of the research and medical
establishments (not to mention the diet, exercise, and cosmetic surgery
establishments) proceed almost as if increasing understanding of the
process of aging and progress in the treatment of disease could post-
pone death indefinitely. It is as if the process of decay we can plainly
observe is something we *should* surely be able to learn to control: the

17. Edna St. Vincent Millay, "Dirge Without Music," in *A Treasury of Great Poems,* ed.
Louis Untermeyer (New York: Simon and Schuster, 1955), p. 1167.
18. Ernest Becker, *The Denial of Death* (New York: Free Press, 1973), p. 283.
19. Becker, *Denial of Death,* pp. 269, 285.

very idea that we could not is a kind of affront. And this mood is mirrored by patients who are taken by surprise when their doctors cannot tell them what is wrong or what to do about it. In our technologically-minded society, it is almost unthinkable that a bit more money and the right expert could not produce an answer.

Our very successes have, of course, contributed mightily to this mind-set. One researcher, who has discovered the biochemical clock that leads to aging in cells (and has had laboratory success in resetting and stopping these clocks — of use, respectively, in reversing aging and in producing it, say to kill cancer cells), is confident that treatments effective in extending human lives will be available in the first quarter of the twenty-first century, and that our descendants, appropriately treated, might anticipate living, say, two hundred years.[20] Impressive indeed, though not just exactly the same thing as defeating death. And not as impressive as the longevity attributed to the antediluvians, whose histories nonetheless ended, reliably and relentlessly, "and he died."

Similarly, knowledge of hygiene and antibiotics and multitudinous medical advances have, where this knowledge can be applied, significantly reduced the death rates in young children and have certainly extended other individual lives as well, though without producing the dramatic increase in average longevity that might once have been anticipated. There always seems to be a backlash: increasing pollution thwarts hygienic efforts; resistant microbes and new viruses lead to the resurgence of familiar diseases like tuberculosis and the emergence of new ones like AIDS; medical technology may prolong dying instead of prolonging living (as we shall explore further below). Still, something seeks to persuade us that, if we die of diseases, surely we ought by conquering diseases to be able to defeat death. Given that we fail to do so, a sense of shame attaches to the whole idea of death and the vulnerable, decay-prone bodies that die (a shame with curious parallels to the shame attached to our fallen sexuality).

A yet more extreme attempt to delay death is that of cryogenic burial — putting someone, perhaps a little before actual death, into a deep freeze, in the hopes that when a cure for what ailed her is discovered, she could be thawed, healed, and given a new lease on life. For a

20. Michael Fossel, "Resetting the Age Clock," *Stanford* 24:3 (July-August 1996): 68-73.

time the idea was quite a fad, with freezing and thawing demonstrated on dogs and with people like Timothy Leary signing up for the future. Before Leary died in 1996, however, he deliberately chose not to undergo cryogenic burial, and the business has come on hard times.[21] No doubt, though, some analogue or "new, improved version" will appear; and the point is not to condemn what seems more like an extreme extension of the art of healing than a defeat of death. It is, rather, to affirm that it is indeed not a defeat of death and to raise the question of whether such ventures are really an optimal use of energies and resources.

To raise such a question is not to deny the importance of the body and the legitimacy of caring for it and using reasonable means to prolong life. Jesus healed the sick; he did not say that their bodily problems were insignificant. The Christian takes embodied existence seriously. Unlike the Greek Idealists and their heirs, she does not seek to make death of little consequence by looking upon the body as a sort of prison house of the soul, with the rational spirit being freed by death to return to its own natural element. As has often been observed (especially following Cullman), Christ did not, like Socrates, face death with cool equanimity, but wrestled in prayer in the Garden of Gethsemene, longing to be delivered (Matt. 26:36-46 and par.; also Heb. 5:7) — and this, even though he was sinless. Though a Christian may be fully aware of her mortality and of the Christian hope for something better, which militates against frantically clinging to life at all costs, yet her desire is "not to be unclothed [to be divested of the body] but to be further clothed" (2 Cor. 5:4).

Death Shaping Life

Death avoided obscures our vision of the individual who dies as unique and responsible agent — losing her in distant masses, in natural processes or meaningless shouts against those universal processes, in the physiological substrate manipulated by physicians and scientists. In a sense, that is the purpose of the avoidance; or, more precisely, the pur-

---

21. David Colker, "Leary Severs Ties to Cryonics Advocates," *Los Angeles Times*, May 9, 1996, p. B3.

pose is to keep from myself the disruptive awareness of the fact that *I* must die. Moreover, I must die alone: no one can accomplish my dying for me.[22] Hence, when the avoidance recedes and the fact of death is allowed its place in shaping my living, it proves an intensely individualizing reality, setting my life off from all other lives. Death casts its shadow on the whole of life.[23] Humans can no more die like animals than they can live like them; for though animals instinctively fear and seek to escape death in moments of danger, people anticipate it in moments of calm reflection as well as in times of existential panic.

Death as Rendering Life Vain

If death is an absolute end, utterly without remainder, we would have to agree with Camus that the only really serious philosophical question is why one does not commit suicide.[24] Not that answers of a sort cannot be provided to the question, under certain circumstances, especially if one is young and healthy and exuberant, or if one adheres to a kind of biological determinism and explains that one is governed by a life-instinct. Or, of course, one can speak of one's responsibilities for others; but talk of responsibility sneaks in categories that should logically be banned from a universe in which nothing matters in the end. Death as utterly final does not just end life but negates it altogether, turns it into "a tale/Told by an idiot, full of sound and fury,/Signifying

22. Tolstoy speaks of the sudden encroachment of the reality of his own death upon Prince Andrew before battle: "For the first time in his life the possibility of death presented itself to him — not in relation to any worldly matter or with reference to its effect on others, but simply in relation to himself, to his own soul — vividly, plainly, terribly, and almost as a certainty. And from the height of this perception all that had previously tormented and preoccupied him suddenly became illumined by a cold white light without shadows, without perspective, and without distinction of outline" (*War and Peace, Great Books,* vol. 51, p. 439).

23. Martin Heidegger, the first great philosopher to make death the fundamental category of philosophy, said that our whole existence is "being unto death" *(Sein zum Tode).* See the helpful summary in Anthony C. Thiselton, *The Two Horizons: New Testament Hermeneutics and Philosophical Description* (Grand Rapids: Eerdmans, 1980), pp. 176-78.

24. See Albert Camus, "Absurdity and Suicide," in his *The Myth of Sisyphus,* trans. Justin O'Brian (New York: Vintage, 1955), p. 3.

nothing."[25] Even if one does not take an absolutely doctrinaire position in these matters, though, but simply sees death as, more than likely, terminating one's personal identity or capacity for action, the suspicion that how one lives could not really matter very much easily arises. If it does not matter, then why not try to maximize personal satisfaction: "Eat, drink, and be merry, for tomorrow we die." "All is vanity," says the book of Ecclesiastes again and again: one might as well enjoy life as best one can.

The adequacy of the logic of self-indulgence is explicitly rejected by Jesus, precisely on the grounds that death is not the end, but that following one's death, one's soul shall be required of one (Luke 12:19-20). The unrepentant would be wise to *wish* death final. But in any case, logic and philosophy aside, something common to people of all ages and belief systems rebels against the thought that nothing whatever will remain of them. Let there be, at least, a stone tablet, a great pyramid, a noble arch; an unforgettable line of poetry or work of art; let there be children to carry on one's name; let there be something remaining to testify that one's life was not, after all, utterly vain. And do not look too far ahead, to the day when the arch falls, the painting crumbles to dust, the last member of one's line also dies.[26]

25. William Shakespeare, *Macbeth*, 5.5.26-28. Or again, Shelley: "Alas! that all we loved of him should be,/But for our grief, as if it had not been,/And grief itself be mortal!" (from "Adonais," in Untermeyer, *Great Poems,* p. 737).

26. In the case of the pyramids, one must note that these edifices were not substitutes for personal immortality but designed to facilitate it: an article about the Great Pyramid significantly entitled, "Cheops, a 'God on Earth,' Lived to Die," details how the megalomaniacal pharaoh, apparently consumed by the knowledge that he would die, oriented much of his existence to seeking to make sure his personal power would be unabated after his death (*New York Times Magazine,* June 6, 1954, pp. 10-11+). Shakespeare did not maintain illusions of that kind and yet trusted his work would survive: granting that a dear one would age and die, he claimed with what might sound like overmuch assurance, "So long as men can breath or eyes can see/So long lives this, and this gives life to thee" (Sonnet #18, in Untermeyer, *Great Poems,* p. 275). Woody Allen was more pragmatic and, finally, more realistic. Having contemplated the option of gaining immortality through his work, he famously concluded that he would prefer to obtain it by not dying.

Death as Making Time and Its Gifts Precious

Quite contrary to the position that death makes life meaningless and so one might as well do as one pleases, is the view that transience confers value: if life had no end, we would neither cherish the good things we have nor achieve what we can, since every worthy deed could always be postponed. If we wish to be wise, we must learn to count our days (Ps. 90:12). (Note that this is a view that, while obviously appropriate for those who believe that their use of time will be judged, is also frequently held by those who have no such conviction but who do not play out to the end the implications of death being utterly final.)[27] Romantic poets have long written of fleeting youth, of great loves lost to death, of noble aspirations cut off: in this realm the experts are not the scientists with their techniques of management, but those who have gifts of expressing human hopes, longings, and despair. They dignify lived experience. The more moralistically inclined, oriented more to duty than to experience, have spoken both of the crass folly of failing to amend one's life while one can and of the responsibility to "redeem the time":[28]

> Oh! Grant me grace, O God, that I
> My life may mend, sith I must die.[29]

Or again, in the words of the old hymn:

---

27. Hence it has been shrewdly observed that "the pious exhortations to think of death and the profane exhortations to make the most of youth almost meet" (J. Huizinga, *The Waning of the Middle Ages* [1949; Garden City, NY: Doubleday Anchor, 1954], p. 141). While the application is general, the context of Huizinga's remark is the *ars moriendi* literature of the late Middle Ages, in which contemplation of death was strongly advocated. Denis the Carthusian, for instance, advised the noble, "when going to bed at night, he should consider how, just as he now lies down himself, soon strange hands will lay his body in the grave" (ibid., p. 138; see also the medieval drawings reproduced in *A History of Christianity: Readings in the History of the Early and Medieval Church*, ed. Ray C. Petry [Englewood Cliffs, NJ: Prentice-Hall, 1962], pp. 486-88).

28. Pascal unites the thoughts in giving the analogy of a man in a dungeon with but a single hour to learn what his sentence is, but that hour enough to earn its repeal if he discovers it. That man would act unnaturally if he frittered away the time on some indifferent pursuit (*Pensées*, #200).

29. Robert Southwell, in Enright, *Oxford Book of Death*, p. 25.

Give every flying minute,
Something to keep in store;
Work, for the night is coming,
When man works no more.

Anna Coghill

The known reality of a limit for both ourselves and others can bestow upon life not absurdity but a sense of seriousness and even of gratitude that escapes us when we presume that everything will continue unchanged indefinitely, if not forever. An emotional response is not wrong, but a true expression of death's impact. "Indifference to death makes mankind's monsters; proper attention to it, its saints."[30] (The idea of limitless time in this life as much removes us from the realm of God's judgment, and hence of a larger context giving consequence to our lives, as does the idea that death is an absolute end: time as God's creation and gift has significance; time as mere duration does not. "All flesh is like grass. . . . The grass withers, and the flower falls, but the word of the Lord endures forever" [1 Pet. 1:24-25].)

Death as Interpreting Discipleship

Perhaps the most specifically Christian of the ways in which contemplating death can shape our living is engaging the manner in which the New Testament transforms the brute fact of death from something that confronts us once and for all (as, of course, it in one sense does, Heb. 9:27), to something that characterizes daily life: "I die daily," said Paul (1 Cor. 15:31). A plain negative suddenly takes on a positive and active connotation, even while retaining its tone of judgment and loss. Jesus said that his disciples must take up their cross — an instrument of death — daily (Luke 9:23; cf. Matt. 16:24; Mark 8:34). In our baptism, we die to sin (Rom. 6:2-4). We are to be conformed to the death of Christ (Phil. 3:10). And — in a surprising phrase — we are told to "let the dead bury the dead" (Matt. 8:22; Luke 9:60). In texts like these, death retains its clear link to sin and the effects of sin and limitations to bodily life;

---

30. Marvin Barrett, as quoted by G. Tom Milazzo, *The Protest and the Silence: Suffering, Death, and Biblical Theology,* and excerpted in Martin E. Marty, ed., *Context* 26:7 (April 1, 1994): 2.

and as such it arouses dread; but it is nonetheless used as a metaphor for something that does not consume the totality of the person. We are to reject the hubris of our first parents and submit ourselves obediently to limits. We are to be willing to undergo persecution. We are, with whatever violence necessary, to put evil away from ourselves.[31] And, very significantly, we are not to allow the fact of physical death or the proprieties surrounding it to consume us or deflect us from our discipleship: the implication is surely that physical death need not have an ultimate claim. *We* are to do these things: there remains a "we" to do them. And the reason is that, while the wage of sin is indeed death, "the free gift of God is eternal life in Christ Jesus our Lord" (Rom. 6:23). Because of Christ, we need not be like those "who all their lives were held in slavery by the fear of death" (Heb. 2:15): the disciples who were terrified in the midst of a storm before Jesus' death and resurrection (Matt. 8:23-27; Mark 4:35-41; Luke 8:22-25) were fearless after them (Acts). But precisely because death is not the absolute end for the Christian, it can be used as a figure for those proximate endings that we must embrace, however wrenching they may be. "Death" and the dread it evokes remains an important symbol for the demands made by this life.

Death Embraced

The "normal," almost automatic response to the immediate threat of death is fear and an effort to preserve one's life. Even a morose individual who longs for life to be over will almost certainly duck if suddenly threatened by a falling boulder.[32] However, at least two kinds of considerations lead people actively to desire death. The first is the trauma, psychological and physical, of this life: going on one more day can seem to be too much to bear. And the second is the hope that some-

31. In this sphere, the interrelationship of the physical body, σαρξ (flesh) in the moral sense, sin, and death, becomes significant (see, for instance, somewhat enigmatic texts like Rom. 7:24 and Col. 2:11-14): the sins of the flesh work death, yet we also experience curbing them as a kind of death (Rom. 6).

32. Given our view that the Fall corrupts all human faculties, those of mind and body alike, one might take special note of Camus's remark about this instinctive avoidance of death: "The body's judgment is as good as the mind's, and the body shrinks from annihilation" ("Absurdity and Suicide," p. 6).

thing better really will follow this life. As Paul himself wrote, contemplating whether he preferred to live or to be put to death, "to depart and be with Christ . . . is far better" (Phil. 1:23). Physical life is not an absolute value for the Christian: one may rightly sacrifice oneself for a worthy cause. What, then, shall we say to those who do not go on to conclude with Paul, "but to remain in the flesh is more necessary for you. Since I am convinced of this, I know that I will remain" (Phil. 1:24-25)? What do we say to those whose horror of life exceeds their horror at the thought of death?

Suicide

The generally harsh view the church has taken of suicide goes back to Augustine, who thought it necessary to combat vigorously those who were actively courting martyrdom in the hopes of winning a more glorious resurrection.[33] And surely there is something worth combating, and something of questionable motivation, in pursuing self-destruction for the sake of glory. Yet the brutally harsh judgment of suicides that led, for example, to their being denied burial in consecrated ground, may seem excessive to those acquainted with human desperation. At the very least, we might make some analogy with those who, because of the external pressure imposed by torturers, no longer act as free and responsible agents.[34] No doubt there are also internal pressures, due to psychological misery or physical pain, that have the same effect (though, essentially by definition, if a person is asking herself whether that point has been reached, it has not been). We might also argue, as does Barth, that to make suicide an unforgivable sin puts too much weight on a single act and fails to take into account the whole of the preceding life: many people, after all, die suddenly, in the midst of unrepented sin.[35] It would seem that only if the person deter-

33. "No man should put an end to this life to obtain that better life we look for after death, for those who die by their own hand have no better life after death" (Augustine, *City of God,* 1.26; see 1.17-27).

34. See above, pp. 38-39. Particularly painful is the increasing incidence of suicide among children, some too young to have a clear sense of the finality of death, but not too young to be utterly miserable.

35. Barth, *Church Dogmatics,* III/4: 401-6.

minately, responsibly, and consciously rejected the possibility that God's grace could sustain her in her present trial, might suicide constitute apostasy — a judgment related to the church's traditional labeling of despair (acedia, sloth) as a deadly sin. But the state of the heart cannot be known with certainty from the perspective of an outside observer. The circumstances that might make suicide most understandable to such an observer, like the horrors of persecutions, wars, famines, and death camps, instead seem generally to jolt those who experience them into heroic efforts to live.[36] The impulse to take one's life is by no means reliably related to external pressures.

Suicide is not in fact expressly condemned in Scripture, apart from the not-unreasonable assumption that the Sixth Commandment also excludes self-murder. The suicides Scripture recounts (most prominently, those of Saul and his armor-bearer [1 Sam. 31:1-6; 1 Chron. 10:1-13], Ahithophel [2 Sam. 17:23], and Judas [Matt. 27:5, but cf. Acts 1:18]; other possible instances are somewhat more ambiguous) are, however, sobering; for none of these people was engaged at the end of his life in a course that could be considered pleasing to God. Also, Job declined even in the midst of great suffering to take his own life, and Paul actively forestalled the intended suicide of the Philippian jailer (Acts 16:25-29).

Given our conviction of the relational character of the divine image, it is also significant that the effect of suicide on those left behind (not to mention the implications of, so to speak, seeking to force God's hand) is very considerably more destructive than that of death from other causes. Suicide seemingly willfully wrenches apart the relational fabric of existence, calling into question those components of others' lives that the suicide's life has touched and leaving survivors feeling impotent and guilty. Thus, the devastating outcome for others at least reinforces the conclusion that there is something not just pitiable or unbalanced, but also sinful and wrong about taking one's own life. As Bonhoeffer has remarked, under conditions of the Fall, our whole existence is so marked by death that we have life itself not as a gift but as a commandment.[37] To live has become a duty that we are not free simply to abandon.

36. That effect is striking enough to have provoked some to advocate sarcastically the prescription of persecution as a remedy for suicidal despair (*Oxford Book of Death*, p. 84).

37. Dietrich Bonhoeffer, *Creation and Fall* (New York: Macmillan, 1959), p. 55. In a moving passage Charles Williams once suggested that the person contemplating suicide does not really want death but life; she wants to kill what makes her life a living death.

Euthanasia and Assisted Suicide

Many who oppose suicide as such nonetheless grant more leeway in cases where an individual's death from disease or injury is imminent (by which some of them mean not the estimated six months remaining by which the medical establishment defines "terminal" illness, but a briefer period of hours, days, or a very few weeks). Indeed, under circumstances in which death is simply being hastened either by omission of some medical procedure or, say, by generous administration of morphine for pain relief, they would decline to consider such omission or action as constituting suicide at all.[38] With this latter judgment we would gladly concur. We would go further and affirm not only that one is not required to employ all available medical technology to prolong the life of the dying, but that one is justified in stopping futile procedures already begun, including nutrition when it can be supplied only by technical means: it is a commonplace that our current ability to sustain certain bodily functions long after any possibility of any even marginally meaningful recovery is past has become an emotional and financial disaster for relatives, not to mention a form of officially sanctioned torture for persons still capable of registering pain.

Let us go on record as opposing most vehemently some of the common mythologies about pain, from the conviction that suffering is basically good for people — an exercise in "soul-making," which they ought to turn to their profit — to the naïve belief that doctors can in fact always give consistently adequate pain relief, so there is no excuse (unless it be a crass, economic one) for those who press for euthanasia in desperate cases. Some people do manage pain heroically and wring spiritual good out of it, which we surely agree they should insofar as they can; and we certainly admire the courageous. Other people, however, whether because of lesser spiritual or psychological or social resources or sharper and more prolonged suffering, are embittered and destroyed by pain. (To deny that suffering is basically good for people is *not* to say that it is meaningless or must be relieved at all costs: these are separate, even if related, issues.) Most people's pain can be managed by sufficient quantities of analgesics or by sedating them into at least apparent insen-

---

38. For a discussion of the complexities here, see Robert N. Wennberg, *Terminal Choices: Euthanasia, Suicide, and the Right to Die* (Grand Rapids: Eerdmans, 1989).

sibility. However, to give just a single example, for a considerable fraction of people, enough morphine to ease pain will produce hallucinations sufficiently terrifying that the sufferer would choose the pain over the hallucinations. We have less control in these matters than we often like to think, or than our best-case examples lead us to believe.

Even though the ideas of "letting die" or of acting in such a way that death can be foreseen as a result, while not being directly intended, are subject to certain ambiguities (as, for instance, when a diabetic suffering from cancer but not imminently dying declines to take her insulin), most ethicists find these ways of proceeding uncontroversial as a general rule. We can be committed to fighting premature death without being committed to persisting in a battle that is already lost. Christians in particular value life as God's good gift to be cherished and cared for; but they do not see it as an ultimate (see, e.g., Matt. 16:25; Mark 8:25; Luke 9:24; 17:33; and also the church's tradition of honoring martyrs, even if courting martyrdom has been discouraged). Much more problematic are active euthanasia and assisted suicide — in any case, but most particularly for those not immediately dying; and "unplugging" or ceasing feeding those who are in a "persistent vegetative state" — not, perhaps, in every case suffering, but highly unlikely ever to regain consciousness.

Few of us can fail to be moved by the eloquent pleas for relief of those suffering terribly, and the pleas made by those who care for them.[39] Many of us fear for ourselves, should we one day be in a condition of protracted and unrelieved agony — most especially if death *cannot* be counted on to deliver us soon. (Note that in such cases, death *not* being imminent strengthens the argument that relief is needed.) These appeals to mercy seem compelling. We do not doubt that, under particular circumstances, they will continue to be heeded, whatever ethicists, theologians, or the law of the land may say. Nonetheless, we would (somewhat reluctantly) hold that ethicists, theologians, and the law of the land should continue their prohibition of active euthanasia and assisted suicide. For one thing, especially in not immediately terminal cases, a period of intense suffering that would not in fact continue,

39. See, for example, Harriet Goetz, "Euthanasia: A Bedside View," *Christian Century* 106:20 (June 21-28, 1989): 619-22. Similarly, Kenneth Vaux, "Debbie's Dying: Euthanasia Reconsidered," *Christian Century* 105:9 (March 16, 1988): 269-71.

could lead a person to take her life in the moment's desperation; or something might later develop in the person's life for which she would willingly bear the suffering. Or it may be that not physical suffering but fear of losing one's faculties and dignity due, say, to Alzheimer's Disease, or of being a burden to others, becomes the dominant motivation for requesting help in dying.[40] Very frequently it appears that not the actual facts of one's physical condition but rather one's psychological state drives the desire for death, with many desperately ill or very severely handicapped people struggling to live and many much less ill people longing to die. Often, people feel it to be a sort of duty not to burden relatives (a feeling some relatives will consciously or unconsciously abet). Perhaps they would feel gratified about being able to leave their dear ones a substantial inheritance rather than devouring everything with medical bills. Without questioning the sincerity of any of these motives, we suggest that they give far too little reverence to life and treat the fabric of human relationships — all too easily torn by utilitarian considerations, legitimated by social mores — too casually. And once we start to argue that it is more "reasonable" that we end our life than continue it, we have cast the whole discussion in the wrong terms, for what makes it "reasonable" that we should exist at all?

For example, poet Nancy L. Swann writes in response to a recent discussion of euthanasia,

> I am a person with a chronic disease, which will eventually kill me in a particularly unpleasant manner unless I am fortunate enough to die of something else first. But if I were ever to request assisted suicide, it would not be because of the hereditary form of emphysema that runs in my family but because of depression — which has always been my bête noir. . . . Imagine how fascistic the oft-repeated argument . . . seems to me — that I have a moral obligation to 'off myself' if keeping me alive starts to cost money. (It does.) Since I am a poet and not much else besides a loving mother of a grown daughter, few would argue that my life is all that useful. Yet once we start to tell the ill and the dying that it is

---

40. We do not consider it incidental that famed "suicide doctor" Jack Kevorkian has already assisted a person in the early stages of Alzheimer's (Robert Steinbrook, "Support Grows for Euthanasia," *Los Angeles Times,* April 19, 1991, p. A1+).

their duty to die and rid society of an undesirable, we are well down the slippery slope to the Reich.[41]

As ethicist Allen Verhey put it, contra the argument that we grant people their proper rights and freedom in legitimating assisted suicide, "When we provide social legitimation for the option of suicide, we may increase options, but we also effectively eliminate an option, namely, the option of staying alive without having to justify one's existence."[42] That is a critical option for anyone who is for any reason vulnerable; and surely the whole Christian tradition has sought to protect the vulnerable.

The case of the comatose is quite different but nonetheless complicated, not least at the level of defining death so that organs can then be "harvested" for use by others in need of a transplant. (Naturally, that need pushes in the direction of pronouncing people dead sooner rather than later.) Cessation of heart and/or lung functioning will no longer do, for we can keep these functions going indefinitely by mechanical means. Total brain death is a commonly accepted and uncontroversial criterion. But what about neo-cortical death: the patient has a flat EEG but may be able to breath on her own because the brainstem is still functioning.[43] In a famous case, Nancy Cruzan, who spent nearly eight years in a coma after an automobile accident, finally died twelve days after her parents obtained a court order allowing her feeding tube to be removed, against the vehement protests of right-to-life advocates.[44] The trouble is the slight possibility that the vegetative state is not permanent after all, illustrated by another woman in apparently very similar circumstances who suddenly woke up after nearly three months (and after doctors had actively tried to convince her relatives to allow them to make use of her organs).[45] Such recoveries of consciousness are admittedly rare — two to three percent — and do not come without

41. Letter published in *Christian Century* 113:28 (Oct. 9, 1996): 949.

42. "Choosing Death: The Ethics of Assisted Suicide," *Christian Century* 113, no. 22 (July 17-24, 1996): 716-19.

43. See the helpful discussion in Wennberg, *Terminal Choices*, chap. 6.

44. Robert Steinbrook, "Comatose Woman Dies 12 Days after Life Support Is Halted," *Los Angeles Times*, Dec. 27, 1990, p. A17.

45. Terence Monmaney, "'I Think She Was Touched by an Angel,'" *Los Angeles Times*, Oct. 5, 1996, p. A1+.

lasting disabilities. Thus, the issue of advance directives (a living will or, better, durable power of attorney for health care, which specifies one's desires in such circumstances) is relevant: at least such a directive obviates the need for "substituted judgment," by which another individual seeks to act as she believes the affected person would have wished (a process prone to error, self-interest or neurotic anxiety, and over-reliance upon chance remarks — which latter are especially problematic, since persons often change their minds about what measures they wish taken when their life is actually in jeopardy; that is, they cling more tenaciously than they earlier thought they would). At the very least, apart from a very explicit advance directive, it would seem that one ought not to withdraw support precipitously.

We support use of advance directives but would caution against their becoming a way of seeking to ensure certain "rights" construed in a simply individualistic way. Surely such directives should be prepared in the context of interaction with those who will be most closely affected by one's death or disability. It is not, in our judgment, humanly responsible for a Christian to fail to consider that those who love one may deeply need not to let go too quickly and be forever tormented by doubts.

We must reemphasize, in any case, that advance directives are no panacea. For instance, we have read of a situation in which a husband is suing the doctors who mistakenly failed to heed an advance directive and kept his wife alive during a medical crisis. While she has a rare genetic degenerative disease, she is *not* now in terrible pain, has perhaps many more years to live, and, her husband admits, would now say that of course she wants to live. However, he claims, were she to have decided when she was fully competent if she wished to live in her current state, she would have been emphatic that she did not. It would seem to us that what constitutes a proper outcome in such a case is scarcely transparent.[46]

In any case, the push for euthanasia or assisted suicide may be driven by mercy, but fear may also masquerade as mercy. And it is not as if there is nothing to fear in the process of dying, even though Christians believe that death itself has been vanquished by Christ. However,

46. See Sheryl Stolberg, "Kept Alive, but to Live What Kind of Life?" *Los Angeles Times,* Oct. 22, 1996, p. A1+.

certain resources can be brought to bear against the fear, resources that may be lost by a flight to euthanasia — and thus, in a vicious spiral, increase the felt need for euthanasia. The first is simply the practice of active care, willingness to be present and involved with the suffering person, not out of the pity that demeans but out of a recognition of common humanity and mutual interdependence.

Contrast this lovely passage from Oliver Wendell Holmes with that attitude which so resists suffering that it would rather end it permanently than engage it:

> He used to insist on one small point with a certain philological precision, namely, the true meaning of the word 'cure.' He would have it that to cure a patient was simply to *care* for him. I refer to it as showing what his idea was of the relation of the physician to the patient. It was indeed to care for him, as if his life were bound up in him, to watch his incomings and outgoings, to stand guard at every avenue that disease might enter, to leave nothing to chance; not merely to throw a few pills and powders into one pan of the scales of Fate, while Death the skeleton was seated in the other, but to lean with his whole weight on the side of life, and shift the balance in its favor if it lay in human power to do it.[47]

If we refuse to ration *care*, we will find it less easy to talk about rationing *resources*, or to say glibly that while we can no longer afford to give optimal treatment to everyone, at least we can provide a quick way out.[48] We do not deny, of course, economic realities, but we do reject a utilitarian calculus applied to human life. That rejection leads to the second positive resource Christians have, which is a deep humility before God's hidden purposes, a humility that will not deny the value of any human life, not even one's own at the moments one wishes most to

---

47. From his *Medical Essays*, quoted in John Franklin Genung, *The Working Principles of Rhetoric* (Boston: Ginn and Company, 1900), p. 51.

48. See Steinbrook, "Support Grows for Euthanasia." See also the reflections of David B. McCurdy ("Saying What We Mean," *Christian Century* 113:22 [July 17-24, 1996]: 708-9), who is concerned that while discussion of the problem of denial of life-saving treatment because of economically motivated rationing is important, such denial should not be called "involuntary euthanasia," since the term "euthanasia" ought to be preserved for actions motivated by mercy and compassion. Failing to use the term precisely further confounds an already difficult debate.

be free of it. This humility will not equate the meaning of a life with its visible productivity, with capacity for pleasure and freedom from pain, or even with the presence of human relationships, for God himself has promised never to leave or forsake us (Heb. 13:5). Thus, it will not readily give up on life — again, not even on one's own. And then, finally, the Christian will simply admit, in the face of all the cries for "death with dignity," that death is not a dignified experience. It is not intrinsically benign. We do well to moderate its agonies; and we are not required to submit to spending our final days covered with tubes, surrounded with machines, and isolated from the presence of our friends; but we do not do well so to naturalize death that we expect it to be innocuous. Sometimes simply labeling a thing accurately gives new power to face it.

Death, the Funeral, and the Grave

Rituals surrounding death and burial rightly mark the significance of the earthly life now past. Treating the body with dignity (according to cultural norms of propriety)[49] likewise honors life: the revulsion most of us feel at the desecration of a corpse suggests a primitive understanding that we cannot treat death or the dead disrespectfully without somehow threatening similarly disrespectful treatment of the living, even if our cold logic tells us that "the person is no longer there" in the dead body. Throughout Scripture, from Jacob's request that he be buried in his own land, in his ancestral burying place (Gen. 47:29-30), to the considerable emphasis given the new tomb provided for Jesus (Matt. 27:60; Mark 15:46; Luke 23:53; John 19:41), proper treatment of the corpse is assumed to be important.[50] To be denied burial in one's ancestral tomb (e.g., 1 Kings 13:22) or, worse, to be denied burial at all

49. We would consider the choice between burial and cremation, for instance, to be primarily a cultural rather than a theological matter. However, violation of cultural understandings can be of theological import if, for instance, a given culture defines cremation as a rejection of belief in the resurrection of the body.

50. Such concerns are, of course, common to other cultures as well: for instance, the whole of Sophocles' *Antigone* revolves around the issue of proper burial of the dead. Those at least as far back as Neanderthal buried their dead, with seemingly obvious provision for a life to come (see *Who We Are,* p. 384).

(Ps. 79:3; Eccles. 6:3), is a serious threat; while even a measure of loving extravagance in preparation of the body for death can be praised (e.g., Mary's anointing of Jesus, John 12:1-8). Rules of uncleanness surrounding death also maintain the aura of seriousness. That such rituals and rules do not have an *ultimate* claim (e.g., Matt. 8:22 and Luke 9:60 on letting the dead bury the dead; and the assumption made by many that the priest in Jesus' parable passed by the man lying injured on the road because, were the man dead, the priest would be defiled and unable to carry out his duties, Luke 10:25-37) does not mean that they have *no* claim. These points must be pressed in a culture like our own, in which avoidance of death on the one hand and its commercialization on the other may conspire to make the bereaved vulnerable to truly bizarre extravagances or lead them to go to the opposite extreme and omit observances that have always been important to the human family in one form or another.

Of course, potential for exploitation is hardly new. Already in the late second century, Hippolytus could write against making any exorbitant charge for the cemetery, and insist that its upkeep be underwritten by the bishop, lest visitors be burdened by a charge.[51] In the nineteenth, Charles Dickens knew about psychological exploitation: he has an undertaker argue that it is sheer reasonableness to pay more for a funeral than a birth

> "because the laying out of money with a well-conducted establishment, where the thing is performed upon the very best scale, binds the broken heart, and sheds balm upon the wounded spirit. Hearts want binding, and spirits want balming when people die: not when people are born." [Then, following a long list of funeral finery that could be purchased,] "Oh! do not let us say that gold is dross, when it can buy such things as these."[52]

Crass, indeed. But it would seem to take the technological and pragmatic mind-set of later centuries to make possible the particular vulgarity of the stained glass casket illuminated from within by a battery;

---

51. *The Apostolic Tradition of Hippolytus*, trans. Burton Scott Easton (New York: Macmillan, 1934), p. 53.

52. Charles Dickens, *Martin Chuzzlewit*, in *The Works of Charles Dickens*, vol. 1 (New York: Collier, 1880), p. 1039.

the drive-through body-viewing establishment with five separate windows for those who are pressed for time but still want to do their duty; and the mortuaries whose advertisements assure potential patrons that their services are indispensable, since planning a funeral involves "forty-seven different jobs."[53] And it takes the self-centered and in this case truly terminal triviality of baby boomers to demand tombstones shaped like beer mugs or Harley-Davidsons, or the already-patented "Personalized Face Creation Urn" for cremains.[54]

Insofar as mortuaries and similar establishments help manage the mechanics in a society where even the laws governing handling of bodies are complex, well and good. Insofar as wakes and funerals are relocated from homes and churches to often-distant funeral parlors, yet further removing death from sight and the bereaved from the community, not so good. When people's vulnerabilities are preyed upon, we rightly object. And when cosmetics, embalming, and promises of endless, peaceful rest in settings offering "perpetual care" help us indulge our longings to deceive ourselves and obliterate all sense of judgment and resurrection to come, the net result is very bad indeed. "Forest Lawn does everything," the slogan has been; but in the final analysis, as far as changing the brute fact of death is concerned, Forest Lawn does not really do anything. Our hope comes not from technology of whatever sort but only from the promises of God in Christ. We cannot with impunity declare death innocuous, nor by any strength of our own render it so.

53. "Death, Be Proud," *Christian Century* 85:19 (May 8, 1968): 635; "Move Over, Forest Lawn!" *Christian Century* 86:36 (Sept. 3, 1969): 1149. The scathing earlier treatments by Evelyn Waugh *(The Loved One)* and Jessica Mitford *(The American Way of Death)* have not eliminated such abuses (as Mitford's 1998 update entitled *The American Way of Death Revisited* shows); nor are they likely to disappear, given the pressures of guilt, conspicuous consumption, and genuine grief.

54. Stephen Prothero, quoted in *Wilson Quarterly,* Spring 2001, and thence by Martin Marty in *Context* 33:16 (Sept. 15, 2001): 1. More Prothero: "In Orlando, Florida, the ashes of a fireworks expert were blasted with Roman candles into the night sky. The cremated remains of a Marvel Comics editor were mixed with ink and made into a comic book. Villa Delirium Delftworks made cremains into commemorative plates, and another firm (Eternal Reefs, Inc.) offered to turn ashes into 'ecologically sound' coral reefs."

Private Enemy #1

A Sermon Preached by Marguerite Shuster
at Knox Presbyterian Church, Pasadena, California
Christ the King Sunday, 1987

But in fact Christ has been raised from the dead, the first fruits of those
who have died. For since death came through a human being, the resur-
rection of the dead has also come through a human being; for as all die in
Adam, so all will be made alive in Christ. But each in his own order:
Christ the first fruits, then at his coming those who belong to Christ. Then
comes the end, when he hands over the kingdom to God the Father, after
he has destroyed every ruler and every authority and power. For he must
reign until he has put all his enemies under his feet. The last enemy to be
destroyed is death.

I COR. 15:20-26 (NRSV)

> Humpty Dumpty sat on a wall.
> Humpty Dumpty had a great fall.
> All the king's horses and all the king's men
> Couldn't put Humpty together again.

Death is like that. The shell of this life shatters, cracks, bursts, crumbles, with a sudden clatter or a sodden thud, and all the king's horses
and all the king's men cannot put it back together again. Not the king's
horses or men, nor the king's technicians or psychologists, nor the
king's statisticians or poets.

Goodness knows they've tried. They've postponed it — a little, for
some. They've subordinated it to the population growth rate. They've
sanitized it — a lot, at least in our affluent society. They've covered it
with rouge on bloodless skin and Astroturf on raw earth. They've eulo-
gized particular deaths in great literature and death in general as that
which makes life precious. They've even sought to turn it into a friend

by dubbing it "the final stage of growth."[55] But shattered shells don't
grow, heal, come back together — not with the efforts of all the king's
horses and all the king's men.

Death is no friend. It's an enemy. If it ever seems a friend, it's only in
the face of other enemies of life like suffering and sorrow and pain.
Death is the *great* enemy, private enemy #1, the one enemy I can by no
wit or skill or virtue escape. It will pursue me every moment of my life,
stalking me patiently; and whether it springs suddenly from ambush
or just strolls up when I can no longer muster strength to flee, it will
have me.

Worse than that, before it has me, it will have people I love. Poet e. e.
cummings puts the rage eloquently:

Buffalo Bill's
defunct
            who used to
            ride a watersmooth-silver
                                    stallion
and break onetwothreefourfive pigeonsjustlikethat . . .
he was a handsome man
                        and what i want to know is
how do you like your blueeyed boy
Mister Death[56]

More eloquent still is the incomprehension of a twelve-year-old son
of a man I once knew, at the sudden death of his thirteen-year-old
brother from meningitis. He started on a poem one evening, this
twelve-year-old, and worked steadily the next day, spending two hours
pecking it out on a borrowed typewriter. Part of it went like this:

I looked up to him,
I twelve and HE "A BOY THIRTEEN",
He was five feet and nine inches tall,
I remember very well looking up and there

---

55. See the book with that subtitle edited by E. Kübler-Ross.

56. Quoted in Jerry A. Irish, *A Boy Thirteen: Reflections on Death* (Philadelphia: Westminster, 1975), p. 21. The omission is the word "Jesus," which admittedly improves the
poem but which I do not feel free to speak as an oath.

HE was with the train window down, his head
a little ways out with the wind blowing
his red hair as he watched the Alps
passing by,
He was my brother,
My <u>only</u> brother,
One I could play Baseball with,
Someone I could talk to,
In Germany he had bought a camera,
A single lense reflex,
He had alot of new things going on,
Then on Feb. 6 He died.
He my only brother the one I planned to
backpack with, the guy I wanted to sled with,
the person I looked up to, the boy that
played baseball with me, the guy with a
new camera, my brother who I could talk to, the
one who could eat as no one else, my brother that
was five feet and nine inches tall, tall and thin with
red hair "THE BOY THAT WAS THIRTEEN."
He died because he happened to breath in some bacteria
that probably can only be seen under some special microscope,
I guess all I can say is I loved him and needed him and that
I don't understand.[57]

How do you like your blue-eyed boy, Mister Death? I loved him and needed him and I don't understand.

Death is an enemy. Death is a marauding enemy. Death is the enemy that swallows up everything and remains unsatisfied, swallows what I love as well as what I do, swallows what you love and what you do. An enemy. *The* enemy. The last enemy to be destroyed, says Paul. It'll be around for a while yet.

Note that Paul links death, the enemy, with those demonic forces that rule this present darkness: when he speaks of every rule and authority and power, verse 24, he is using the same terminology he employs when speaking of the principalities and powers, those demonized

---

57. Irish, *A Boy Thirteen*, p. 17 (spelling and punctuation are that of the boy who wrote the poem).

structures of life and society that, though in some sense they hold things together, also hold them away from God. The whole creation, says Paul in Romans 8, groans in bondage. Or, to change the figure, it's as if the creation were a huge truck, driven by a powerful engine, but whose steering wheel had locked. It can't make the proper turns. It jumps off the road. Because of its power, it keeps plowing through the underbrush, leaving destruction in its wake. It goes on; but it has no capacity to turn around and get back on the road.

The whole world operates like that today. Death is a part of that system, almost personified, as if it had a will of its own, a will set against the will of Christ — which, in that it is a part of the kingdom of darkness, it in a sense does. "How do you like your blue-eyed boy, Mister Death?" We are in the grip of forces that are beyond us.

But — and here is a very interesting point — the fact is that while Scripture says really a lot (more than we usually notice or admit) about the demonic and about principalities and powers as sources of evil; the Bible also emphasizes human sin as the source of evil; and it will do both right in the same passage. Take my text as an example. I've just pointed out that death is counted among the demonic enemies of Christ's rule: Christ will deliver the kingdom to God the Father "after destroying every rule and every authority and power. For he must reign until he has put all his enemies under his feet. The last enemy to be destroyed is death." But only a few verses earlier, we find the source of death in sin: "death came through a human being"; "all die in Adam."

Death, you recall, was the penalty for Adam and Eve's disobedience of God. Whether the primary spring of that disobedience was sensuality, as the Eastern Orthodox Church has suggested — the fruit was good for food and a delight to the eyes — or whether the primary spring was pride, as we in the Western Church have believed — Adam and Eve wished to be as God, knowing good and evil — is not the crucial point here. Here, the point is just that their sin resulted in death for them and for all their descendants: God drove them from the Garden and barred the way back with a flaming sword, lest they gain access to the Tree of Life. "You are dust," said God, "and to dust you shall return" (Gen. 3:19).

Two questions — at least! — arise here: What is the relationship between death as the penalty for sin and death as the tool of a demonic enemy? And how is it that we all die in Adam?

The figure I like to use in response to the first question is the relationship between a traitor and an enemy in wartime, taking our sinfulness as the traitor within us and the principalities and powers as the enemy with which we should be doing battle. The fact that we may be traitors does not preclude there being an outside enemy. Rather, it assumes that there is an outside enemy with whom we ought not to be allied. Hence, in the Garden, we find not only a man and a woman and a tree, but also a snake, the representative of the enemy. We find a Tempter — external evil — as well as sinful yielding to temptation — internal evil. These are by no means alternatives, of which we must choose only one. On the contrary, Scripture plainly brings them together. Sin gives Satan a claim on us: the wages of sin is death (Rom. 6:23), and death is the devil's business. So too, for us to be delivered from death, both sin and Satan must be defeated. Thus in old baptismal formulas, where the symbolism suggests being cleansed from sin, dying to sin and rising to new life, the person also promised to renounce the devil and all his works. Let me repeat the link to my text: it puts death in a list of demonic enemies like rule and authority and power — the "principalities and powers" Paul discusses elsewhere — *and* says death came by humankind, that all die in Adam.

That brings us to the second question: why does Adam and Eve's sin bring death to all of us, and not just to themselves? In a way, even asking the question shows how individualistically inclined we are. We are affected by, and affect, others all the time, for better and for worse. In fact, virtually everything we do affects others, and is affected by them. And single, far-distant events can have lasting consequences, consequences that cannot be undone. At the biological level, we can imagine some set of genetic mutations in our first parents that would have given us all three hands, and we would think nothing of it; or, our burgeoning population can and does destroy dozens of species of plants and animals every single day, leaving our world changed forever. At the intellectual level, having once learned to do certain things that shouldn't be done — splitting atoms is probably one of them — we do not know how to forget how to do them. So our world is changed, forever. And at the moral level — well, Adam and Eve sinned, and all humans have been sinners ever since. We are born sinners, with our wills inclined to evil. If you need evidence, watch any baby with an unbiased eye. They are the most utterly self-concerned creatures imaginable. It has been well said that a wicked man is but a child grown strong. Only a naive romanticist will insist that we start out in pristine innocence. No, however we explain it, we are born sinners, which means that from our first moment, we are subject to death; and all the king's horses and all the king's men cannot do a thing about it. How do you like your blue-eyed boy, Mister Death — or your brown-eyed girl, or your gray-haired grandmother, or your tall slender dad? They're all the same to private enemy #1, Mister Death.

All the king's horses and all the king's men. . . . But my text isn't about the king's horses. My text isn't about the king's men. My text is about the King — King Jesus. King Jesus, who is no petty tyrant with a petty, partial domain, grudgingly shared with other monarchs. King Jesus who must reign until he has put all his enemies under his feet. All his enemies — even death.

> For since death came through a human being, the resurrection
> of the dead has also come through a human being; for as all
> die in Adam, so all will be made alive in Christ. But each in his
> own order: Christ the first fruits, then at his coming those who
> belong to Christ. Then comes the end, when he hands over the
> kingdom to God the Father, after he has destroyed every ruler
> and every authority and power. For he must reign until he has
> put all his enemies under his feet. The last enemy to be
> destroyed is death. (1 Cor. 15:21-26)

The end will come when, and only when, all the enemies have been defeated. The end will come when, and only when, all those in Christ have been made alive. No rebellion can finally stand against King Jesus.

Note the dual focus again: Christ subjects the enemy death to himself so that it has no more dominion. Christ gathers the believing sinner to himself, covering the sinner's disobedience with his own perfect obedience, bearing the penalty of death himself that the sinner might live. Yes, by a human being, Adam, came death; but also by a human being, Christ Jesus, comes the resurrection of the dead — the defeat of death the powerful enemy, the rescue of those who have reaped death as their just wage. "Death of death, and hell's destruction," says the hymn.

"Too good to be true," says the skeptic. "Mere poetry, wishful thinking, and neurotic denial. Death reigns everywhere you look. Nothing's changed since the beginning of time. 'The fate of the sons of men and the fate of beasts is the same; as one dies, so dies the other.... All go to one place; all are from the dust, and all turn to dust again' (Eccles. 3:19-20). Eat, drink, and be merry; or make what you can of life; or tidy things up as much as you wish — as you like; still, Mr. Death will not pass by your door."

But you're looking in the wrong place! says Paul. Death does not reign everywhere you look. Christ rose! And if death could not hold him, neither can it finally hold those who belong to him. He is the first fruits — not the whole harvest, but the promise of the whole harvest to come. No one would long celebrate a single sheaf of grain if it held no hope for more to come. No one would long celebrate one man's resurrection if it held no hope for others. The resurrection of the dead has come, says Paul. It's just that it takes place in an orderly way: first Christ, then all who belong to him, when he has finished his kingly work of subduing all the rebellious powers. If they could not destroy him — and they could not — then he will not allow them to destroy us. After all, that's why he came.

And so, when Lew Smedes wrote some years ago about the death of his mother, he wrote of her awareness of being a forgiven sinner, an heir not only of Adam's death, but of Christ's life.

> She was bone-tired, so her words came slow: "Lewis, I am so thankful, so thankful, that the Lord forgives all my sin." "Can you think of any sins in particular, Mom?" I asked, teasing a little maybe, but serious. "No, I can't think of any now. But I know I'm a big sinner." ... The way she felt it was the way she said it: "I am a sinner." It is the way you feel it when you sense that life is lived before the face of God. She dared to accept guilt and shame. But she also dared to count on grace.[58]

Death of death, and hell's destruction, for all who believe.

So too, to close with part of a final poem, wrote John Donne, addressing death the demonic power.

> Death be not proud, though some have called thee
> Mighty and dreadful, for thou art not so,

---

58. Lewis Smedes, "The Art of Dying," *The Reformed Journal* 26 (September 1976): 2.

For those whom thou think'st thou dost overthrow
Die not, poor Death, nor yet canst thou kill me. . . .
One short sleep past, we wake eternally,
And death shall be no more. Death, thou shalt die.[59]

Mister Death, enemy #1, you are no match for King Jesus.

59. John Donne, "Holy Sonnets" #10, in *The Complete Poems of John Donne*, ed. Roger E. Bennett (Chicago: Packard, 1942), p. 269.

Biblical Vocabulary Relating to Sin

More than fifty words in the Hebrew (if one includes specific as well as generic terms) and more than a dozen in the Greek are used in the Bible to describe sin.[1] The very breadth and scope of the vocabulary gives a sense of how large a place sin has in the biblical view of things. Of the Hebrew roots, חטא, פשע, and עון are the most commonly used (and are sometimes used together, e.g., Exod. 34:7; Ps. 32:5). All of them have a secular as well as a religious sense, and none of them is exactly equivalent to "sin." חטא means to be mistaken, to be found deficient or lacking, to miss a specific goal or mark. It does not take into account the inner motive of an act but only its formal quality, and hence the biblical writers sometimes add the phrase ביד רמה ("with a high hand"; see, e.g., Num. 15:28-30) to take the idea out of the simply formal sphere. It is closely related in its root meaning to guilt, punishment, and the compensation (sin or guilt offering) it requires. פשע is the least formal of the terms. The noun should be translated "rebellion" and involves the willful, knowledgeable violation of a norm or standard; and sometimes, in the context of a challenging attitude towards God, it has a sense of violating something with numinous value, something holy. עון means "error" or "iniquity" and is the most religious of the three terms;

1. These observations, as well as the following discussion, rely heavily upon Robin C. Cover and E. P. Sanders, "Sin, Sinners," *Anchor Bible Dictionary*, 6:31-47; W. Günther and W. Bauder, "Sin," *New International Dictionary of New Testament Theology*, 3 vols., ed. Colin Brown (Grand Rapids: Zondervan, 1978): 3:573-87; Quell, Bertram, Stählin, and Grundmann, "ἁμαρτάνω, κτλ," *TDNT* (Grand Rapids: Eerdmans, 1964-1974), 1:267-316.

it is closely related to guilt and punishment and, indeed, may have more than one of these connotations in a single passage. Other Hebrew words involve criminal wrongdoing or wickedness, ethical or moral badness, or the kind of "crossing over" that may constitute a religious transgression. To disobey God is to despise, spurn, refuse, or reject his rule (five different terms); to reject religious values is to be godless or profane, wicked or irreverent, or wanton (three terms). Some sins are designated by words describing how loathsome and abhorrent they are to God, and apostasy is spoken of in the language of sexual promiscuity. The prophets inveigh against criminal violence, dishonesty, treachery, oppression, and injustice; and in other contexts cultic errors count as serious sins. Furthermore, terms for trouble, calamity, and sorrow often overlap with words suggesting sin, reinforcing the inevitable connection in Hebrew thought between sin and hardship or suffering, not just for the sinner but for the whole community. (One can see the loss of nuance when the LXX uses only two words, ἁμαρτία and ἀδικία, for almost the whole range of Hebrew terms.)

The initially secular content of most of the Hebrew vocabulary for sin gains theological significance when seen in the light of a Law and covenant of God that take in the whole orderly functioning of the society and are by no means restricted to a limited religious sphere (see, for instance, Dan. 11:32). For the most part, that vocabulary points more to an intellectual conception of sin than to one that emphasizes its irrational aspects (with the exception of a few terms, including the important פשע, and also מרה [be contentious, refractory, rebellious] and שגה [go astray, err]). There are certain lines along which human life *should* move. What might seem to be insignificant or non-culpable actions become important if they nonetheless violate God's norm. "Sin," then, has both legal and theological content in the Old Testament, and it has both social and theological import. It destroys communion both with God and with the human community, setting up a process of destruction that will continue until the sin is somehow dealt with.

In the New Testament sin is basically any activity or stance opposed to God, the rejection of God's claims by a self-assertive humankind. Because God loves and cares for people and because his law therefore takes in relationships to people, sins against people are also sins against God. The most commonly used and comprehensive term for sin in the New Testament is ἁμαρτία and its cognates, which can refer to almost any kind of error; but its biblical context of opposition to God means it should not to be seen as meaning *innocuous* error (as some of the expositions derived from its literal sense of "missing the mark" suggest). It rather involves guilt, brings separation from God, and has a demonic character (see John 9:31; 1 John 3:8). Indeed, according to Romans 8:3, the purpose of the Incarnation was to deal with ἁμαρτία: (ὁ θεὸς τὸν ἑαυτοῦ υἱὸν πέμψας ἐν ὁμοιώματι σαρκὸς ἁμαρτίας καὶ περὶ ἁμαρτίας κατέκρινεν τὴν ἁμαρτίαν ἐν τῇ σαρκί, "God . . . sending his own Son in the likeness of sinful flesh, and to deal with sin . . . condemned sin in the flesh"). Paul (unlike the writers of the Synoptics) almost always uses the word in the singular, with a connotation of hostility to God; and he sometimes speaks of it as a power or an active agent (especially in Rom. 5-7; James Dunn remarks on a kind of ambivalence in Paul's language about sin that reflects an ambivalence in the experience of sin: it is always a power exercising great compulsion; but sometimes it seems to arise more from within, other times from without;[2] see also Heb. 3:13 for ἁμαρτία as a sort of agent). The way it encompasses other terms may be seen in 1 John 3:4 — Πᾶς ὁ ποιῶν τὴν ἁμαρτίαν καὶ τὴν ἀνομίαν ποιεῖ, καὶ ἡ ἁμαρτία ἐστὶν ἡ ἀνομία, "Everyone who commits sin is guilty of lawlessness; sin is lawlessness"; and 1 John 5:17 — πᾶσα ἀδικία ἁμαρτία ἐστίν, "all wrongdoing [unrighteousness] is sin."

Next in importance to ἁμαρτία, in the New Testament terminology, is ἀδικία — "unrighteousness," usually against a fellow human being. The word has a legal overtone and refers particularly to the outward and visible characteristics of that which is sinful. The criterion for determining unrighteousness is by contrast with God's righteousness (Rom. 3:5; 9:14). Other terms involve everything from lawlessness (ἀνομία), disobedience (παρακοή), trespass (παράπτωμα), transgression (παράβασις), and debt in the sense of sin against God or neighbor (ὀφειλέτης); to impiety (ἀσέβεια), wickedness (κακία), evil or depravity (πονηρός), and evil desire (ἐπιθυμία, which should be taken broadly of human yearnings opposed to God's law and claims, not understood only in a sexual sense); to somewhat milder ideas of lack, stumbling, and going astray or deceiving oneself. In each case, though, God's order, norm, or standard has been breached.

2. James Dunn, *Romans 1-8, Word Biblical Commentary*, vol. 38a (Dallas: Word, 1988), p. 390.

Subject Index

Adam: as personal name, 9; example of, 188

Adam and Eve: immaturity of, 41; representative capacity, 12-13, 27; unique significance, 7-8, 206

Adam, First: 7-8, 45n.16, 76; and temptation, 40-41, 171

Adam, Second: 7-8, 15n.27, 28-29, 76; obedience of, 16, 19; and temptation, 40-41, 55

Advance directives, 250

Animals: died before Fall, 73-74; docility in Eden, 77; do not sin, 53; linked to humans, 78; suffering of, 78-79

Apostasy, 143; and suicide, 245

Arminianism, 197n.35; and civil righteousness, 213n.6; Dutch, 189; Wesleyan, 189

Art: and nudity, 69-70

Atheism: protest, 91-92

Authority: and God's law, 52; and learning, 51

Biochemistry: and sin, 121-23

Body, 243n.41, 243n.42; importance of, 238; not source of sin, 60-61, 106, 118n.48, 202n.49; to be treated with dignity, 252

Brainwashing, 38-39

Burial, 252-53; cryogenic, 237-38

Care: in serious illness, 251

Causality, 190, 192n.22; not applicable to sin, 37, 87; God's, 88, 190

Cause: versus reason, 79

Character, 186-87

Children: and parents' guilt, 208; as sinners, 166-67, 168

Choice, 13, 37, 113, 190-91, 192-93, 194; contrary *(liberum arbitrium indifferentiae)*, 197-98; between evils, 46-47, 91; and loss, 33, 42; and tragedy, 45

Church: corporate imagery, 208

Civil disobedience, 111

Clothing, 66-70

Common grace, 213-14, 225

Concupiscence, 60

Conscience, 20, 47, 60, 206; essential to humanness, 16; and law, 111; and sickness, 119-20; and sin, 103, 113, 118, 139

Consciousness: of responsibility,

192n.23, 233-34; and sin, 15, 37, 42; and vegetative states, 249-50

Conversion, 180, 227

Corporate personality, 207-8

Covenant, 6-8, 12, 17, 264; of grace, 8n.11, 28; of works, 8n.11, 27-29

Creation: as good but marred, 3, 5, 15-16, 73, 75, 77-80, 91n.9, 258

Creationism: versus traducianism, 202n.49

Crime: and sickness, 124; and sin, 110-12, 216; violent, 140; white-collar, 140, 149

Cross, 9; not tragic, 47; and will of God, 92

Cryogenic burial, 237-38

Culpability: blindness to, 114; and calculation, 139-41; and compulsion, 138; degrees of, 138-39, 140, 142; and knowledge, 139

Culture: and sin, 51, 120, 169

Cynics, 147n.28

Death (physical), 231-62; and demonic forces, 257-58, 259; as enemy, 232, 255-62; as interpreting discipleship, 242-43; as making life vain, 239-40; as making time precious, 241-42; medical definition, 249; as mercy, 230n.3; as necessary, 73; predates Fall, 10, 73-74; related to sin, 75-78, 79-80, 169-70, 258; threat of in Genesis, 3, 32, 24, 26n.51; universal, 80, 170

Death: threefold meaning, 24-26

Decalogue, 52, 103, 109, 145

Desire: not always wrong, 107-8

Determinism, 87, 124n.62, 184-85, 201n.47

Disobedience: and God's authority, 10, 20, 24, 34, 43, 45, 49-51, 58, 72, 104, 108, 177; and knowledge, 51

Divine image, 6-7, 10, 188; and fall, 59, 160; and infants, 168n.23; and racial prejudice, 153; and women, 156

Donum superadditum, 16n.30, 59-61

Doubt, 34, 54, 108

Eastern Church, 52-53, 197

Eden: expulsion from, 27; location of, 10-11, 77; meaning of, 10-11, 12, 15, 80

Environment: and behavior, 122-23, 191, 214; and sin, 38, 43, 121-22, 188, 202-3

Euthanasia, 246-52

Eve, 34, 43, 52, 58

Evil: not necessary for good, 90-92; not to be justified, 93; not to be used as means, 94; power and, 218; unity of, 136

Evil (moral): banality of, 141; chosen as evil, 184; and demonic powers, 40; as irrational, 43-44; as irreducible and prior to sin, 46

Faith, 54, 186, 219, 227, 229; and evil, 96

Fall: historicity of, 9-10; not coerced, 40; objections to, 4; as pride and unbelief, 52-59; as revolt, 52; as sensuousness, 52-53; and sex, 62; theological importance of, 5-6

Fatalism, 137, 184, 209

Felix culpa, 89-90

Feminism: and sin, 57-59, 157-58

Finitude: and sin, 37, 42, 119, 121, 157

Flesh, 16n.30, 57, 60, 106, 223-34, 243n.31. *See also* Body

Flood, 82

Freedom (human), 38, 88, 185; and Adam and Eve, 198n.37; destroyed by sin, 190; varied meanings, 190

Funeral, 252-54

Gender: roles, 58, 155n.47; and sin, 58, 155-58

Genetics, 123; and sin, 38, 101, 121, 126, 201

God: author of sin? 87-90; immutability, 70-72; mercy, 72; nature of, 5; sovereignty of, 86-87; will of, 18; wrath of, 70-72

Guilt, 47, 54, 117, 125, 135, 139, 177, 183, 201; alien, 205-6; of children, 208; and psychopathology, 119n.52; and shame, 64; solidarity in, 210; felt by victims, 192

Habit, 185n.9

Heart, 194, 215-16, 225-26

Heroism: and sin, 140-41

History: as fallen history, 80-83, 92; primal, 7, 8-10; as problem, 8-10

Holocaust, 93, 151, 210, 218

Idealism: Greek, 11

Ignorance: sins of, 121, 139

Immaturity: and sin, 37, 41, 89n.7

Imputation of sin, 203-5

Individualism, 209, 222

Individuality: human, 13-14

Knowledge: related to obedience, 51-52

Language: corruption of, 116; influence on perception, 120, 163; and race, 151-53

Law: God's, 28, 52, 83, 103-4, 109-10, 143, 216; human, 110-12, 168n.22, 216, 247

Legalism, 104

Liberalism, 13, 182, 189

Love, 66; and Law, 109-10; not emphasized in Genesis 3, 64

Matter: not inherently evil, 60

Milgram experiments, 164

Modesty, 66-70, 147n.28

Money: and sin, 149-51

Monogenism, 200

Moral agency, 38-40, 44, 124

Mortal sin, 142-43, 145

Motives, 167, 171, 198, 215, 227

Natural justice (justitia naturalis), 59-60

Nature: linked to fallen humanity, 77-80; subject to curse, 72-73

Nazism, 163-64, 210

Nudity: and art, 69-70

Obedience: Christ's, 26, 28-29, 41, 103, 119, 260; human, 13, 16n.30, 17, 18, 50-51, 62

Original righteousness, 14-17

Original sin, 159-81; and Greek Fathers, 177; imputation of, 203-5; as "late" concept, 171-72; as pride, 55; Roman Catholic view, 157; transmission by heredity, 200-202; transmission through environment, 202-3; as wound, 79

Paradox of moralism, 166

Pelagianism, 13, 16n.20, 188-89, 197n.35, 202

Power: and evil, 218; and sin, 131, 155

Pride, 34, 52, 54, 55, 176, 217, 226, 227; and clothes, 68; and legalism, 104; and psychological views, 56-57; and racism, 153; and women, 157

Probation, 17-21

Progressive revelation, 172

Providence: versus tragedy, 47

Psychology: behaviorism, 123; and pride, 56-67; and sin, 129

Race: and sin, 151-54

Radical depravity, 160-67, 212; and degrees of sin, 163

Reason, 167n.21; corruption of, 114n.36, 162; limits of, 18, 51, 53, 184n.6, 215, 248; and natural justice, 59-60

Reparations, 207n.64, 209

Repentance, 44, 187

Representation, 12-13, 28-29, 80, 206

Responsibility, 47, 80, 101, 117, 125, 182-83, 184-85, 186, 187, 190, 192, 206, 209

Resurrection, 10, 79, 93, 47, 261

Revenge, 136n.5

Righteousness: of Christ, 13, 203, 204, 224, 227

Romanticism, 141, 166, 188

Satan: author of sin, 87; and death, 259; fall of, 40; as "God's Devil," 92; as Tempter, 22, 35. *See also* Serpent

Science: blind to moral values, 218; and the Fall, 14, 56, 73-76; and objectivity, 162; and sex, 147; and sin, 162; as source of death as well as life, 51n.6, 165, 218

Scrupulosity, 23, 142, 167

Self-centeredness, 166; of children, 168; as essence of sin, 34; and the intellect, 106-7; and psychological views, 104-5; and racism, 153; and religion, 107; and sensuality, 106

Self-deception, 114-15, 161, 177-78

Self-help, 195

Selfishness. *See* Self-centeredness

Self-justification, 115, 178, 180, 215

Self-righteousness, 224

Self-transcendence, 105, 108, 191, 192

Sensuality, 52-53, 106, 107, 258

Serpent, 82n.52; approach to Eve, 43, 53, 58; and origin of sin, 23, 46; as symbolic of Satan, 22, 32, 40, 41, 259

Seven deadly sins, 144-45, 169, 176-77

Sex: and sin, 20, 53, 62, 64-66, 140, 146-49

Shame, 147n.28; and clothing, 68; and death, 237; and Fall, 62-64

Sickness: biblical data, 120-21; and crime, 124-25; as resultant from Fall, 119; and sin, 117-27, 201

Sin: degrees of, 137-43; dependent on virtue, 141, 163; and fear, 133-34; and finitude, 37, 42, 119, 121, 157; and ignorance, 121, 139; inexplicable, 126-27; and the insignificant, 49-51; mortal, 142-43, 145; nature of, 53, 102-10, 113-17; origin of, 42-43; and power, 131-33, 155; process view, 53; and race, 151-54; resistance to idea, 99-101, 175-77; and sex, 20, 53, 62, 64-66, 140, 146-49; and sickness, 117-27; and sins of omission, 108-9; transmission of, 200-205; "unforgivable," 142-43, 161; venial, 142-43, 145; and violence, 53, 140

Sincerity, 220n.26

Snake. *See* Serpent

Stranger: care for, 154n.43

Suffering, 3, 74, 76, 78-79, 228, 246-48; and good, 90-91; not to be justified, 85, 94; and tragic vision, 45-46, 48

Suicide, 239, 244-45

Temptation: ambiguity of term, 21n.44, 23; distorts truth, 21-23; of Jesus, 28, 35, 40-41; in primal history, 21-23; to self-reliance, 30-31

Ten Commandments. *See* Decalogue

Theocracy, 111-12

Theodicy, 84-96; and human freedom, 92-93; and tragedy, 46

Total depravity: and Formula of Concord, 161n.4. *See* Radical depravity

Traducianism, 202n.49

Tragedy: as alternative to Fall, 44-48; as Greek substitute for sin, 45

Tree of Knowledge of Good and Evil, 17-21, 26, 34; fruit not bad in itself, 50; as "mother of science," 51n.6; as sacramental, 18-19

Tree of Life, 12, 26-27

Unbelief, 34, 53, 54, 104

"Unforgivable sin," 142-43, 161

Venial sin, 142-43, 145
Vicarious action, 13, 28
Vice, 218
Vice lists, 143
Violence: and sin, 53, 140
Virgin birth, 201n.48

Virtue, 23, 41, 45, 90, 104, 141, 163, 212-18, 220, 223, 225

Will (human), 191-93; bent toward evil, 193-95, 198; Farber's view, 195-97
Work, 71-72

Name Index

Allen, Woody: on immortality, 240n.26
Aquinas, Saint Thomas: on death, 25n.49; on seven deadly sins, 144
Auden, W. H., 48, 90, 96
Augustine, Saint: on children as sinners, 168n.23; on concupiscence, 60; on creation as reflecting foreknowledge of Fall, 77n.9; on death, 25n.49, 231, 232; on degrees of sin, 137n.6;on evil, 91n.9, 92n.13, 93; on freedom, 199; on grace, 16n.30, 204n.57; on hidden sin, 217; on impotence of will, 196; on nature of sin, 49n.2, 101, 102, 104; pear incident, 183; and Pelagius, 188; on sex, 65, 147n.28; on suicide, 244; on tragedy, 46; on transmission of sin, 200, 202n.50; on Tree of Knowledge of Good and Evil, 50; on virtue, 212n.1, 213, 215n.10

Baillie, Donald, 187n.11
Bandura, Albert, 122
Barr, James: on Genesis 3, 26n.52, 49n.2
Barth, Karl: on Adam's sin as connected to ours, 205; on evil as necessary for good, 91n.9, 94; on nature of sin, 102, 109, 131; on probation, 18n.35; on suicide, 244; on war, 110n.29; on world as provisional, 76
Bavinck, Herman: on categories of sin, 157n.24; on common grace, 213n.6; on pride, 217n.18
Bayle, Pierre: on freedom as gift, 93
Becker, Ernest, 236
Benét, William Rose, 141
Berdyaev, Nicolas: on Eden, 42n.10; on moral dignity, 195n.29
Berkhof, Hendrikus, 75-76, 108
Blake, William, 152
Boman, Thorleif, 11n.19, 68n.16
Bonhoeffer, Dietrich: on Fall, 18, 68, 82n.52; on life as duty, 245; on responsibility, 117n.47
Brock, Rita Nakashima, 158
Brown, Robert McAfee: on evil, 93; spoof of Kant, 184n.6
Brunner, Emil: on creation as reflecting foreknowledge of Fall, 77n.38; on death, 230n.2; on nature and extent of sin, 113n.35, 165; on pride and unbelief, 54n.15; on virtue and vice, 218

Buber, Martin: on Job, 95n.25; on sin and evil, 136
Bunyan, John: on integrity of the self, 40

Calvin, John: on common grace, 215n.6; on degrees of sin, 137n.6; on free choice, 194n.28; on God's will, 93; on location of Eden, 11; on original righteousness, 14; on patriarchs, 82n.49; on transmission of sin, 200; on total depravity, 160; and theocracy, 111
Camus, Albert: on innocence, 115n.41; on pride, 55, 57; on self-preservation, 243n.32; on suicide, 239
Chesterton, G. K., 95, 203
Clement of Alexandria: on contrary choice, 197n.35; on Fall and immaturity, 41n.8; on virtuous pagans, 213
Cowper, William, 180
cummings, e. e., 57, 256
Cyprian, 79

Dante Alighieri, 11n.17, 19n.38, 47, 115, 186, 197n.36, 201n.47
Delitzsch, Franz: on creation as reflecting foreknowledge of Fall, 77n.38
Donne, John, 261
Drummond, Henry, 109
Dubarle, A. M., 62n.1, 205

Edwards, Jonathan: on covenant of works and final judgment, 29n.53; on disposition and act, 16n.31; on moral sincerity, 220n.26
Eichmann, Adolph, 118
Epicurus, 234
Eusebius: on virtuous pagans, 213

Farber, Leslie: on willing, 195-97
Farrer, Austin, 192n.22

Fiering, Norman, 197n.35
Flacius, Matthias, 113n.35, 160n.3
Francis de Sales, Saint, 107

Gestrich, Christof, 21n.42
Goethe, Johann Wolfgang von, 106-7
Gregory of Nyssa: on Fall, 52, 77n.38
Gustafson, James M., 153n.40

Haught, John, 74-75
Heidegger, Martin: on death, 239n.23
Housman, A. E.: on theodicy, 85n.3
Heim, Karl: on choice, 198n.37; on guilt, 56-57; on Satan, 94, 205
Henderlite, Rachel, 153n.40
Hick, John: on immaturity and the Fall, 41n.8
Hippolytus, 253
Hocking, W. E.: on sin, 105, 106
Holmes, Oliver Wendell, 251
Hordern, William, 182n.1

Johnson, James Weldon, 34, 82
Jones, L. Gregory: on reparations, 207n.64
Justin Martyr: on free choice, 197n.35; on serpent as Satan, 22n.45; on virtuous pagans, 213

Kant, Immanuel: categorical imperative, 103; on radical evil, 43n.11, 97, 100n.4, 163, 216n.15; on responsibility, 184
Kaufman, Gershen: on shame, 63
Keillor, Garrison: on "badness," 130
Keller, Evelyn Fox, 124n.62
Kierkegaard, Søren, 92, 185, 219n.24
Koestler, Arthur, 117
Kübler-Ross, Elizabeth, 233, 235
Kuhn, Thomas, 162
Kuyper, Abraham: on common grace, 214

Leibniz, Gottfried Wilhelm: on theodicy, 90

Lewis, C. S.: on evil, 19n.38; on repentance, 187; on those who "live for others," 165

Lifton, Robert Jay: on brainwashing, 38-39

Luther, Martin: anti-Semitism, 163; on death, 231; on Devil, 92; on self-justification, 115; on sex, 106, 147n.28; on sin, 104, 167, 178, 217; on will, 191-92

MacDonald, George, 177

Mather, Cotton, 71n.26, 178, 180

Mauriac, François: on Holocaust and "progress," 164-65

May, Rollo, 162, 166, 196

May, William, 55n.17, 110n.29

Menninger, Karl, 100n.4, 127n.68

Miller, Alexander, 162

Milton, John: on death, 25n.49; *felix culpa,* 89; on integrity of self, 39; on limits, 199n.40; on pride, 217n.18; on Satan, 104n.13, 143; on sin, 50, 125, 135n.1, 144n.19; on theodicy, 85n.3; on Tree of Knowledge of Good and Evil, 51n.6

Moore, Hannah, 132-33

Mowrer, O. Hobart, 119n.52

Murray, John, 213n.6

Niebuhr, Reinhold: on original righteousness, 14-15; on original sin, 159; on power, 150; and racial prejudice, 153n.40; on self and reason, 53

Nietzsche, Friedrich, 55, 59, 220

Odo of Tournai, 87n.5

Origen, 52, 76n.34

Otto, Rudolph: on Job, 95n.25

Pannenberg, Wolfhart: on original righteousness, 14

Park, Andrew Sung: on *han,* 79

Pascal, Blaise: on death, 232, 241; and dignity, 15, 97, 161; on evil, 141; on ignorance, 139; on pride, 217n.19; on reason, 184n.6; on religion as source of evil, 165; on transmission of sin, 200; on truth-telling, 69; on our wretchedness

Pelagius, 13, 188-89, 202

Peters, Ted, 157n.49

Piaget, Jean: on self-centeredness of children, 168

Plato: on evil as privative, 102

Polanyi, Michael, 162, 215-16

Quell, G.: on sin and guilt, 205-6

Rahner, Karl: on death, 233n.10

Ramsey, Paul, 153n.40

Ricouer, Paul: on desire, 199n.40; on evil, 118n.48; on responsibility, 183n.2, 192n.23; on unease in world, 66; on wrath of God, 25n.50

Robinson, H. Wheeler, 207n.65

Rosenstock-Huessy, Eugen, 207n.64

Sade, Marquis de, 147

Sayers, Dorothy: on choice, 197n.36; on moralism, 196; on punishment, 126n.67

Schleiermacher, Friedrich: on God as Author of sin, 87n.5

Schopenhauer, Arthur, 81, 193n.26

Shakespeare, William: on corrupted good, 165n.17; on death, 240n.26; on responsibility, 201n.47

Shaw, George Bernard, 141

Smedes, Lewis, 261

Spurgeon, Charles, 54, 133-34, 167-68

Suchocki, Margaret, 53-54

Swann, Nancy L., 248

Swift, Jonathan, 64-5, 167n.21

Taylor, Jeremy, 34

Thielicke, Helmut: on sin and loneli-
    ness, 163n.3
Thomas, Lewis: on death, 232
Thomson, Oliver, 215

Van Leeuwen, Mary Stewart, 155n.47
Verhey, Allen, 249

Watson, John Broadus, 123
Watts, Isaac: on clothes, 68
Weber, Otto: on creationism and
    traducianism, 202n.49
Weil, Simone: on evil, 115n.40

Wesley, John: on faith, 219
Whitefield, George, 72n.29
Wiesel, Elie, 96
Williams, Charles: on creation, 95; on
    Fall, 80, 83n.53, 162; on sex, 63; on
    suicide, 245n.37; on tragedy, 47
Williams, Daniel Day: on racial preju-
    dice, 154n.42
Wink, Walter: on corporate personal-
    ity, 207n.65
Wolff, Tobias, 178-79

Zimbardo, Philip, 164

Scripture Reference Index

OLD TESTAMENT

Genesis

1–11	8, 9n.15, 10n.16
1–5	9n.12
1	3, 5, 74n.32
1:26	59n.27
2	9
2:7	72
2:17	19, 24
2:23-34	20
2:25	62
3	4, 7, 8n.11, 9, 22, 53, 172
3:1-7	30-36
3:1-19	21n.44
3:4	54
3:5	55
3:6	53
3:7	53, 62
3:8	62
3:9	9
3:11	70
3:12	47, 206
3:12-13	81
3:15	40, 72
3:16	58, 155, 155n.47
3:16-19	70
3:17	73
3:19	25, 72, 231, 258
3:20	71
3:22	20, 26, 27
4	53
4:7	71n.27
4:8	81
4:9	81
4:23	81
4:24	9n.12
6:5	81, 172
6:11-12	82
8:21	28, 172
9:2	74
9:5	82
9:6	59n.26, 74
9:12-13	19
11	7n.9
12	7n.9, 18
12:10-20	139
13:10	12
15:6	203n.55
22:1	21n.44
47:29-30	252
50:20	93

Exodus

3:14	70
9:12	88
9:34	88
12:49	154n.43
13:16	208
15:26	120
20:2	103
20:3-17	52
20:5	208
20:15	103
21:24	136
21:28	78
22:21	154n.43
23:25	120
33:18-20	85
34:7	117, 263

Leviticus

4:2	139
4:13	139
4:27	139
5:15	139
12	66
14	120
15:16-18	65
18:15	8n.11
19:34	154n.43
20:1-3	102
20:15	78

24:20	136	29:12	149n.31	137:8	209
26:40	209			137:9	209
		2 Chronicles		139:6	95
Numbers		6:36	172	143:2	172, 219
15:22-31	121			145:17	96
15:24-29	139	**Ezra**		148	72n.29
15:28-30	263	7:17-18	115n.38		
35	138			**Proverbs**	
35:15	154n.43	**Nehemiah**		4:23	194
		9:2	210	10:15	149n.31
Deuteronomy				11:4	149n.31
10:19	154n.43	**Job**		11:28	149n.31
14:29	154n.43	12:16	86	13:22	149n.31
23:19	149n.31	14:1-4	66	16:4	86
24:19-22	154n.43	14:4	172	20:9	172, 194
25:17-19	208	15:14-16	172	21:1	88n.6
29:14-15	207	18:13	120	21:4	217n.18
32:35	38	25:4	172	22:4	149n.31
		31:33	8n.11	24:11-12	108
Joshua		38–41	95		
7	208			**Ecclesiastes**	
		Psalms		3:19-20	261
1 Samuel		14	172, 173	5:19	149n.31
8	111	15:5	149n.31	6:3	253
15	209	19:12	183	7:20	172
21:5	65	19:12-13	139	7:29	14, 14n.24
31:1-6	245	26:2	21n.44		
		32:2	203n.55	**Song of Solomon**	
2 Samuel		32:5	263	7:10	7in.27
11–12	138	49:6	149n.31		
11	121	51:4	102	**Isaiah**	
11:1-15	128-34	51:5	66, 183	1:18	152
12:13	102	51:7	152	5:20	94
14:17	20	58:3	66	11:7	73
14:20	20	79:3	253	42:10-11	72n.29
17:23	245	79:8	208	43:27	17in.30
		90:12	241	46:10	86
1 Kings		94:14	83	48:8	66
3:13	149n.31	98:7-8	72n.29	51:3	12
8:46	172	104:21	74	53:6	172
13:22	252	107:17	120	55:8-9	95
		112:1-3	149n.31	59	173
1 Chronicles		130:3	172	64:6	219, 226
10:1-13	245	131:1	85	65:25	73

Jeremiah
6:7   172
7:4-5   17
7:6   154n.43
9:23   149n.31
13:23   185
16:11-12   209
17:9   113, 172
31:31-33   194
32:18   208

Lamentations
3:31   83
4:7   152
5:7   209
5:16   209

Ezekiel
5:6   137n.7
8:15   137n.7
14:23   96
18   208
18:1-4   208
28:13   12
31:8   12
31:9   12
31:16   12
31:18   12
36:26   194
36:35   12
45:20   139
47:23   154n.43

Daniel
2:38   82n.51
4:35   87
11:32   264

Hosea
6:7   8n.11

Joel
2:3   12

Jonah
3:7-8   78

Zechariah
7:10   154n.43

INTERTESTAMENTAL LITERATURE

2 Esdras
3:21   171
4:30   171n.30
7:116-18   171
7:118   4n.2

Wisdom of Solomon
2:24   22n.45

2 Baruch
23:4   171n.30
48:42-43   171n.30
54:15   171n.30
54:19   171n.30

2 Enoch
30-31   15n.26
32   15n.26

NEW TESTAMENT

Matthew
1:21   173
4:1-11   28, 35, 40
5:17-20   143
5:19   135
5:22   137n.6, 144
5:23   137n.6
5:27-28   137
5:28   23, 144, 147
5:43-48   214
6:12   172
6:13   21n.44

6:21   150
6:24   150
7:11   173
7:17-18   186
8:22   242, 253
8:23-37   243
9:2-8   120
9:12   119
10:28   25n.49
12:31   142
12:33   186
12:34-35   186
12:35   159
13:22   150
14:5-10   163
15:11   139
15:18-20   139
15:19   159
16:22   41
16:23   41
16:24   242
16:25   247
17:27   111
19:8   14n.24
19:14   208
19:20   104, 144
19:21   150
19:24   150
22:15-22   111
22:37-39   104, 216
23:23   104
23:35   5, 8, 208
25:14-30   109
25:31-46   108, 154n.43
26:36-46   238
26:41   121
26:53-54   35
27:3-6   163
27:5   245
27:60   252

Mark
1:12-13   40
2   120

2:1-12	120	12:47-48	139	15:20	139
2:17	119	13:1-4	46, 170	16:16-24	112
3:29	142	13:1-5	120	16:25-29	245
4:19	150	16:8	214	17:6	82n.51
4:35-41	243	16:13	150	17:30	139
6:22-28	163	16:19-31	214	17:32	162
7:14-23	139	16:21	107	19:23-27	112
7:34	91	17:33	247		
8:25	247	18:16	208	**Romans**	
8:34	242	18:21	104, 144	1	169, 173, 173n.33
10:14	208	18:22	150	1:18	24, 117
10:21	150	18:25	150	1:21	114, 139
10:25	150	19:11-27	109	1:26	113
12:13-17	111	20:20-26	111	1:29-31	143
12:30-31	104, 216	23:34	139	2	173, 173n.33
14:38	121	23:53	252	2:13-14	173n.33
15:46	252			2:14	215
		John		2:15	215
Luke		1:29	173	3	173
2:1	82n.51	3:6	201n.48	3:5	265
2:52	119	5:14	120	3:10	199
3:38	8	8:36	199	3:10-17	173
4:1-13	28, 40	8:39-41	201	3:18	173
5:17-26	120	8:44	22, 173, 201, 205	3:20	28
5:31	119	8:51	25n.49	3:23	102n.11, 173
6:32-35	214	9:1-3	46	4:3-12	203n.55
6:33	215	9:2	120	4:6-8	203
6:43-45	186	9:3	120	4:7-8	203n.55
8:14	150	9:31	265	5-7	265
8:22-25	243	12:1-8	253	5	4n.2, 7
9:23	242	12:19	82n.51	5:12	170, 172, 200n.45,
9:24	247	12:31	40		204, 205
9:60	242, 253	19:11	137n.7	5:12-14	174
10:19	22n.45	19:41	252	5:12-19	204, 205n.58, 211
10:25-37	48, 253			5:12-21	205
10:27	104	**Acts**		5:16	204n.57
11:4	173	1:18	245	5:17	204
11:13	173	2:5	82n.51	5:18-19	8, 204
11:51	8	2:23	87	5:19	204
12:4	25n.49	4:19	111	6	243n.31
12:10	142	4:24-30	86	6:1-2	90
12:19-20	240	5:29	111	6:2-4	242
12:20-21	150	13:10	201	6:16-19	186, 204
12:34	150	15:18	86n.4	6:16-22	199

6:17	113	9:16	198	1:24-25	244
6:19	113	11:7	59n.26	2:6-11	35, 55
6:23	75, 79, 170, 174,	11:27-29	27	3:2-11	220, 221-29
	231, 243, 259	11:29-30	120	3:3-6	223-24
7	194	12:12-26	154	3:4-7	165
7:9-10	24	15	4n.2, 7	3:7-11	228-29
7:10	8n.11	15:17	26	3:10	242
7:12	143	15:20-26	255-62	4:8	19
7:13-25	184	15:21-22	204, 205		
7:14-24	106	15:22	7, 207n.65	**Colossians**	
7:15	124	15:24	257	2:11-14	243n.31
7:17	124	15:26	232	2:13	24
7:20	124	15:31	242	2:15	40
7:24	243n.31	15:45	7, 9n.12, 76	3:10	59n.26, 69
8	201	15:49	7		
8:3	28, 265	15:56	25n.49, 78, 174	**1 Thessalonians**	
8:7	113			4:13	231
8:8	95n.24, 186, 219	**2 Corinthians**			
8:17	201	1:3-7	90	**1 Timothy**	
8:19-23	73	3:17	199	1:9-10	143
8:20	73, 78	4:17	95n.24	1:13	139
8:28	93	5:4	238	1:15	44
8:29	59n.26	5:19	203, 203n.55	3:1	107
9:14	265	5:21	203	3:3	150
10:4	109n.27			3:8	150
10:5	8n.11	**Galatians**		4:2	113
11:32	10, 88, 89	3:6	203n.55	5:6	24
11:33-34	95	3:22	173	6:10	150
12:3-8	154	5:19-21	143		
12:10	154			**2 Timothy**	
12:19	38	**Ephesians**		2:12	95n.24
13:1-7	103, 111	1:4	13	3:12	47
13:8-10	109	1:11	86		
13:14	69	2:1	24	**Titus**	
14:13-23	139	2:1-3	174	1:7	150
14:23	103, 219, 219n.24	3:20	36	1:15	70
		4:18	113		
1 Corinthians		4:24	59n.26, 69	**Philemon**	
1:18-25	162	5:12	69	18	203
2:14	186	6:12	40		
6:9-10	143	6:14	69	**Hebrews**	
6:12-20	146			2:10	90
8	139	**Philippians**		2:14	40
8:13	103	1:23	244	2:15	40, 243

2:17	119, 173	3:9	59n.26	3:12	8, 36
3:13	265	3:13-18	162	3:15	137
4:15	28, 119	4:1	90	5:16	142
5:2	121	4:11	51	5:17	265
5:7	238	4:17	102n.11		
5:8	90, 119	5:1-3	150	**Revelation**	
6:4-6	142	5:14-15	120	1:5	173
6:11	107	5:16	173	2	207n.65
9:7	139			3	207n.65
9:22	19	**1 Peter**		6:16	64
9:27	242	1:24-25	242	9:20-21	143
10:26	139	2:14	215	12:9	22
10:26-27	142	2:24	173	13	111
10:30	38	4:1	90	18-19	82
11:4	8			18:6	209
11:6	219	**2 Peter**		19:8	69
12:24	8	1:4	60n.31	20	40
13:5	252	2:20	139	20:2	22
				20:14	232
James		**1 John**		21-22	12
1:13	21	1:5–2:2	175-81	21:1	74
1:15	170	1:8-10	173	21:4	95
1:17	215	2:17	60n.31	21:5	74
2:10	104, 135	3:4	52, 102n.11, 265	22:2	26
2:23	203n.55	3:8	205, 265